Manage IT as a Business

How to Achieve Alignment and Add Value to the Company

Manage IT as a Business

How to Achieve Alignment and Add Value to the Company

Bennet P. Lientz

Anderson Graduate School of Management
University of California, Los Angeles, California

Lee Larssen

The Strategic Edge

Amsterdam · Boston · Heidelberg · London · New York · Oxford
Paris · San Diego · San Francisco · Singapore · Sydney · Tokyo

ELSEVIER
BUTTERWORTH
HEINEMANN

Elsevier Butterworth–Heinemann
200 Wheeler Road, Burlington, MA 01803, USA
Linacre House, Jordan Hill, Oxford OX2 8DP, UK

Recognizing the importance of preserving what has been written, Elsevier prints its books on
acid-free paper whenever possible.

Library of Congress Cataloging-in-Publication Data

Lientz, Bennet P.
    Manage IT as a business: how to achieve alignment and add value to the company / Bennet P. Lientz
and Lee Larssen.
        p.   cm.
    Includes bibliographical references and index.
    ISBN 0-7506-7825-9 (pbk. : alk. paper)
    1.   Information technology—Management. 2.   Information technology—Economic
aspects. I.   Larssen, Lee. II.   Title.
    HD30.2.L54 2004
    004'.068'4—dc22   2004005623

British Library Cataloguing-in-Publication Data
A catalogue record for this book is available from the British Library.

ISBN: 0-7506-7825-9

For information on all Butterworth–Heinemann publications
visit our Web site at www.bh.com

04 05 06 07 08 09 10   10 9 8 7 6 5 4 3 2 1

Printed in the United States of America

Contents

Part I
Govern and Plan Information Technology

Chapter 1
Introduction

Chapter 4

Develop Your Strategic IT Plan

Part II

Manage the People and the Work

Chapter 5

Manage Risk and the Project Portfolio

Chapter 6

Manage the IT Staff

Chapter 7

Manage the Work

Part III
Direct and Coordinate IT

Chapter 8
Coordinate Business Unit Activities

Chapter 9
Direct Outsourcing and Manage Vendors

Chapter 10

Communicate with Management

Chapter 11

Software Packages and System Development

Chapter 12

Implementing Change in IT Management

Part IV

Address Specific Challenges

Chapter 13

Personnel and Staffing Issues

Chapter 17

Vendor and Outsourcing Issues

Preface

THE SITUATION IN IT TODAY

Many IT projects and efforts fail to deliver the benefits to the business that were promised. IT is often viewed with skepticism, distrust, or distain. Critical processes lack adequate supporting systems. Yet, IT managers and staff work hard to meet the needs of the business in terms of satisfying department and business needs. Systems are put in place; network operations are reliable and stable. The result is a misalignment of IT with the business. There have been a number of books written on IT alignment. These often do not provide detailed direction or steps to take. Then there are other books that deal with IT management. However, these present the view of IT as reactive to requests. They treat IT management from a technical and business view. They ignore the politics and the real world of IT. This book provides a down-to-earth approach for better managing IT and achieving increased alignment with the business.

HOW DID WE GET HERE?

At the start IT was often a part of accounting. It was viewed as strange and technical. Most of the early systems provided no direct support for business work and processes. Instead, users would do the work and then record the results after the fact. IT responded to many requests and managed the backlog of work. Programming was difficult and complex.

Online systems and microcomputers changed things. IT got closer to the work. People performed the work using systems. This was a fundamental change as it put IT close to the business. E-Business, ERP, and other systems then took this a step by replacing some of the labor and manual effort and automating the transactions and work.

Business managers have had many bad experiences with technology that did not deliver the benefits that were claimed. Systems that were to cut paper, save time, increase productivity, and reduce costs failed to deliver. In many cases, things actually got worse. This is not unusual today.

Yet, with technology advances and more and expanded use by the business, IT management often did not catch up. Many IT groups today are run and managed about the same as they were 20 years ago. They take requests in from users. They assign resources to the requests. Much of the resources of IT are dedicated to support and maintenance.

Let us summarize some of the problems associated with IT.

- New technology promises benefits that are not delivered.
- Systems are implemented that are not used properly and fail to yield the benefits.
- Many IT projects are started and often either fail or run severely over budget and behind schedule.
- Users often resist change and new systems.
- There is miscommunication between IT and the business.
- IT plans are often not taken seriously by either IT or the business.

That is not to say that IT is bad or that IT does not deliver. IT managers and staff toil endlessly to satisfy needs. Yet, sometimes they are as frustrated as the users and managers. They would naturally like to see more success and then recognition of their efforts.

PURPOSE OF THE BOOK

The goals of this book are to:

- Show how to align IT and the business.
- Gather and use lessons learned to cumulatively improve IT performance.
- Develop methods that make IT more proactive in helping the business and its processes.
- Measure IT activities using realistic performance measurement.
- Show how to improve the communications with management.
- Build a more positive, collaborative approach within IT.
- Create teamwork with business departments and staff in doing work together.
- More effectively manage vendors.
- Avoid negative surprises.
- Ensure that more projects are completed on-time and within budget.
- Assure that benefits from systems projects and work result in tangible benefits.

- Establish a strategic IT plan that is effective and used.
- Indicate approaches to increase effectiveness and reduce IT costs.

Nothing in this book requires you to spend money. Rather, over 200 specific guidelines and methods are provided for you to employ.

Specific problems that are addressed in this book include:

- Misalignment of IT and the business. IT often tends to be reactive to the individual business request.
- Poor IT project selection. Projects are selected for tactical, not strategic reasons.
- Mismatch between where IT resources go and where the needs are. Critical processes do not receive sufficient resources and attention.
- Focus on intangible benefits. Focusing on intangible benefits can lead to the wrong work being performed.
- Misallocation of IT resources. Too much of IT resources are consumed in maintenance, operations, and support activities.
- Cope more effectively with political and cultural factors.

APPROACH OF THE BOOK

The approach in this book is focused on how to improve IT work, performance, and alignment. There has been enough written about the problems and generalities of "what." The following themes are pursued:

- Creation of more proactive approach for IT.
- Alignment of IT to the business through business processes, planning, and work.
- Implementation of realistic measurements of IT and IT-related work as well as processes.
- Establishment of a low overhead IT planning approach.
- Collaboration and communications as focal points.
- Stress on tangible benefits from IT work.
- Improved methods of IT resource allocation.
- Proactive management of risk and issues related to IT work.

ORGANIZATION OF THE BOOK

The book is organized into four parts.

- Part I—measure, plan, and control of IT.
- Part II—manage IT resources and work.
- Part III—coordinate vendors, business units, and management.

- Part IV—deal with detailed and frequently encountered IT issues and problems.

Each chapter in the first three parts is divided into the following sections:

- Introduction—this provides background for the material in the chapter along with considering the traditional approaches followed for the work.
- Specific sections for the subject of the chapter that provide guidance.
- Alignment with the business—how the methods of the chapter help you to align IT with the business.
- Manage risk—specific ways to deal with risk.
- Examples from three organizations of different sizes and types.
- Lessons learned—detailed guidelines on how to carry out the methods.
- Performance measurement for the specific area—provides a scorecard for evaluation of your work.
- Summary.

The last part of the book addresses specific, commonly encountered problems. For each issue we consider:

- Background of the issue.
- Impact(s) of the issue.
- Prevention of the Issue.
- Detection of the issue.
- Actions to take regarding the issue.

AUDIENCE OF THE BOOK

There are a number of people who will find this book useful and many have found the techniques to be valuable in the past.

- Senior management who oversee IT.
- Business managers involved in the processes.
- IT managers and staff.
- Project leaders of IT-related projects.
- Individuals involved in change management, process improvement, Six Sigma, and process improvement.
- Consulting, ASP, and vendor managers and their staff.
- Technology developers.
- Students involved in learning information technology.

ABOUT THE AUTHORS

Combined, the authors have over 45 years of hands-on experience in IT. We have managed nine IT groups of different sizes. We have consulted with over

95 IT and business groups in over 40 countries. When we started, we tried to apply traditional methods and techniques. When these failed, we began to improvise new methods. This book is a culmination of this experience. Our overall goal is to give you specific, tangible tools that help you manage and do IT work more efficiently and effectively, and to benefit the business more.

The techniques in this book have been implemented in over 60 organizations around the world in over 20 industries ranging from government, transportation, logistics, banking and finance, insurance, aerospace, high technology, manufacturing, real estate, utilities, natural resources, engineering, petroleum and energy, and medical care. The methods work and feedback on them have also served to enhance the methods further.

FEATURES OF THE BOOK

Some of the key features of the book are:

- Coverage of all aspects of IT—planning, management, operations, software development, technology selection and improvement, process change, and support.
- Over 250 specific guidelines for IT management.
- Specific steps to align IT with the business.
- Scorecards and methods for measuring IT performance as well as vendor, management, and user involvement.
- Critical success factors for greater IT success.
- How to address key issues in IT management.
- How to oversee vendor work.
- How to develop an effective IT strategic plan and planning process.
- How to identify suitable projects that will deliver tangible benefits and align the business to key processes.
- How to improve communications within IT, with the business, and with users.
- How to maximize the return on your IT investment.
- How to get more effective user involvement in IT work.
- How to control and direct maintenance, enhancement, and support.
- How to deal with resistance to change and new IT systems.
- How to build better relationships with vendors.
- A simple, down-to-earth, common sense writing style.
- Extensive tables, lists, checklists, and charts for your faster use of the material.

Part I

Govern and Plan Information Technology

Chapter 1

Introduction

ISSUES WITH INFORMATION TECHNOLOGY AND MANAGEMENT

Information systems and technology have now been around for almost 50 years. During this time, we have all seen many improvements in hardware, communications, and software. Miniaturization, continuously improved price-performance, and automation of more complex work are three specific areas of change. That is the bright side.

The dark side is the fact that the percentage of information technology (IT) projects and work that fail remains very high. Depending on which survey you read, you find that less than 40% of IT projects fail to deliver tangible benefits; less than 50% are completed on-time and within budget. A high percentage never are completed. Unfortunately, these numbers have not changed for the past 20 years. This is despite improvements in technology, new methods, and techniques that have been created. In this regard, many methods for management of IT and doing the work in IT have often promised much and delivered little. Methods come and go. People grasp a new concept hoping that this is the "magic bullet" for IT success. Yet, failure continues; success remains elusive.

Here are some specific problems with IT and IT management today.

• IT is not perceived as being aligned to the business. Many IT groups seem to work on marginal projects and work. IT works on the wrong stuff.

• Too much of IT effort and resources are consumed by support and maintaining the existing IT systems and technology.

• IT becomes too easily enamored with new technology—to the detriment of meeting real needs.

- IT is often too reactive to events and demands, rather than being proactive. Thus, IT never seems to get ahead of the curve.
- Many IT projects that are completed do not result in any changes or benefit.
- IT and IT work seem to be disconnected from process improvement.
- Benefits from investment in new technology are often not perceived to accrue.
- The entire investment in IT over the past 20 years has been called into question by some researchers and others.

The impact of these issues on the business is substantial. It is widely perceived and accepted that businesses depend upon their key processes for revenue and profits. Successful IT will implement systems and technology that directly support key processes. Thus, the fate of the business is linked to IT through the business processes. This is the core of alignment of IT to the business. Successful firms, for example, Wal-Mart and Toyota, attribute much of their success to the welding of systems and processes together. Firms that failed, for example, K-Mart, Chrysler in the 1990s, and others, did not integrate their systems and processes. The result was that the inventories did not match the needs, higher costs, and loss of market share.

SOME PAST ATTEMPTS AT IMPROVING IT

There have been many attempts to improve both IT and business processes. It is useful to examine some of these since they reveal characteristics of the problems that IT management faces today.

- *Outsourcing*. This idea is not new. It began in the times of Egyptians and Romans. Machiavelli wrote about mercenary armies in his book, *The Prince*. Outsourcing has become popular recently for IT work. There is local outsourcing as well as international outsourcing. Has outsourcing lowered IT costs? Sometimes, but not often. Has outsourcing solved many of the IT issues that were stated above? No. It just changed some. Outsourcing is only a part of an answer if it is structured and managed.
- *Software packages*. The purpose of getting a software package is that you get the benefits of the software faster and there is less risk than with system development on your own. True, but packages have many limitations including lack of general flexibility. Many software packages have been implemented with few benefits because the underlying business processes were not changed.
- *New technology*. Whether it be wireless, PDAs, PCs, etc., there is often excessive hype with any new technology. Management and IT grasp the new technology often without thinking through the consequences. The results are failure, lack of faith in IT, and lost opportunities. Technology must be managed more closely.

EFFORTS AT IMPROVING BUSINESS PROCESSES

Now let's turn to methods to improve business processes. After all, these are relevant here since IT is supposed to improve the business through effecting changes and improvements in the business processes.

- *Reengineering*. This was the notion of radical changes to processes. Start with a blank piece of paper. It did not work because the processes had to keep functioning during the change. Moreover, processes are often highly constrained by the supporting systems and technology.
- *Industrial engineering*. The idea here is to measure and change how people perform work in the processes. The problem here is after making improvements, many processes deteriorated as people reverted to their old ways.
- *Total Quality Management and Six Sigma*. These are two different, but related concepts that emphasize measurement. The problems with these methods are that there is substantial training cost and a long learning curve to get started. Then often, the benefits do not cover the costs.
- *Information systems*. We throw this in here because the concept is that implementing a new system will fix a process.

There is an underlying theme to many process improvement methods. That is, they are independent and not related to systems and IT. Take a look at the list and you see that they are one-dimensional for the most part. Effective process change depends on changes in multiple areas, such as:

- Processes and transactions;
- Procedures;
- Policies;
- Systems and technology;
- Organization;
- Employees and their roles and responsibilities;
- Measurement.

Success in process improvement has most often come with employing a combination of the above factors—adopting a multi-dimensional approach.

There are two factors to consider in process improvement that relate to the scope of what is to be done. The first is the process itself. It is often a mistake to take on an entire process. Most processes are burdened with exceptions, workarounds, and shadow systems (informal systems that departments have created on their own). If you attempt to address all of this, you will be mired down and likely fail.

The second problem with process improvement is time. Most process improvement efforts are wound down after changes have been made. Yet, just like our bodies, houses, clothes, etc., processes deteriorate. One example is when new employees are hired, they are often not formally trained in the business processes.

Another example is when new work appears that does not match what went before. Typically, there are senior employees who wield great informal power who can effect how the work is done. We will call these people "king and queen bees."

A BRIEF REVIEW OF IT GOVERNANCE

What is IT governance? Governance is more general, but includes management of IT. Governance of IT includes the roles and responsibilities of management, the business, and external governing boards and steering committees. In the past, IT governance was not viewed as significantly different from IT management since IT was viewed as a support organization.

If we go back in history over the past 40 years, we find that initially IT was often embedded in finance and accounting or some other department. Hardware power and software sophistication were pathetic. It took months to create and debug or correct problems in relatively small software programs. The only technology infrastructure was in the systems organization. The IT organization served as an intermediary between departments and the computer systems since the system interface was so primitive. As such, IT or Information Systems as it was often called then, was reactive. There were no resources to go out and seek out the best opportunities. The limited capability of the software and hardware meant that only selected small parts of processes could be automated. The remainder of the process was left manual. The process was often either split into manual and automated parts, or overlapped and redundant where the manual process was completed and then the results were entered into the computer system.

Overall, the traditional IT governance picture was that shown in Fig. 1.1. In this figure, you can see the business department at the top controlling its employees who are working in the process. The process is a separate entity since part of it is manual and part automated. Below the process you can see the application software and software tools. Supporting this are the hardware, software, and network infrastructure composed of technology components. On the left you can see IT planning and on the right are IT measurement and control. There are several observations from this diagram.

- IT governance is focused on strictly IT activities.
- In this approach, IT does not plan or measure for the process. The business defines its needs to IT. IT often accepted what was given as fact.
- There is a disconnect in that there is no role for implementing changes to the process after the IT systems and work have been completed. No one has responsibility for achieving the benefits of the IT investment.

Why is IT governance importance? Because if we consider just traditional IT management, we get the lower part of Fig. 1.1 with all of the limitations. Going

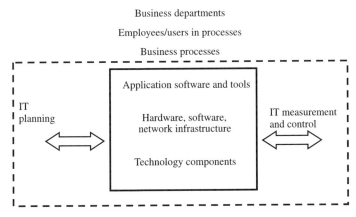

Figure 1.1 Traditional IT Structure

into more detail, IT governance includes the following elements:

- Oversight and direction for IT.
- The role of IT in the organization.
- Roles and responsibilities of both IT and business units in IT activities.
- Planning and measurement of IT and processes.
- Management of the IT portfolio and projects.
- Resource allocation across various IT activities.
- Direct management of the IT effort.

TRENDS AND CHALLENGES IN IT GOVERNANCE

IT was and often is largely a reactive organization. IT managers and staff have been trained to begin with user requests. These are then prioritized based upon technology feasibility, availability of the appropriate IT staff, benefits, and costs. With its technical knowledge and experience, IT was often tasked to develop not only plans and costs, but also benefits. This often led to the following problem.

Issue of benefits: Benefits were defined by IT, but business units and departments were not often held accountable for achieving the benefits. The impacts were that there were and still are many systems implemented for which there were few, if any tangible benefits.

Another problem related to the identification and selection of the projects for IT. In a reactive mode where IT depended upon requests, the requests often came from single departments. Logically, most departments would request systems work to address specific narrow business activities in their own departments. This led and still leads to another IT issue.

Issue on IT impact: Much of the IT effort was marginalized into less important projects rather than cross-department processes and work.

It is now more widely accepted that the major benefits from automation are achieved by addressed business processes that cross department. Improving these processes has a multiplier effect across the organization.

Now let's turn to the system development and package implementation activity in IT. Given a reactive mode, IT staff was sent out to user departments to investigate the request and propose a solution. There were and are many issues here.

Issues related to requirements and system approach:

• IT staff often accepted what users stated at face value. It was assumed that users (1) understood their problems; (2) had an idea of what was needed in terms of a system; (3) were willing to make changes with a new system.
• Requirements often focused on what users said they wanted.
• The system solution was often framed in terms of a new system. Little thought was given to alternatives such as policy change, procedure modification, etc.
• Automation was sometimes perceived as a golden bullet that would solve a variety of non-IT issues.
• All aspects of the business activity were analyzed including exception transactions.

In retrospect, it is not surprising that even today many projects deliver results that are not beneficial to organizations or processes. There are some basic lessons learned that can be gathered from 40 years of IT work.

• Requirements can only be gathered when you know where you are going. Without a firm vision of the future process, it is very difficult to determine the road to travel to get there.
• While upper management and some middle managers may want change and a new system, employees who have been doing the work in the same way for many years do not see the need for any change. IT often did not take into account resistance to change—another common ingredient for system failure.
• The scope of the solutions to business problems was far too narrow—being focused on delivering a new or modified system.
• Looking at all transactions is not only wasteful, but also impossible. In most business processes, there are just too many exceptions to address.

Gathering requirements was and is an exhaustive and time-consuming effort. Contributing factors were the completeness of requirements to include exceptions, the need to get user signoff, and standardized methods such as interviewing.

Interviewing to gather requirements has turned out to be a big disappointment. Some people do not know the process, but give information as if they do. Other people tell the IT staff what they want to hear. There is little or no validation of the interview findings in the work. IT staff relied too much on information provided by supervisors and a few key employees. We will call these key employees "king and queen bees." These are individuals who have been in the department for many years. They seldom take vacations. Junior employees rely on them for instructions. King and queen bees have tremendous informal power in departments and they often relish the power. So when IT shows up to consider automation, it is not surprising that they are often resistant to change. They see, often correctly, that automation will reduce or eliminate their power that has been built up over the years. Many IT managers and IT management do not take this resistance into account.

A WINNING APPROACH FOR IT GOVERNANCE

If we were to write another IT management book along traditional lines, it would not address the problems that have been discussed above. Our purpose is to provide you with proven methods and techniques for IT governance and management for the 21st century as opposed to traditional IT management. Obviously, there will be similarities as well as differences between the new and traditional approaches. The methods in this book have been tested and validated in over 50 organizations in 20 countries. They work because they are common sense and draw upon lessons learned from the past.

The goal is to achieve more effective governance and management of IT. This means that IT resources are more proactively employed and deployed to support key business processes and initiatives.

More detailed objectives of this book are:

- To help align IT to the business and processes.
- To effect lasting process improvement and change.
- To better control and direct resources.
- To support the measurement of both processes and IT.

In terms of scope, we will include the following elements:

- Assessment of new and current technology and methods.
- Measurement of IT and processes.
- IT planning and control.
- Managing risk.
- Specific steps to align IT to the business.
- Resource allocation and budgeting.
- Managing the portfolio of IT work.
- Managing IT projects.
- Directing IT support and operations.

As part of scope, we include the politics of IT governance and management. Why is IT often so political?

- IT projects involve changes to systems and then to business processes.
- Changes in processes affect both the informal and formal power structure within and between departments.
- Many people feel comfortable with the way things have been and so resist change.
- Many instances of IT failure are traceable to not addressing resistance to change and change management.

The bottom line here is that IT is not only linked to business processes, but also to change management. This is shown in Fig. 1.2. Here the dashed line shows the expanded scope of IT governance as compared to the dashed line in Fig. 1.1.

The table in Fig. 1.3 gives a comparison between traditional and modern IT management and governance. Here are some comments on the differences:

- In traditional IT, each piece of work is viewed on its own. This focuses on the uniqueness of the work so that there are fewer opportunities to see patterns and reuse what was done in the past. In modern IT, the attention is on seeing patterns and similarities to minimize the amount of new work.
- In traditional IT, the response to requests was most often some system solution. In modern IT, the attention is on solving the problem—which often may not require a system.

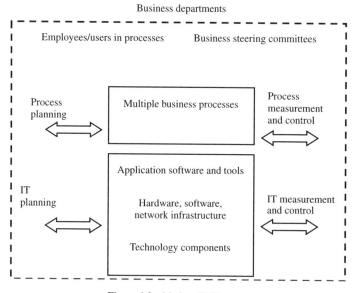

Figure 1.2   Modern IT Structure

Area	Traditional	Modern
Approach to work	Reactive	Proactive
Attitude	Each project is different	Many similarities; aim for cumulative improvement
Solutions	Systems	Procedures, policies, systems, etc.
Scope	Restricted to systems	Includes processes as well as systems
Scope of IT projects	Systems	Process change and systems
Process improvement	Not included most of the time	Included
Change management	Not included	Included
Resources	Tend to be dedicated to specific work	Greater flexibility and management control
Outsourcing	By area on an individual basis	Viewed as strategic
Alignment of IT with the business	No formal approach	Formal approach through processes
Role of IT	Technical, support	Coordinating as well as supporting
Measurement role of IT	Not applicable	IT coordinates measurements

Figure 1.3 Comparison between Traditional and Modern IT Management and Governance

- The scope of modern IT management and governance includes the measurement and coordination of business processes. There is a reason for this being in IT. Critical processes cross multiple departments so that there is no one owner except general management. While ownership can rest with the business, IT is the appropriate place for process coordination since IT crosses all departments and has in-depth knowledge of the processes. Now whether the people in your IT group today can do this is a different question.
- Resource allocation today and in the future must be more dynamic as opposed to dedicating resources to work or projects so that the people are unavailable for other critical work.

BENEFITS OF THE APPROACH

The audience for this book includes managers, consultants, and business and IT staff involved in IT as well as students in the field. There are a number of benefits of the approach and the book for you.

- *More successful IT.* Using the methods, organizations have shown that IT can be more successful and better aligned to the business than when following traditional methods.
- *More comprehensive.* The method is more comprehensive since it includes process improvement, project management, change management, as well as standard IT activities.

• *Common themes.* There are common themes throughout the chapters. One theme is collaboration and collaborative work. This is key to resolving IT-related issues and to getting cumulative improvement. A second theme is that of models, outlines, or templates for much of what is discussed in terms of methods. A third theme is measurement.

• *Realistic.* The approach is realistic and deals with the real political world surrounding IT.

• *Scalable.* It has been shown to be scalable from small organizations to large, multinational organizations, involving literally thousands of IT staff.

• *Cumulative.* The methods described in each chapter are structured to be improved through experience over time. Cumulative improvement of IT is a goal of modern IT governance.

• *Easy to implement.* The methods in this book can largely be implemented on a small or larger scale right away. There is no need to bring in an army of outside help or to buy some software.

There are some basic truths here as well.

• You can be very successful in IT work and yet still fail the business. How can this happen? You work on the wrong projects, less important work, or politically neutral work. So there is little or no benefit.

• To get benefit from IT investment, you not only have to implement a system, but also a new process. But wait. It does not stop there. You also have to change the orientation of the people and managers toward the work to fit with the new process.

ORGANIZATION OF THE BOOK

The book is divided into four parts as follows:

• Part I—Govern and plan IT. This includes governance, technology assessment, planning, and measurement.

• Part II—Manage the IT effort. Specific chapters address the project portfolio, the IT staff, projects, and work.

• Part III—Direct and coordinate IT. This encompasses coordinating business unit participation in IT, managing outsourcing, management communications, and system development and software packages. A chapter is also included on implementing the approach.

• Part IV—How to address key IT-related challenges. The areas include personnel, systems and technology, management, business units, and vendors.

The organization of each chapter in the first three parts follows a parallel structure as follows:

• *Introduction.* This section identifies elements of traditional IT management as well as issues and problems involved. A table will be included that compares the traditional and modern approaches. The technical, managerial, and political goals of the approach are defined.

• *Approach.* This consists of several sections that provide both the general approach for the topic as well as specific guidelines for implementation.

• *Alignment of IT and the business.* This section shows how the methods in the chapter help to align IT and the business.

• *Manage risk.* This is a key area since behind risk are the potential issues and problems that are faced in managing and governing IT.

• *Examples.* There are several examples that are discussed in each chapter. These are combinations of real firms and situations that we have encountered over the years. One is Supreme Oil. This is a multinational energy firm that has several large IT organizations. Another is Tucker County. This is a local government example that involves a middle sized IT group. The third is Shamrock Agriculture that has a small IT group that must meet many challenges. In each of these we consider political as well as technical and managerial factors.

• *Lessons learned.* This section includes tips from applying the methods and approach of the chapter.

• *Performance measures.* To help you assess how you are doing, performance measures using a scorecard approach are provided here.

• *Summary.* This provides an overall view of what was covered.

The chapters in the final part address specific challenges that you are likely to encounter in IT governance and management. For each these include the following:

• *Source.* How the challenge arises.
• *Detection.* How to detect that the issue is present or evident.
• *Impacts and effects.* What the impacts of the problem are if the issue is not addressed.
• *Solutions.* Approaches to deal with the issues.
• *Prevention.* How to prevent the problem from occurring.

There are also several appendices in addition to the Index. The first is called the Magic Cross Reference. This provides a faster way to access materials in the book than the Index for you. There are also websites and magazines that provide much useful information. The third appendix consists of references.

ALIGNMENT OF IT AND THE BUSINESS

As was noted, IT tends to be very specific in terms of activities, projects, and technology. The general business goals, issues, and strategies, on the other hand, are general. The problem in aligning IT and the business has to address the general business factors with the detailed IT factors. The critical success

Factor	Business	Processes	Information technology
Objectives			
Issues			
Strategies			
Action items			
Plans			
Benefits			
Impacts			

Figure 1.4   Alignment of the Business with Information Technology

factor in alignment is through the business processes. This is shown in Fig. 1.4. In this figure, the rows are the ways in which it is desired to align business and IT. The columns are for business, processes, and IT. Note that the table is not filled out. That is what will be done throughout the book in this section. In fact, we will take one area such as objectives and create a table for just this with the rows as individual objectives.

MANAGE RISK

We need to determine a common sense, easy-to-use definition of risk. Risk in mathematical terms consists of multiplying the likelihood of an event or problem occurring by the impact or exposure or loss if the problem occurs. We will use a similar definition. An IT element such as a plan, project, etc., has risk or is risky if it has one or more associated significant problems or issues. Significance is determined by the degree of impact of the issue and the likelihood that it will happen. This will be useful for us since it gets at the factors behind the risk. Why is there risk? Because of the associated issues and problems.

Overall, IT in many organizations has a number of risks that are related to the following issues.

• IT resources are consumed by operations support and work for individual departments on their processes. The impact is that there are no resources available to work on cross-department processes. These tend to be the most critical to the company. This points to the need for a proactive approach to managing IT resources and generating IT work.

• Many IT projects are either not completed, or if completed, do not yield any significant benefits. Behind this is the need to include process improvement and change management with the project management and IT work.

• Business units and their employees do not fully commit to the change and improvement effort. They tend to resist change. The result is that even with the best of effort by upper management and IT, the work will tend to fail.

EXAMPLES

SUPREME OIL

Supreme Oil is a diversified, large energy exploration, producing, and developing company with operations in over 20 countries. The IT organization is split. There is a headquarters IT group. There are separate IT groups for each major business activity, including exploration, development, refining, distribution, and retailing. Supreme has implemented a number of standard systems as well as several packages. Yet, there are a number of business issues. The geological and engineering groups are not supported in an integrated manner. This has resulted in losing bids on new properties for drilling as well as overbidding on marginal properties. Management has complained that they do not think that they get enough from their investment in IT.

TUCKER COUNTY

Tucker County is a local government that supports over 10,000,000 residents. The IT organization is centralized and has been run for years in a reactive mode. The IT group has started a number of projects, but few ever finish. The technology that is used is not up-to-date. Business units are starting to go out on their own with respect to IT. The IT group is losing control of the situation. From the user department view, IT is not responsive.

SHAMROCK AGRICULTURE

Shamrock is a cooperative that supports farmers in many areas including milk production, feed production, retailing, headquarters operations. The IT group works very hard, but is small. Their work is appreciated and is of high quality, but there is just too much work to do. There are insufficient financial resources to increase staff substantially.

As you can see, these are very different organizations with a variety of issues and problems. Yet, they all suffer from the same general problems.

- There is a need to align business and IT.
- There is a need to measure IT to determine the value of IT.
- A better approach is needed for governance, organization, and management of IT.

LESSONS LEARNED

- Change of an IT group from the traditional to the modern model does not come overnight. A basic lesson learned from our experience is that it is best for the change to come through IT rather than through top-down imposition of rules and policies.
- One useful approach for analysis is to see the impact of what would happen if the current situation in IT were to continue. Another part of this approach is to also consider the opportunity cost of what other types of work could have been and could be done if resources were redirected. This is a very good way for people to see beyond their current situation.
- When considering changes in IT governance, a useful first step is to evaluate the current governance and management. In this task, there are several goals. One is to identify the problems and issues that need to be addressed through the change. The second and, probably more important, from experience is to get people to recognize the impact of not changing as well as to see the need for change. If these goals are not met, the best efforts by management to effect change will often be wasted.
- There are useful charts that can be prepared from readily available information. These include:
  - The mix of requests by source—management, process improvement, user request, etc. This can indicate reactiveness.
  - The mix of IT resource hours by type of work—development, enhancement, maintenance, support, etc. The more effort that goes into support, the fewer the resources are available for new work.
  - Analysis of started projects—completed on time, completed within budget, completed and yielded tangible benefits, etc. This helps to begin to question how project ideas are evaluated and selected.

PERFORMANCE MEASURES FOR THE IT ORGANIZATION

In this section, we discuss and provide scorecards for measuring the performance of areas and topics that relate to the chapter. In this chapter, we cover the measurement of the current IT organization. Fig. 1.5 gives a set of performance measures for IT. Before commenting on the individual measures, let's cover how this would be carried out. In doing performance measurement, the purpose is to gain consensus so that improvements and future actions can be taken with widespread support. Thus, the scorecard is not used by a few IT managers or staff. Rather, users, managers, and IT jointly participate and discuss the elements. The idea is to gain consensus through the scoring process. Note that this is totally

Area	Score	Comments
No. of IT employees		
No. of employees		
Ratio of IT employees to total		
Percentage of projects generated proactively		
Percentage of resources dedicated to projects		
Average duration of projects		
Percentage of projects that yield real benefits		
Percentage of projects completed on time		
Percentage of projects completed within budget		
Percentage of total resource hours on projects that yielded tangible benefits		
Percentage of project ideas turned down		
Common issues across projects		
Use of templates		
Turnover of IT employees		
Transfer of knowledge from vendors		
Common plans with vendors		
Common issues database with vendors		
Average time to resolve IT-issues		
Average time to resolve vendor-issues		
Templates for presentations		
Meetings for issues and lessons learned		
Documentation evaluation method		
Requirements checklists		
Process measurement and score cards		
Process plans		
Coordination role for issues, lessons learned, templates		

Figure 1.5   Performance Measures for Information Technology

different from standard voting. The political benefit for this is to gain more support for change. Thus, you can either come up with a score of high–medium–low or a numerical score of 1–5, where 1 is low and 5 is high. By having the scoring elements available for discussion in a neutral way, you can get more opinions and views surfaced.

Now let's turn to the individual elements.

• No. of IT employees—objective number, but it forces you to think about people in departments doing IT work.
• No. of employees—used for ratios and overall measurement.
• Ratio of IT employees to total—indicates coverage of IT employees.
• Percentage of projects generated proactively—if this is low, then it is likely that this is a more reactive IT group.

- Percentage of resources dedicated to projects—this should be high, reflecting control over support activities.
- Average duration of projects—this should be less than one year; too many long projects typically spell problems for an IT group.
- Percentage of projects that yield real benefits—this will be generally lower than the next two percentages.
- Percentage of projects completed on time.
- Percentage of projects completed within budget.
- Percentage of total resource hours on projects that yielded tangible benefits—this measures the resource allocation effectiveness.
- Percentage of project ideas turned down—it is hoped that this is high so that there is selectivity.
- Common issues across projects—this is an indication that issues are more proactively managed.
- Use of templates—this indicates the use of standardized methods within IT.
- Turnover of IT employees—this should be moderate; too low may mean trouble in terms of new methods; too high may indicate instability.
- Transfer of knowledge from vendors—this is subjective.
- Common plans with vendors—this is important as a sign to show control over outsourcing.
- Common issues database with vendors—indicates a collaborative approach.
- Average time to resolve issues—IT.
- Average time to resolve issues—vendor.
- Templates for presentations.
- Meetings for issues and lessons learned—this indicates if there is adequate attention for issues and lessons learned.
- Documentation evaluation method.
- Requirements checklists—this relates to templates.
- Process measurement and scorecards.
- Process plans—this will be covered later in detail; a process plan is an organized approach for how a process will be changed over time.
- Coordination role for issues, lessons learned, templates.

SUMMARY

Information systems and technology have risen in importance to the performance of the business processes of organizations. Thus, the business, technical, and political success of companies is perceived to depend increasingly on IT. With this increased importance, it has become more evident that traditional management of IT as a narrow, reactive support activity is neither sufficient nor responsive to the greater and more sophisticated demands placed on IT.

In order for a company to succeed, IT must be aligned and fully integrated into the business processes. Resource allocation, portfolio management, project management, process improvement, and change management must all work together to support sustained process improvement. That is the modern goal of IT as opposed to goals of the past related to efficiency. Here efficiency is replaced by effectiveness.

Chapter 2

IT Oversight and Governance

INTRODUCTION

In the last chapter, IT governance was defined along with trends and business objectives. Here you will see how specific business elements such as objectives, vision, etc. can be related to Information Technology. After this, the roles and responsibilities of the IT organization can be addressed. The purpose of this chapter is to provide you with guidelines so that you can define the alignment between IT and the organization as well as to see and implement more effective IT governance.

Let's consider IT governance and management in the traditional setting. In the previous chapter, IT was originally seen as a support organization that responded to specific business demands. IT was a reactive organization, much like a public safety organization, such as a fire or police department. IT oversight and governance was typically in the hands of the manager to whom the IT group reported. IT, as such, was often insulated from much of the business since systems work was more time consuming and complex. Once IT supported finance, accounting, payroll, and some operations functions, there was little left over for other work.

Management expectations of IT and systems was fairly limited. If you read the literature of 20–30 years ago, you find that many upper level managers had little understanding of IT. There was only a limited view of how dependent the organization was on systems and technology. In fact, systems was often viewed as a way to perform manual work faster. Thus, the expectation of management was that IT be an efficient, low-cost service provider. Most IT projects were selected based upon management judgment on what was needed. This was often based on what vendors offered and what other similar firms were doing. People paid lip service to benefits, but benefits were seldom enforced. After all, many processes did not heavily interact with systems. You often did the work and then input the results of the work into the computer system.

Technology advances, new software systems, and the drive of firms to be more productive, efficient, and competitive changed all of that. Management began to realize that the critical success factors for business profitability and growth lay in the performance of business processes rather than the business departments. Attention began to center on how to improve the business processes. In parallel, systems became available that could perform more of the work in the business processes. Enterprise Resource Planning (ERP) systems are just one example of a class of systems. Others existed in transportation, logistics, manufacturing, distribution, and retailing.

With the availability of systems and the realization of the importance of business processes came the desire by management to make the business processes through information systems and technology. This resulted in several fundamental changes in management thinking, including:

• IT began to be seen as very important to the business. IT could not be left alone to manage itself or be managed by one person with his or her own local interests.

• With success in a number of firms, the benefits of integrating business processes with systems became evident.

The result was to change the nature of IT governance, oversight, and management. How to carry out effective modern governance of IT is a major theme of this chapter.

GENERAL PURPOSE AND SCOPE OF OVERSIGHT

The goal of efficiency for IT is still present in many organizations. Yet, it has become less relevant and important. Efficiency is more of a constraint than an objective.

The major goal of IT oversight and governance is to ensure that IT is effective in improving and sustaining the performance of the business processes and infrastructure within the organization.

Effectiveness is a very general word. The word effective means to bring about a desired result. This means a business result. Thus, management expectations that formerly reviewed budget and schedule of IT work change toward getting benefits and results from the IT effort after a new system or capability has been installed. These two things are far different in the following ways:

• Getting an IT project completed within budget and on schedule, while still important, becomes secondary to getting tangible business results and impacts.

- IT success is no longer what IT does, but on what IT was able to change and improve.

Look at these two bullets and you can see a fundamental shift in thinking. IT used to be like a highway department. It built roads for people. People were then responsible on their own for getting the benefits of the road. This is the traditional support role. Things have changed. Now IT effort goes beyond the road into transportation planning and effectiveness. This is a much bigger scope. Here are some elements of how the scope of IT effort has changed.

- *Business processes.* Process change and improvement now are expected to go hand-in-hand with an IT project. Otherwise, many would argue, "Why do the project at all?"
- *Nature of IT projects.* In the modern world of IT, there is neither sufficient resources nor time to take a reactive approach and wait for requests. IT projects must be generated more proactively.
- *User requirements.* Traditionally, users defined their requirements. After all, since they have been doing the work for many years they know what they want. But the reality is different. Many employees fear change and want to have the new process work the same as the old—only with a new system. Then there are no benefits—only costs. In the modern world, user requirements become jointly defined by managers, IT, and employees. They are too important to be left to a few king or queen bees.
- *Measurement.* Traditionally, there has been little real measurement of the business processes. Total Quality Management (TQM) and Six Sigma emphasize measurement, as do other newer methods. Measurement becomes essential for IT work and for processes.

This is not to say that most organizations have adopted this new purpose and scope of IT governance. Many have not. Most are in a "Catch-22" world in which management expectations for benefits are high, but the role and governance of IT has not changed. This has created many problems within IT and with management, including:

- IT is not given responsibility to change processes. Business staff sees no need for change. Systems are put in and benefits are not achieved.
- In the more limited role of traditional IT, IT staff often tries to meet user requirements by carrying out these without question. Yet, many requirements are often political and aim at ensuring that there is no real change to the ways that the work is performed.

Figure 2.1 summarizes some of the differences between traditional and modern IT governance. Using this table and the above discussion, you can answer the question, "What is IT success?"

IT success occurs when key business processes are improved to a state of being effective, efficient, and flexible to meet new demands.

Factor	Traditional	Modern
Systems	Separate, single dept. focused	Integrated, multi-dept. systems
IT goal	Efficiency and cost control	Effectiveness
Responsibility	Complete IT work on time and within budget	Achieve business benefits and do the work within schedule and budget
IT oversight	Single manager who is responsible for IT	Upper management
Ideas for new IT work	Reactive	Proactive

Figure 2.1   Some Comparative Factors Relating to Traditional and Modern IT Governance

This is far different from the traditional definition of success in which IT managed their budget, resolved problems, and delivered what was requested in a timely and low-cost manner. Very different indeed, eh? This very definition of success has many ramifications and implications on processes, the roles and responsibility of the IT organization, the roles of the business units, and how IT is governed.

There are many implications if you take this discussion and definition of success into the IT organization itself. Some of these are:

• Systems work cannot be done as an art. There must be greater structure and predictability.

• There should be cumulative improvement in IT performance on projects. This helps to make IT more responsive to business changes with limited resources.

• Selection and adoption of new technology has to be done with more care due to the direct effect on the business processes.

• The ways in which IT does work in terms of support, requirements, handling requests, planning, etc. must be altered to reflect process improvement, measurement, and change management.

THE ROLE OF BUSINESS PROCESSES

You have seen the importance of business processes. So it is appropriate to pause and examine some of the characteristics and behavior of processes. A *business process* can be defined as a set of rules, procedures, and policies that the organization follows to achieve specific purposes. Any organization has many processes. They can be classified in different ways.

• *Within or across departments.* Smaller processes may function within a department. People outside of the department only see the results and may often not be aware of what work is going on. Cross-department processes tend to be more critical and involve many people in different geographic and organizational locations.

• *Standalone or interdependent.* Today, there are far fewer standalone processes that function independently. More and more the trend is toward integrating processes into process groups.

• *Informal or formal.* Processes that depend heavily on systems tend to be much more formal. Many manual processes are informal.

Most processes are composed of several categories of work. There are the common transactions or tasks that constitutes the greater part of the work volume in the process. There are exception transactions that are handled outside of the normal work. These exceptions often require specialized attention. Typically, there are many types of exceptions in processes—more than normal, common transactions.

The following are resources that support and sustain a process.

• Facilities and work layout;
• Average employees who often do the standard transactions;
• Supervisors and king and queen bees who have special expertise and formal or informal power in the organization;
• Formal systems;
• Informal procedures;
• Workarounds. These are procedures that get around limitations in the process or systems;
• Shadow systems. These are informal or formal systems that have been created within the business department to help do the work. The department staff tends to be very dependent upon these;
• Policies that govern the work;
• Procedures and rules for the work;
• Guidelines for how best to do the work;
• Training materials for the business process;
• Measurement methods for the process;
• Supporting process for dealing with problems, new or unplanned work.

Keep this list in mind as we consider the life cycle of a process, E-Business, and issues and deterioration of business processes.

What is the life cycle of a process? Here are some simple stages.

• *Definition and startup.* A process is created here. Often this is informal and casual. New small businesses do this all of the time. Definition of the process may be carried out with care or haphazardly and reactively. Most of the items in the list above are not included.

• *Formalization and some automation.* Here the volume of the work mandates that there be increased efficiencies. Computer systems are created or bought to support the process. The planning and care of structuring the process is generally far less than that of implementing the new system to support the process.

• *Process change and adaptation.* A process is a living and changing entity that is affected by changes in the nature of the work and by changes in any combination of the resources in the above list.

• *E-Business.* At this stage the process becomes totally formalized and automated. There are few, if any, exceptions. Shadow systems and workarounds are absorbed into the automation.

Now you can see the appeal of E-Business and why it is a continuing trend despite the dotcom bust. E-Business offers the best hope of formalizing and making a low-cost, efficient process.

Processes tend to deteriorate over time. Figure 2.2 gives a list of how deterioration can occur in each of the resource areas of the above list. When you think that many processes endure multiple signs of deterioration at the same time, you can see why many business processes run into trouble and do not serve the management or the organization effectively. But wait! The real situation may be far worse than this. Different processes decay and rot at different rates. One deteriorated process can impact other interfacing and related processes. It is like the spread of a disease.

There are political factors at work here too. King and queen bees as well as some supervisors may relish power and so it is in their self-interest that there be no change or improvement to the work. A king or queen bee has the knowledge to do the exception work. Other employees have to come for directions. They like and even love exceptions—the more the better. Power relates to job security. If they share the knowledge and support the automation or elimination of exceptions, then they lose power and also their job security is eroded.

Couple the king and queen bees to the fact that many people naturally and genuinely want to do things the same way and you have a key problem in process improvement and automation.

> **While management may want change and IT may rush in to implement IT solutions, unless the potential resistance of the regular employees, supervisors, and king and queen bees is proactively addressed, there will be failure.**

Experience shows that it is not enough to have management and IT together. You have to have grassroots support for change and improvement. Otherwise, if the employees do not succeed in wearing down a project and causing it to fail, they can wait until the new system is in and make the process revert in part or whole, back to the way it was. For some, their favorite song is "Memories." Is this too negative and pessimistic? Of course, there are many people who want change. However, there are also many instances where change has been derailed. Here is

- Facilities and work layout
  - Work can be relocated causing the staffing to change, affecting morale
  - No investment is made at upgrading facilities so the work space is run down
- Average employees
  - New employees are hired, but are not trained in the process. They make mistakes
  - There is a lack of supervision so that procedures are not followed Information in databases can deteriorate
- King and queen bees
  - They sustain and increase their power by focusing on exceptions
  - They do not share their knowledge and obstruct developing guidelines
- Formal systems
  - Key programmers may leave
  - Multiple people work on the system over time, making each future change more difficult
- Informal procedures
  - They do not become standardized so that there are different, inconsistent versions
  - People tend to rely more on the informal procedures
- Workarounds
  - Failure of the system to keep pace with the change in the work generates more workarounds and shadow systems
  - Workarounds are not formalized so that there are more errors
- Shadow systems
  - The person who developed or supported the shadow system leaves. The system fails. No one can fix it
  - Employees do not want to make changes since they would have to change their shadow systems
- Policies
  - Policies do not adapt to new conditions and so become irrelevant
  - Policies fail to be consistent with actual practice
- Procedures and rules
  - Procedures are not written down
  - Procedures are neither updated nor maintained
- Guidelines for the work
  - No guidelines are produced. There is total dependence upon the king and queen bees
  - Guidelines are not documented or reviewed
- Training materials
  - Training materials are not updated
  - There are training materials for the system, but not the process
- Measurement
  - The only measurements that are used is labor cost and IT cost. Hence, you cannot determine the state of the process
- Supporting process
  - Supporting processes are not documented
  - Supported processes are managed and used by other groups and so are not controlled

Figure 2.2   Examples of Deterioration in Business Processes

an example. Look at the many ERP implementations where changes were made to the system so that the process would not have to be changed. Then management wondered why there were no benefits. Give us a break!

After reading this, you are left with the following inescapable conclusions.

1. **Businesses depend upon their business processes for success or failure.**
2. **Processes are dynamic over time and subject to deterioration like everything else.**
3. **Managing business processes is an absolute key to business success.**
4. **Information systems and technology represent the best hope for structuring processes and for dealing with deterioration.**
5. **Management must proactively direct and govern IT so that processes are supported.**

These seem totally obvious to us in an academic sense. Then why do so many companies fail or run into trouble? Why are there so many examples of management malfeasance and fraud? Because the processes are not properly structured, managed, operated, and measured. Some managers take painstaking steps to keep process details confidential and private. Key processes should be totally transparent and visible.

What are some of the challenges that relate to managing business processes? Here are some.

- You have to get grassroots support for change in the work as well as in recognizing the problems and their impacts on the current work.
- You have to regularly measure processes to see if there is substantial process deterioration.
- Just because you completed an IT project successfully means little. You have an ongoing program to ensure that there is no fallback and reversion.
- In addressing a process, you have to focus on the common work. If you get drawn into the world of dealing with exceptions, you will never finish the project. There are just too many exceptions and new ones come up all the time.

THE MISSING ROLES OF IT GOVERNANCE THAT CAUSE BUSINESS FAILURE

Let's start with the roles that are needed to support the implications directly on IT and those stemming from the focus on business processes. A list is given in Fig. 2.3. These are ten critical activities.

Are these items needed? After all, many of these are not performed now. The approach that you should consider is to answer the following question for each of these, "What happens if the specific function is not performed?" Carrying out this

- *Measurement.* Measuring of business processes, IT work, and related activities. Measurement is essential to management to help set priorities and determine where there are problems
- *Business process and IT planning.* IT plans that are not sensitive to the business processes may end up being wasted
- *New opportunity identification.* Proactively identifying new opportunities for IT work that support improvements in the processes
- *Process improvement.* Supporting and implementing process improvement and change
- *Change management and coordination.* Helping to identify and deal with resistance to change
- *Project selection.* Greater selectivity in determining which projects to recommend and to do
- *Issues management.* Being more proactive in identifying and coordinating the management of issues
- *Wider project scope.* Expanding the scope of projects to include process improvement, change management, and measurement
- *Process planning.* Developing process plans to determine the future long-term direction for business processes
- *Lessons learned and guidelines.* Here lessons learned are gathered for both IT and the business processes to improve and provide guidelines for both the business and IT

Figure 2.3 New Roles for Modern IT Governance and Management

discussion with our clients has been one of the most successful ways of generating enthusiasm for change. If these things are either not done or not carried out in a structured way, the results will either be inconsistent or there will be no benefit.

Are IT groups ready to carry out these responsibilities? A few do this now. Some are gradually moving in this direction. However, many are not. They are more traditional. Are the people that are currently in IT the ones to do these things? Probably not. Some can be trained, but there will have to be change based on our experience in implementing these roles.

Do these roles belong in IT? Start with another question. Should these roles be performed? The answer is clearly yes. Next, ask the question, "What organization is qualified to perform these functions?" Well, let's see. The organization would have to cross the company. It would have to have a great deal of systems and process knowledge. There are only a few options beside IT.

- *Outside consultants or outsourcing.* These are core activities that are not routine. They are performed regularly. While consultants can assist in putting these into place, the functions are really internal.
- *Internal auditing.* They could do some of the functions, but lack the IT knowledge. They also compromise their independence by being so proactive.

• *A new group.* This has been tried in the past many times. Most of the time the result is failure. There are too many turf wars, political conflicts, etc.

Thus, you tend to be left with IT by default. Maybe, the Information Technology group should be renamed to be Information Processes and Technology. The phrase Information Technology is too confining for the scope of the new "IT." Another popular choice is "Information Services."

MODERN GOVERNANCE OF IT

Having discussed the changes and new functions that have to be done as well as the current work, we can turn to considering how IT oversight and governance would work. One issue is the reporting relationship for the IT organization. Today, IT is viewed by many organizations as so important that IT reports to either the CEO, COO, or CFO. The IT manager is titled Chief Information Officer (CIO). That is consistent with the new roles for IT and process coordination.

That addresses the day-to-day reporting, but it still leaves the question of oversight unresolved. An approach that has been used is that of an IT Steering Committee. This concept has met with mixed success. The implementation may start off well, but if there are no major issues, managers put subordinates into the committee and the decision-making ability of the committee tends to deteriorate. There are other problems associated with a single IT Steering Committee, including:

• One manager can assume a dominant position in the committee. The result may be that the wrong projects are approved. Evaluations and decisions may be biased toward that manager.
• Managers may start to micromanage the IT group. This raises even more issues.
• Managers may not be available when needed to deal with issues. High-level managers have many commitments.
• Some of the issues that the Steering Committee has to deal with are at too low a level.

What do you need for oversight of IT? First, you need a high-level group to deal with major issues, problems, opportunities, and direction. Second, you need a group that deals with issues and opportunities at a lower level first to filter and resolve some of the less major situations. Third, you need a group that can oversee specific initiatives or projects to address policy, procedure, and process issues that are specific. Thus, there are three types of groups. Two are permanent. The last may be created and then disappear with the completion of the project and process change and measurement.

For convenience let's refer to the three committees as follows:

• *Executive Steering Committee.* This group is composed of very senior management and does not meet very often. Perhaps, it only meets a few times a year. Its duties are listed in Fig. 2.4.

• *Operational Steering Committee.* This group is permanent and is composed of a few higher level managers and a cross-section of middle level managers. The duties of this group are given in Fig. 2.5.

• *Project Steering Committee.* This is a temporary group that oversees a specific large-scale process project. Duties are listed in Fig. 2.6.

There is the obvious hierarchy here. Project steering committees report through a coordinator to the Operational Steering Committee. The Operational Steering Committee in turn reports into the Executive Steering Committee, which has the ultimate authority next to the CEO and Board of Directors.

* Review the results of analysis of potential and current projects
* Approve and authorize new projects and work
* Determine which processes have the greatest needs for change and are most critical to the business
* Review the budget for IT
* Deal with major issues and opportunities
* Ensure that there is upper management support for process improvement
* Carry out a summary review of process, IT, and business plans

Figure 2.4   Duties of the Executive Steering Committee

* Perform the initial review and decision making on issues related to processes and IT
* Perform the first review of budgets, schedules, and plans
* Work to resolve most issues that arise in businesses, IT, and from projects that relate to business processes
* Recommend new project initiatives for future work
* Provide a link between business departments and IT on one side and the Executive Steering Committee on the other
* Review and approve process plans
* Review and approve the IT strategic plan
* Review and approve business unit automation plans

Figure 2.5   Duties of the Operational Steering Committee

* Ensure that there is grassroots support for process improvement and change
* Address specific issues that relate to the project
* Involve a wide base of employees in the decision making so that there is a widespread sense of ownership

Figure 2.6   Duties of the Project Steering Committee

Having these three types of committees can help deal with the issue of project ownership and sponsorship. Often, a project starts with the CEO or COO being the project sponsor. Then things change. Managers may come and go. Other priorities arise. The sponsor may fall into disfavor, dragging down the projects and work that are being sponsored. The sponsorship lapses. A basic lesson learned is that it is dangerous and unwise to rely on one sponsor.

Do these three levels of oversight represent too much of a burden? Is there too much overhead? Experience shows that this does not happen if the roles and responsibilities of the committees are defined and understood by all.

The overall point is that oversight can be established with a reasonable effort that is consistent with what many organizations already have in place. Later, guidelines will be given for implementation.

MODERN ROLES AND RESPONSIBILITIES OF IT

There also needs to be a role in IT that acts as a coordinator with the committees. Is this too much of a burden? Not really. If you think about it, this coordination role that includes the items listed in Fig. 2.3 is really an alternation to the concept of the "Project Office." The Project Office is traditionally the repository for project management and coordination of projects. So this just expands the role.

Overall, IT roles change from support into more of a coordination role. If you look at the user roles discussed in the next section and listed in Fig. 2.7, you can see that there is a coordination effort required.

- Ongoing training of employees in the business processes
- Development and maintenance of training materials for the process. This includes the system procedures developed by IT, but embedded in the process training materials
- Development of operations procedures and guidelines for the business process Again, this includes the systems procedures
- Identification of issues and problems along with their impacts in the current work
- Support in the inclusion of shadow systems in the new process
- Support in the reduction, control, and elimination of exceptions
- Participation in the definition of the new business process
- Determination of benefits of the new process and how these benefits will be achieved
- Participation in data conversion, testing, and requirements definition
- Active roles in implementation planning
- Definition and implementation of short-term changes or Quick Hits to the process to pave the way for long-term change
- After implementation, participation in the measurement of the processes and identification of problems and issues
- Participation in process planning for the long-term future process

Figure 2.7 Potential Responsibilities of Business Departments in Projects

What happens to the support activities? Obviously, they continue. However, there is a trend to outsource some of the more routine IT activities. The acquisition of software packages as opposed to doing new development is another example of this outsourcing. Outsourcing of network and PC support, training, and the help desk are other examples.

MODERN ROLES AND RESPONSIBILITIES OF BUSINESS UNITS

Business units are involved in IT governance as well. In the past, business units typically supplied the human resources and management to the process. They would request help from IT when they perceived a need. Processes tended not to be measured except in general terms or when some problem surfaced. If there was a problem, then there would be a major cleanup effort and then calm. Most business managers and employees are tied up in the daily operations of a department. They see the process as just work that has progressed the same each day. Unless there was an innovative manager or someone in upper management who spotted an opportunity, there were few changes. After all, things were running smoothly so why rock the boat? This approach led to a number of problems, including:

• Innovation in the work depended upon the individual manager. Processes that did not need major attention got attention. Others that were critical, but had managers that liked the status quo were left alone.

• Individual managers looked after the processes in their own groups, leaving cross-department processes alone. After all, why incur the political risk and cost?

• IT could not generate project ideas without the involvement of the business manager. Many business managers did not want to start new IT efforts due to the risk and potential failure as well as the fear of the effects of change.

• There was no proactive measurement of the work so there was little hard, or even subjective information to indicate that there were problems.

In the modern setting with the governance approach above, it is clear that there must be changes. A key is to define where the responsibility for generating ideas for improvements and changes to the work originates. In the modern approach to IT governance, this can be a combination of IT, the line managers overseeing the process, the employees involved in the work, and the steering committees. There must be more openness and transparency so that people are willing to identify problems in the work. This replaces an atmosphere of fear of "whistle blowing for change."

Business departments need to be actively involved in the measurement and criticism of processes and work. IT can provide coordination for measurement of processes, but the knowledge lies in the people and supervisors doing the work. If you adopt this approach, you begin to degrade the informal power of the king and queen bees who relish and seek to preserve the status quo.

Once a process or group of processes have been identified as the basis of a project, then the role of the business unit expands as well. Figure 2.7 gives a list of what is logical for business departments to perform. Once you look at the list, you are likely to say, "They will not want to do these things." Or, "They do not have the skills to do some of these things." These statements may be true of the current situation, but many of these are carried out jointly with IT staff and others. Moreover, when you implement these new roles, you will be selecting one user area to serve as a model. In the end, the business department staff has to carry these things out since they have the knowledge, they are the direct beneficiaries of the work, and it is in their self-interest to do so. What if they refuse? Then you have to ask if the project is really feasible. We have had several cases where good project ideas that were needed were not started because of the users being unwilling to fully participate in the change effort. We will examine these issues in more detail later.

IT GOVERNANCE AND BUSINESS VISION, MISSION, AND OBJECTIVES

An overall framework for IT governance and management has been laid out. Much of the remainder of the book will discuss implementation and the framework in more detail. Here it is important to begin the alignment analysis of IT with the business. This begins at a high level that is relatively fuzzy and uncomfortable.

Let's give some background first. Most companies spend quite a bit of time and money developing mission and vision statements. They appear in annual reports, plans, and are posted on walls. Employees are often given pep talks about the mission and vision. Many times this falls on deaf ears. An average employee has a hard time grasping how their daily routine work relates to some fuzzy mission and vision statement. Management sometimes is frustrated because they do not see the mission and vision used. Work just seems to go without change. The challenge in this section is several-fold.

- You want to make the mission and vision relevant to IT and business processes, and especially projects.
- Aligning the business and IT requires that you relate the mission and vision to IT.

You will see how to achieve this so that, at a general level, IT and the business alignment or lack of alignment will be visible. In the steps and approaches that are presented, the emphasis is on doing this in a short time with collaborative effort.

At the general business level, there are many fuzzy words. People think of mission, vision, etc. differently. So it is necessary to have some definitions first.

- *Stakeholders.* These are internal and external entities that are interested or involved in the activities of the organization.
- *Vision.* The vision of an organization is where it wants to be in 3–5 years. The vision is where you want to go—not how to get there.
- *Mission.* The mission of an organization is how in general terms it will try to reach the vision.
- *Business objectives.* Business objectives are more specific goals that support the mission.
- *Business issues.* These are problems and opportunities that impede or impair the attainment of the business objectives and, hence, the mission, and the attainment of the vision.
- *Business strategy.* The business strategy is how you will attain the business objectives while handling the business issues.

Here is a vision statement extracted from a real organization.

XXX is a government agency that is committed to providing high-quality, personalized experience to the public that provides superior service that exceeds expectations. We provide streamlined delivery of information and services on a cost-effective basis. We support high morale among our employees. We enhance the working and home environment of our residents.

If you examine each sentence and phrase, you can extract the elements of the vision given in Fig. 2.8. Note that the company probably had not done this before. So you may find some strange entries and determine that there are gaps. This is a side benefit of defining your change management objectives—completeness and validation of business planning elements.

An alternative is to establish measurable vision elements. Here are some examples that relate to specific areas:

- Services provided:
  — Range of services provided at a future date versus current services,
  — Percentage of services provided that are personalized.

- High quality service
- Personalized service
- Streamlined service delivery
- Cost-effective operations
- High employee morale

Figure 2.8   Sample Vision Elements

- Performance/workload related:
  — Number of customers/calls/transactions handled per person per time period,
  — Number of customer complaints per person per time period,
  — Total volume of work/total number of employee hours,
  — Average time per customer call.
- Cost/revenue related:
  — Total revenue at a particular future date,
  — Total profitability at a future date,
  — Average cost per transaction for a time period,
  — Average revenue generated per customer prospect for a time period,
  — Average revenue generated per customer,
  — Percentage of operating costs in labor hours.
- Technology related:
  — Percentage of the work and transactions that are automated,
  — Percentage of work in a transaction that is manual for specific transactions.
- Customer related:
  — Customer/client/patient retention,
  — Average number of visits per patient per time period,
  — Level of customer satisfaction as revealed by surveys.
- Quality and biotechnology related:
  — Number of patents filed per unit time,
  — Number of drugs and new treatments per unit time.
- Employee related:
  — Turnover of employees per time period,
  — Total revenue divided by total number of employees,
  — Total costs divided by the total number of employees.

Now turn to the mission statement. Remember that the mission indicates how generally the vision will be attained.

XXX seeks to provide a full range of government services through both in-person service and automation based networks and systems. Service performance is actively measured and tracked along with extensive problem follow-up. Employee input and participation in service activities are valued and encouraged.

Doing the same with these sentences, you can develop the mission elements listed in Fig. 2.9.

- Full range of IT-supported services
- Measurement of customer satisfaction
- Employee participation

Figure 2.9   Sample Mission Elements

Next, you can make a list of critical business processes. Space does not allow us to make a complete list for Tucker County. Instead, the following three processes will be considered as examples.

- Birth and death records;
- Change of name;
- Voter rolls and registration.

Another list is that of major business units and departments. Here we will include only the recorder office, the elections office, and IT. In a real situation, like the business processes you will have many more.

Another element of business planning is that of business objectives. You often have to read annual reports or presentations made by upper management to glean the objectives. Here are several that will be used as an example.

- Increase investment in systems and technology to better serve the public;
- Reduce clerical workload and activity;
- Control cost of services.

But the business objectives and, hence, the vision and mission, cannot be achieved quickly or immediately due to business issues. Here are some relevant business issues.

- Employees have political power through their union organization.
- Some of the existing computer systems are quite old, impeding change.
- A past previous effort at modernization of processes failed.

With these issues, the problem is how to work toward the objectives. This is where business strategies come into play. Here are several business strategies:

- Implement new technology in departments that support change;
- Use established methods and technology;
- Involve employees in the work associated with change.

Here are some useful tables that you can create with the lists above.

- *Organization versus business processes.* The entry is the extent of involvement of the business unit in the process. This table tells you which organizations you will likely be dealing with for specific processes. See Fig. 2.10 for the example.
- *Business processes versus business issues.* The entry is the impact of the issue on the process. This and the next two help you to select which processes or activities to go after later either in terms of problems (issues) or goals (objectives and strategies). This is shown in Fig. 2.11.
- *Business processes versus business objectives.* The entry is the importance of the process to the objective. Fig. 2.12 contains an example.
- *Business processes versus business strategies.* The entry is the importance of the process to the strategy. See Fig. 2.13.

• *Business processes versus vision.* The entry is the role of the process in the mission. This is often the volume of work performed that carries out the vision. See Fig. 2.14.

• *Business processes versus stakeholders.* The entry is the value of business process to the specific stakeholder. See Fig. 2.15.

Where are you so far? You have taken the general business factors and applied them to more tangible things that can be related to by IT factors. In the chapter on IT planning later, the detailed steps will be provided. For now let's list some of the IT related tables that will be produced.

Organization	Processes		
	Birth/death	**Name change**	**Voting**
Recorder	Ownership	Ownership	—
Election	—	Indirect user	Ownership
IT	Support	Support	Support

Figure 2.10   Organization Versus Business Processes

Process	Business issues		
	Employee power	**Old systems**	**Previous failure**
Birth/death	Medium	Middle aged	No
Name change	Medium	Middle aged	No
Voting	Medium/high	Yes	High

Figure 2.11   Business Processes Versus Business Issues

Process	Business objectives		
	Systems/ Technology	**Reduce clerical**	**Cost control**
Birth/death	Suitable	Suitable	Moderate impact
Name change	Suitable	Suitable	Limited impact
Voting	May not fit	Limited effect	Little impact

Figure 2.12   Business Processes Versus Business Objectives

Process	Business strategies		
	New technology	**Established methods**	**Employee involvement**
Birth/death	Suitable	Suitable	Moderate
Name change	Suitable	Suitable	Moderate
Voting	Cannot justify much due to infrequent elections	Suitable	Good

Figure 2.13   Business Processes Versus Business Strategies

Process	Vision elements				
	High quality	**Personalized**	**Streamlined delivery**	**Cost-effective**	**Morale**
Birth/death	Possible	Yes	Possible	Yes	Yes
Name change	Possible	Yes	Possible	Yes	Yes
Voting	Difficult due to volume, peaks	No	Not suitable	No	No

Figure 2.14   Business Processes Versus Vision

Process	Stakeholders		
	Public	**Employees**	**Management**
Birth/death	Moderate	Moderate	Some
Name change	Moderate	Moderate	Some
Voting	Infrequent benefits	Limited no. of employees	Some

Figure 2.15   Business Processes Versus Stakeholders

- IT objectives versus processes;
- IT projects versus processes;
- IT issues versus processes;
- IT strategies versus processes.

The approach will be to relate these IT factors through the business processes to the mission, vision, and other business factors. This will then show in a tangible, direct way the alignment or misalignment of IT to the business.

BENEFITS OF EFFECTIVE IT GOVERNANCE

What can you expect when you establish the structure described above and begin to be more process focused?

- There will be an attitude change. As opposed to people feeling helpless and unable to effect change, they can now participate in the change and renewal of processes.
- Employees can see the relationship between the processes, the projects, IT, and the business mission, vision, and objectives.
- There is a more proactive and open approach to identify new opportunities for improvement.
- There will be a wider understanding and support of what changes mean and why they are important.

Perhaps, most importantly there will start to be cumulative improvement as collaboration increases. Templates, project plans, issues management, change management, and lessons learned related to both IT and the business improve over time.

Does this come overnight? Of course not. Experience reveals that a successful approach is to begin to make small changes and proceed in a parallel manner.

ALIGNMENT OF IT AND THE BUSINESS

In this chapter, you have begun to see how the general alignment analysis will work—through the business processes. This is the conceptual part of alignment. However, as you know, you can plan all day and nothing ever comes about.

The tangible part of carrying out alignment in this chapter has been through the structure and oversight of IT. The structure of steering committees and other factors supports the mission and vision analysis above.

MANAGE RISK

What are some potential problems and risks associated with the discussion in this chapter? One is that management does not see the need for change. The company may be doing well financially so that there is no pressure for change. Two important elements here are:

- Identify problems with the current method of IT management and governance.
- Develop the impacts both short- and long-term of the current methods.

Then you can use this to generate interest in improvement. The same applies to employees who do not see the need for improvement. Point out that while the current situation has worked before, it can be improved. Further, you want to show that if things continue as they are, there will be more problems later. Looking at firms like Enron, Worldcom, K-Mart, the dotcoms, and Parmalat you can see in hindsight that had the problems been addressed when they were first known, there would have been more actions to address and fix them, possibly heading off the disasters that followed.

EXAMPLES

SUPREME OIL

Supreme Oil was basking in the glow of higher oil prices and good profits. Management did not see a need for change. Then the government opened up bidding on oil tracts in the ocean. The company used traditional analysis to determine what to bid on and the prices for bidding. It was a total disaster. They underbid or failed to bid on good tracts. They paid too much for bad tracts. What was the cause of failure? They did not use modern systems and technology to support exploration and analysis. Competitors did. This was a real wakeup call to management.

Within two months after the failure, IT was restructured. Oversight and governance of IT was changed and given much more importance. Major new systems were employed. All of the critical processes were examined and a number of new projects initiated to improve the work. After one year, results started to bear fruit in other bidding. Supreme never went back to the old ways.

TUCKER COUNTY

Tucker County was given as an example in this chapter. There was a great deal of inertia that got in the way of improvement. The systems were antiquated, but management and employees just suffered along. IT oversight was minimal and a joke! Unlike Supreme Oil, there was no crisis to trigger change. We had to start small. The approach was to evaluate three critical processes to county operations. Using the performance measurements discussed below, many issues and problems were identified. The benefits of improvements and change became evident. There began to be more interest in systems and IT. Next, the IT projects were reviewed. Many were then cancelled. New projects were created using the mission and vision as well as process analysis presented above.

SHAMROCK AGRICULTURE

Shamrock Agriculture is geographically diverse with many small business units. Each was managed separately. Management at headquarters found that they could not obtain reliable information. Issues that were identified in the business were not addressed. So the first step was to assess the business processes and organization. Work did not begin with IT. After this analysis, it became clear that the only way to instill improvements that would be sustaining would be through automation and improved systems. Attention then moved to IT governance.

LESSONS LEARNED

- If you attempt to impose a structure for IT governance and management without generating support, then the change is likely to be short lived. Thus, a lesson learned is to ensure that there is widespread participation in doing and reviewing the analysis, tables, and lists that have been presented.
- It is tempting to implement all of the approach at one time or to implement changes in IT management top down. These methods have problems. They may

not yield short-term results and so are transitory. A better method is to start with some detailed work and gather support as you go. A major initial goal and Quick Hit is to get management and employees to understand that the way things are now has problems and that the negative impacts of the problems are substantial. Then people are more prepared to accept change. The performance measures below will help you get started.

PERFORMANCE MEASURES FOR IT OVERSIGHT AND GOVERNANCE

There are a number of performance measures that relate to this chapter. The first is to evaluate business processes. Figure 2.16 gives an evaluation table for scoring a business process. Not all of these elements will apply to your situation. You want to use this as a starting point. Note that some elements in the table point to problems and issues that you can then identify. Other elements are objective and just help to support future measurement. After all, you will want to use the same table on a regular basis later after you carry out change and projects.

Next, let's turn to the current IT governance. Figure 2.17 gives a list of questions that can be answered that will help you determine some of the problems and issues with the current IT oversight.

Another evaluation is to assess the current roles and responsibilities of IT, management, and business units. A list of questions is given in Fig. 2.18.

From the discussion of mission and vision you can take advantage of the questions in Fig. 2.19 to evaluate the state of the current mission, vision, and other business elements.

How do you use these tables? The first step is to take a table and select the elements that you feel are appropriate. Then you seek to have people review the lists. This begins to get people interested and involved. Next, you can create some sample tables as well as alternative answers to the questions. Seek feedback on these. Write down people's comments. This is a proven collaborative approach.

SUMMARY

In this chapter we have discussed oversight of IT, the importance of business processes, roles and responsibilities, and have begun to address alignment of IT and the business. This chapter provides a comprehensive view of the roadmap for IT governance. Why is the emphasis upon business processes? Because they are the basis of the business. People, organizations, systems, and technology come and go, but the processes go on. Unless you link IT governance to stable factors, you will find that the sands under IT governance will keep shifting.

Factor	Score	Comments
No. of people directly involved in process by department		
Total no. of people involved in process		
Turnover of employees by dept.		
Turnover of employees in process		
No. of workstations		
Facilities used by process		
Systems provided		
Total cost of IT for process		
Total cost of employees for process		
Total cost of process		
Volume of work performed		
Frequency of transactions		
No. of reported problems by type		
Average time to perform a transaction		
Mix of work performed		
Extent of rework		
% of work in exceptions		
% of work in workarounds		
% of work in shadow systems		
No. of exceptions		
No. of shadow systems		
No. of workarounds		
Quality and completeness of training		
Employees skills		
Quality and completeness of procedures		
Relevance of policies		
Extent of collaborative work in department		
Reliance on key people for the process		
Volume of work/employee		
IT cost/total cost		
Employee cost/total cost		
Volume of work/workstation		
Cost per transaction		
Revenue of process		
Profit of process		
No. of problems/volume		
Revenue per transaction		

Figure 2.16 Business Process Evaluation

- Are multiple managers involved in overseeing IT?
- Are people aware of what IT is working on?
- Is management aware of the allocation of IT resources to work?
- How are potential IT projects and work identified?
- What is the role of the business units in defining and selecting IT work?
- How are requests and problems handled by management?
- Is the oversight of IT consistent over time or does oversight change depending upon the style of the managers?

Figure 2.17   Evaluation of the Current IT Oversight and Governance

- Are multiple managers involved in overseeing IT?
- Are people aware of what IT is working on?
- Is management aware of the allocation of IT resources to work?
- How are potential IT projects and work identified?
- What is the role of the business units in defining and selecting IT work?
- How are requests and problems handled by management?
- Is the oversight of IT consistent over time or does oversight change depending upon the style of the managers?

Figure 2.18   Assessment of the Current Roles and Responsibilities Related to IT

- Is there a defined mission?
- Is there a defined vision?
- Have the mission or vision ever been updated after being created initially?
- Are either the mission or vision used in business or IT decisions?
- Has there been an effort to relate IT to the mission or vision?
- Have the mission or vision been related to the business processes?

Figure 2.19   Evaluation of the Mission and Vision of the Organization

On the other hand, if you provide stability, then you provide the framework for sustainable, effective, and low-effort IT governance. Keep in mind that managers and employees have to do many other things at work. So a key success factor in the approach is to minimize the extent of effort for implementation.

Chapter 3

Technology Assessment, Management, and Direction

INTRODUCTION

Given that this is a book about IT management, you would expect that a chapter dealing with technology would emphasize the benefits of the technology and how it can solve many business problems. And, yes there are many benefits of the technology. After all, technology makes the process improvement and change management possible. However, there is also tremendous waste and misdirection of effort due to technology. Thus, it is important to take a balanced view of new and existing technology.

Let's first turn to the life cycle of technology. Most new technology is generated based on discovery and research as opposed to solving specific business problems. In essence, much of technology (including that not pertaining to computers and automation) is a solution looking for problems. Nothing wrong with that as long as you take a pragmatic and realistic view. In order to be useful, technology often has to fit in with what already is on the market and in use. This puts attention on interfaces. Suppose, for example, that someone invents a new telephone model that can perform many functions such as video, camera, PDA, etc. Each of these functions has to interface with what people have on their existing PCs. Otherwise, you either have to invent even more technology or you find that there is no market for the technology. This is called backward compatibility. Backward compatibility is essential, but it is also a limitation because it places constraints on the extent of new features. Consider 32-bit computers. Basically, they are all backward compatible with the instruction set of the Intel 80386 computer chip that was designed in 1979. This limits the power and capability of the newer 32-bit computers. Initial 64-bit computers have to also be backward compatible to run all of the existing 32-bit software.

When new technology arrives on the market, companies and individuals have to make decisions about it. Some key questions that are sometimes not asked when they should be are:

• *Benefits.* What are the benefits of the new technology to my business activities? Will standard business processes benefit and be changed by the technology?

• *Replacement and stability.* Is the new technology likely to be replaced soon by still better technology?

• *Interfaces.* How will the technology interface to the systems and technology already in place? What will be the integration effort?

• *Long-term support.* What are the long-term support implications of the technology?

• *Management.* How will the new technology be managed, measured, and controlled?

These questions are sometimes not answered. In the 1980s people plunged into buying standalone PCs. Many of these ended up giving little value except for novelty and entertainment.

When new technology is adopted, there is a learning curve. This learning curve can be broken down into phases. This is shown in Fig. 3.1. The phases are:

• *Initial learning.* Here a person gains some understanding and basic knowledge of the technology product. They really cannot do much with it yet.

• *Proficiency.* You start to explore and use the technology. You think about how it can be used in a business setting.

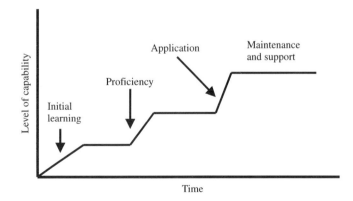

Figure 3.1   Technology Learning Curve

• *Application*. You decide that the technology is worth pursuing further and you consider developing applications and using it in a business activity.

• *Maintenance and support*. The learning has basically stopped and you are now forced to maintain it.

Between the initial learning and proficiency, and between proficiency and application, there are pauses where you essentially get tired and saturated of learning and stop for awhile. Many people acquire some technology and stop after initial learning. Some may have become satisfied with what they have in terms of capabilities. Others may have given up. Notice that the slopes are steeper as you go since you are trying to learn and perform more complex things with the technology.

In terms of mistakes, people tend to make most mistakes in the initial period. As an example, many automobile accidents occur in the first 60 days of driving a new car. That is when you are getting used to the handling, steering, controls, braking, etc., of the vehicle. This is probably a contributing factor to accidents with rental cars since the renter is using the car for the first time on strange roads.

Look at a simple device like a VCR. Many people purchased them and then used them for a few movies. Then they lost interest. Evidence of this is the fact that many VCRs have time clocks that blink 12:00 constantly. The time was never set and you couldn't do time recording from the television. If you look around people's offices and homes, you find quite a few devices—PDAs where it was too much trouble entering the names and addresses, digital cameras where the instructions and manipulation were too complex, kitchen devices that were seldom used, etc.

Whose fault is this? Why did it happen? You could blame the person who bought it. You could blame the manufacturer for making the technology harder to use than is necessary. They may have added a number of marginal features that you don't and will never use. It is estimated that most people use only about 10–15% of the capabilities of word processing and spreadsheet software. But this misses the major point—which is that you must be cautious in selecting new technology.

The life cycle cost elements of technology are substantial and often underestimated. Some of the major costs are listed in Fig. 3.2. Let's consider the maintenance and support effort. After you have installed and built an application using the technology, you begin to realize that the fun is just beginning. Vendors bring out new versions of the technology, new releases of the software, etc. You have to evaluate these and determine if it is worth the cost and effort to migrate to the new version or issue. Many new versions have bugs or problems that have to be ironed out and fixed through service packs and patches. The hopeful, optimistic view is that each new release brings new, useful features. Not always so! When adding some new features, some old features may be deleted. As an example, we use an old version of a calendaring software tool because it is the last version that gives year-at-a-glance. The software is now 6 years old and runs fine.

- *Cost of evaluation and selection.* You have to consider alternative solutions and technologies. You may have to draft reports and presentations to sell the technology. You have to spend time figuring out how the new technology will fit it with what you have and the benefits that will be derived
- *Cost of acquisition and purchasing.* The item that you want may require many additional pieces of hardware, software, or network components
- *Retrofitting the current technology cost.* You may have to change the current technology and upgrade it in order to use the new technology
- *Installation cost.* You have to spend time and money installing it or having someone install it for you
- *Training cost.* There may be initial training and in-depth training
- *Setup cost.* After installation, you often have to setup the new technology in terms of parameters, etc.
- *Application cost.* You incur major costs when you now build an application using the technology
- *Process change cost.* You have to change the business activity to take advantage of the new application
- *Expertise cost.* You may need to hire someone to consult as an expert on the technology since you are learning it for the first time
- *Support and maintenance cost*

Figure 3.2   Cost Elements Associated with Technology Adoption

Technology becomes obsolescent for a variety of reasons. If the vendor does not issue new releases or versions of a product, the product will not meet current and new business needs. Another reason is that nature of the business and, hence, the requirements of the business can change. This occurred with the rise of servers and will happen again with 64-bit computing. A third reason for obsolescence is internal. IT staff who are critical to the old technology may retire or die, leaving no one who has the requisite knowledge. In the agricultural business, this occurred in a mill that makes animal feeds. The person who maintained the production of pellets for the food retired and later died, making maintenance impossible. Had the equipment broken down, the mill would have been out of business since it would not have been able to make pellets. Analysis of current technology pointed this major problem out and helped impel management to seek new software.

What are the lessons learned from this discussion? Here are three.

You have to carefully evaluate any technology before making a commitment.
You have to commit to several stages of learning and work in order to reap major benefits from the technology.
People tend to underestimate the cost and effort in maintaining and supporting technology.

There is another basic lesson learned. That is, there is a cumulative support and maintenance burden to the technology. Over time, you acquire technology, but keep the old technology because it is still needed. You create over time a structure of technology that will be labeled the *technology architecture*.

So should you get depressed and be deterred from new technology? No. You just need to be realistic and pragmatic.

TEN MYTHS ABOUT TECHNOLOGY

Over the years a number of myths have emerged about technology that should be examined.

- **Myth Number 1: New technology solves business problems.**

Unfortunately, many people believe this—leading to excessive and false expectations. Technology is just a tool to help you improve a business process. Most of the time the political, managerial, and organizational factors are as or more important to solving the business problem.

- **Myth Number 2: New technology is always better than what it replaces.**

This is sometimes true, but you cannot assume it to be true. Many assume it to be true. Some new technologies can make things worse. Examples are new car models with major design flaws that cause the cars to turn over, explode, or have high maintenance.

- **Myth Number 3: The pain in a new technology is in learning it.**

There generally is more pain in applying the new technology to get real business benefit. This is where most of the effort lies.

- **Myth Number 4: New technology tends to replace the current technology.**

This does happen. But often, the new technology augments the existing technology. For example, when you buy a DVD player, you do not automatically discard the VCR player.

- **Myth Number 5: New technology is less expensive than the current technology.**

Not necessarily so. The new technology may be more complex to work with and build applications. It may have many more features that require more learning time and effort. Support costs may be higher.

- **Myth Number 6: Technical IT people love new technology.**

Some do. Many are like you and me. They feel comfortable with the technology that they have and are using. They have become proficient in it. Therefore, it is not surprising that technical people may resist learning new technology. Examples are COBOL programmers who do not feel comfortable learning Java or Active Server Pages.

- **Myth Number 7: Most new technology delivers benefits.**

Benefits, and we mean tangible benefits, accrue only when you develop applications for the technology and change the business activity to take advantage of the new technology. These are major points. That is often why many IT groups do not automatically upgrade to new release of office type software.

- **Myth Number 8: It is good to be an early adapter of new technology.**

In some cases where the benefits are obvious and risks are small, this is true. Most of the time it is not. At the early stages of a new technology, there is limited experience with the technology. There are few lessons learned. There may be bugs and problems with the technology. It is better to let others be pioneers. One of our fathers bought one of the early VW buses. It was very unique. People stopped us on the street, wanted to get inside it. It was a major problem getting parts for the thing. It was a nightmare experience.

- **Myth Number 9: With new technology, support requirements are less than that required for the existing technology.**

This may or may not be true. You cannot assume this until you have direct experience or have gathered the experience of others. The complexity of the new technology may actually increase support costs.

- **Myth Number 10: New technology is more complex.**

This is one of the negative views that some have. In some cases, new technology is easier to work with and use. When new technology adds capabilities, it does not necessarily add to complexity.

STEPS IN TECHNOLOGY MANAGEMENT

You need an organized approach for managing technology. If you don't use it or have it, you can run into problems. One problem is that people may purchase new technology in their department without planning. This can result in political battles, drain valuable support resources, and increase the costs of IT. Another problem is that there is no general view or vision of what systems and technology are in use. This can lead to more confusion.

From experience here are some steps to successfully manage technology.

• Assess the technology that you have. It is important to review what you have and eliminate or identify technology that can be replaced or eliminated.

• Identify and track new technology. Politically, you want to be on top and knowledgeable about key technologies that can affect your business.

• Develop a framework for implementing and supporting new technology. An organized approach will require less resources and be more efficient.

• Implement the new technology.

ASSESS YOUR CURRENT TECHNOLOGY

You first want to identify the systems and technology along with the versions that you are using. Figure 3.3 presents an overall table for this. In this table the type indicates whether it is hardware, software, or network based. The next two columns indicate the component along with the version number. The fourth column allows you to identify any problems that are known with respect to support or operation. Typical problems might be the extent of failures, time to repair, effort to repair, etc. Impacts of the issues and problems are given in the fifth column. These should focus on business impacts. The last column is for comments. One comment could be whether there are newer versions of the software.

This table is politically useful since it allows you to participate among both IT staff and business managers. By employing a collaborative approach you can start identifying issues and problems with the current technology from the people who are actually involved in either using or supporting the systems.

When you are creating this table, make sure that you include the support software and tools that are employed. For example, don't just list a database management system. Also include the supporting software.

The next action is to create an overall architecture diagram of the systems and technology. This shows management and employees how the systems and components interrelate and are interdependent. You can use this diagram to list issues as well. Figure 3.4 gives an example of this for a small IT group. Note that this

Type	System	Version	Problems	Impacts	Comments

Figure 3.3 Table for Current Systems and Technology

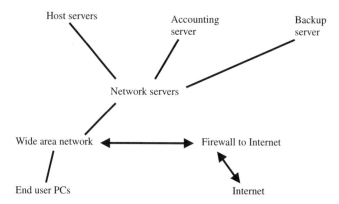

Figure 3.4   Example of an IT Architecture Diagram

diagram is not totally complete. The political purposes of an architecture diagram are:

• To be able to show people where there are issues and problems and discuss their impacts.
• To show where potential new technology would fit into the overall architecture.
• To help indicate to business managers the structure and complexity of the current technology and systems.

This last point is important because many managers do not realize the complexity of support. In several organizations where we have developed the table and figure, the results were dramatic. There was general support for changing and replacing some of the obsolete technology. Remember that for all of the concerns about new technology expressed earlier, there is still a need to replace technology.

You do not do this one time. It is useful to update the table and figure on an annual basis. Go back and revisit issues, problems, and impacts to see if actions taken in the past year improved the situation. Alternatively, some impacts could have increased and the problems become more pronounced.

IDENTIFY AND TRACK NEW TECHNOLOGY

There is far too much technology to track. Moreover, the technology that is potentially useful depends upon the specific industry and business of the organization. From experience, we recommend that you make a list of 10 technologies to watch. Here are some examples.

• 64-Bit computing;
• RFID (radio frequency identification);

- database management systems;
- ERP (Enterprise Resource Planning) systems;
- new handheld devices (cameras, PCs, etc.);
- XML development tools;
- software development tools for your environment;
- network management tools for your communications.

How do you go about identifying the potential technologies for you? Look at some of the articles on the websites that are listed in the appendix. They give articles from vendors as well as IT professionals on trends and specific new technologies.

For each technology, you will want to list the following elements:

- specific vendors and products;
- existing technology that could be replaced or augmented;
- potential business benefit to the department operations;
- trigger factors that would cause you to seriously evaluate and select the technology.

The last bullet item deserves some discussion. A trigger factor is what would get you to become serious about the technology. This gets to the question, "When is a new technology ready for you to adopt?" Here are some answers.

- When there are firms similar to yours who have gotten benefit from the technology.
- When there is a body of knowledge on how to implement and support the technology.
- When there are demonstrated benefits from the technology.
- When the implementation and application effort appear to be reasonable.
- When there are resources in time, money, and people to implement the technology.

As you can see, new technology has to overcome a number of barriers and jump hurdles before you will really adopt it.

What if someone in management or at headquarters imposes a new technology? For example, suppose headquarters imposes a new ERP system. Yet, the trigger factors are not present. What do you do? The best approach is to use trade-offs. You do not want to be cast as a person who is negative on change. This could be fatal to your career. Yet, you do not want to back the new technology wholeheartedly. A moderate, middle-of-the-road approach is to employ trade-offs. Identify what will have to be given up if the technology is adopted. Point out to business managers what the impact and benefit will be to them if the new technology is implemented. Your attitude toward the new technology should be positive neutral. That is, you can see the benefits for the new technology, but you also can see the costs and effort required for implementation, use, and support.

SELECT THE NEW TECHNOLOGY

Some critical success factors for technology selection are listed in Fig. 3.5. Let's make some comments on these questions. In the strategic IT plan objectives, strategies, and action items are identified. New technology should hopefully support these as well as helping to resolve existing IT and business issues. If there is a disruption to the plan and the new technology is inconsistent with the plan, there the entire plan is put into jeopardy. Of course, this may be a good thing if you have a faulty plan.

The second question addresses the pain of not going ahead. This should be considered together with the question on real benefits. New technology is sometimes selected on defensive grounds. That is, all of the major players in your industry are adopting it, so you should too.

The questions of technology implementation on resources, maintenance, and architecture address the implications of the technology on the IT organization. If the IT organization is in the middle of a major implementation, then there are no resources available to proceed now even if there are no benefits. The alternative would be to outsource the effort. We will discuss more later in the chapter on outsourcing.

The ripple effect of new technology can be a major pain. If one manager gets a PDA, then many others will want it as a status symbol. The same is true with PCs. This question helps you to think about the longer-term implications on the managers and employees.

DEVELOP A FRAMEWORK FOR TECHNOLOGY IMPLEMENTATION AND SUPPORT

Once you have selected or have had a technology selected for you, you want to have an organized approach for implementation and support. From experience,

- Does the new technology help achieve the objectives in the strategic IT plan (discussed in the Chapter 4)?
- What will happen if the new technology is not implemented now?
- What impact will new technology implementation have on existing IT and business resources?
- What will the real, tangible benefits to the business be?
- What is the impact of the new technology on the IT architecture?
- What are the long-term support and maintenance implications for the new technology?
- Is there a ripple effect from bringing in the new technology? Will everyone want one?

Figure 3.5   Critical Factors in New Technology Selection

you should begin with operations after the new technology has been implemented. What will the new technology do to the architecture? A reasonable approach is to develop new versions of the table in Fig. 3.3 and the diagram in Fig. 3.4. Then you can see a comparison between where you are now and where you will potentially end up. This allows you to see the benefits of employing the new technology.

The next action is to consider technically what the new technology will have to interface and integrate with. From an IT view this is where the major technical issues will likely be. Can you do this if you have not even purchased the technology? Well, you can ask current customers who have implemented the technology. You can also discuss implementation with the vendor.

From a business view you should address how the business processes will be changed when the new technology is implemented. You can use the same sources as in the previous paragraph. Should not this wait for implementation? No, do it now in planning. You should take a sample transaction in the process. Write down the way the work is done now. Then write down, with the collaboration of business staff, how the transaction would be performed after implementation.

Another action in the framework is to identify specific business and technical questions and issues that will likely occur with implementation and later support. Here is a list to get you started.

- What technical staff would be involved in the implementation of the new technology?
- What will happen with their current work?
- How would process change be handled in the business department?
- What other support software and tools are needed to implement and support the new technology?
- What existing technology will be eliminated, have to be upgraded, or changed?
- How will you determine the success of the implementation effort and the success of the new technology overall?

If you have this framework handy and create checklists for the framework, it will not only make your life easier; it will also provide a means for management, IT staff, and business employees to better and more effectively participate in the planning.

IMPLEMENT THE NEW TECHNOLOGY

Implementing new technology is specific to the situation and the technology. However, some general guidelines are useful. Identify and keep track of unresolved issues and problems involving the technology. If you have a problem that goes unresolved for some time, then there could be potential failure later.

Another guideline is that you work with the business unit on change issues related to the business process with the new technology. If you detect strong resistance, then you might want to question the implementation. In fact, you might want to put it on hold for later when there is a more conducive business environment.

Develop a modular project plan that pulls out all tasks related to integration and interfaces as a separate subproject. This will give these activities more attention. After all, this is a major area of risk.

CRITICAL SUCCESS FACTORS FOR TECHNOLOGY MANAGEMENT

Here are some factors that should be part of your management of technology.

• Bundle business change as well as changes to current architecture with the new technology. Otherwise, the old technology may live longer than needed—raising the support cost. Also, business change is real justification for most new technology so it should always be at the forefront of your thinking.

• Focus on integration and interfaces. These are the most difficult technical issues because the old technology never envisioned the old. Moreover, people who developed the new technology probably did not think about the existing technology in detail.

• Be selective on what new technology to go ahead with. Yes, you want to implement new technology where it has benefit, but there are many choices as well as many ways to proceed with the implementation.

• Seek to eliminate existing technology where you can. Remember here that the existing technology usually extracts a high cost in support.

• Keep in mind that new technology and its selection are often political. Some managers seek to increase their power and/or influence through the technology selection process.

Overall, you should take a minimalist view. The less different technologies you have to install, implement, and support, the more time and resources are available to implement business change and improve support.

ALIGNMENT OF IT AND THE BUSINESS

IT and the business are aligned in the end through business processes and systems. Systems are technology and depend upon technology. Several tables are useful here to assess how effective your alignment is. Figure 3.6 is a table for existing systems and business processes. Here the rows are the major existing systems and the columns are the critical business processes. In the table you can list the problems and limitations of the existing systems on the performance of the specific business process.

Figure 3.7 consists of a table of existing systems and business issues. Business issues were identified and discussed in Chapter 2. The rows are the existing systems while the columns are business issues. The table entry is the impact of the existing system on business issue. It tells you how the problems in the existing systems contribute to the individual business issues.

Taken together these two figures and tables can help you determine where new technology would be useful. You can now get down to more detail by using the table in Fig. 3.8. Here the rows are some of major components of technology. The table entry is the impact of the problems with the technology on the process. An example might be network performance.

There are two additional tables involving new technology. The first in Fig. 3.9 gives the impact of new technology on the existing systems. Using this table and that of Fig. 3.6, you can develop the table in Fig. 3.10 which gives the impact of the new technology on the business processes.

Processes

Systems			

Figure 3.6   Existing Systems and Business Processes

Business issues

Systems			

Figure 3.7   Existing Systems and Business Issues

Processes

Technology components			

Figure 3.8   Selected Technology Components and Business Processes

Existing systems

Potential new technologies			

Figure 3.9   Potential New Technologies and Existing Systems

	Processes		
Potential new technologies			

Figure 3.10   Potential New Technologies and Business Processes

MANAGE RISK

One major risk is that new technologies may be imposed upon you. This may be out of perceived value on the part of some upper-level manager. This can be a disruptive surprise. How do you head this off or at least mitigate the effects? First, you want to indicate to the management that you are positive neutral about new technology. This will put you in a better position to deal with requests or demands. Second, you should point out where the problems and limitations with the current systems and technology are. The tables in the preceding section should be useful here.

Another risk is that you sincerely believe in the benefits of a new technology. You and IT staff members devote considerable time looking at and evaluating the technology. You gradually are becoming more committed to the technology, even if subconsciously. This is a major issue since you are getting ahead of the business and what they are willing to accept. In general, users and business managers will not readily accept new technology unless they perceive, on their own, that there are substantial benefits. Shoving it down their throats will not work—even with upper-management support.

A third risk is in operations, support, and maintenance. Here many people just tend to accept things as they are. They maintain the status quo of the technology. The burden of the technology increases. The flexibility and ability to respond to business needs are diminished. To address this you want to examine critically the existing technology on a regular basis.

EXAMPLES

SUPREME OIL

Supreme was not known for its technology innovation. They were followers. Then a major new idea was conceived—change the gasoline stations into convenience stores to sell more goods beyond petroleum products. This was a major change in IT. It was also a major shift in business thinking. The costs and benefits were obvious, but there was just too much change. In addition, there was no halfway measure. You either implemented the convenience store concept or you did not. Two separate projects were initiated. One was to deal with the business culture to accept the change. The second was to revamp the IT group to implement point-of-sale-related systems. This was a major new initiative. The existing IT staff did not have any experience in this area. The solution was a separate, new IT group to focus on retail sales. The approach was so successful that the profits from non-petroleum sales exceed that of gasoline and related products. Today, the retail concept has been spun off so that there are retail stores that do not sell gasoline.

TUCKER COUNTY

Tucker County IT management and business management were locked in traditional technology. As they received more business pressure from departments, it became clear that technology modernization was needed. Without planning, they plunged into implementing several new systems. The technology network architecture was kept intact. The results were a disaster. All three systems efforts failed. Rather than fall back on traditional IT, a planning effort was begun along the lines of this chapter and the previous one. As a result, the technology infrastructure was modernized first. There was only pain for users, but this was essential if there were to be new systems. The new systems were then installed next along with changed processes.

SHAMROCK AGRICULTURE

As you recall, Shamrock had a small IT group. There was little extra resources for new technology. However, there were a number of pressing business needs and issues that could only be addressed by new technology. What to do? A mixed strategy was adopted. For the new ERP system, consultants were employed. The rule was that the business processes and rules had to be simplified to minimize system customization. Several other new technologies were delayed due to lack of real need. The internal IT staff became focused on critical processes related to retailing. The mill software that was maintained by the existing IT staff was getting old. Here, like the ERP, a package software system was acquired and installed. The installation was managed by the internal IT staff while the work was performed on an outsourcing basis. The overall strategy was a mix of internal and external resources where critical business processes were supported internally.

LESSONS LEARNED

• Each new technology is often viewed as unique. Yet, you can gather many useful facts and experiences from different technology implementations. It is recommended that an effort be made to gather lessons learned from both implementation and support.

• Within business departments there are individuals who are very interested in new technology. IT groups often view these people with disdain or mistrust. To IT they create more problems and issues by surfacing new technology. The attitude should be different. These people can be useful allies in evaluating and selecting new technology. They can also help in getting business support for change. You should get them involved in the development of the tables in this chapter.

PERFORMANCE MEASURES FOR TECHNOLOGY MANAGEMENT

One set of performance measures relates to how you use and evaluate technology now. Figure 3.11 gives a list of factors for how you manage current technology. Most of these questions are self-explanatory. Technology issues should be tracked and kept in a database. Lessons learned from the current architecture need to be gathered. The impact of obsolete systems and old technologies should be measured, not just accepted as is.

Factors for evaluating and selecting new technology are listed in Fig. 3.12. The source of new technology initiatives is important. These should come from a combination of IT and business units involved in the work, as opposed to upper management. After all, that is where the need and benefit are. In terms of benefits, you have to consider the tangible business benefits as well as the support costs and benefits. Assignment of IT resources should be organized along with the decision to use outsourcing.

- Do you have an up-to-date architecture diagram?
- Do you have a list of technology and systems issues?
- Are systems and technology mapped against business issues and processes?
- Is the effort in supporting technology measured down to the individual technology level?
- Do you have a regular review of existing technologies and their shortcomings?
- Do you gather and use lessons learned from technology experience?
- Is there a regular effort to eliminate or replace obsolete technologies?
- What is the business role in technology evaluation and selection?
- At what point does process change enter in the selection of new technologies?
- Is management kept informed about technology issues?

Figure 3.11   Performance Measures for Existing Technology

- How are new technologies introduced into your organization—reactively or proactively?
- Is there a formal process for evaluating and selecting new technologies?
- Do you have an organized approach for watching specific technologies?
- How does management learn about potential new technologies?
- Is there a structured framework for technology implementation?
- Are the real benefits of new technologies measured?
- How are IT resources selected for work on new technology implementation?
- Is there an organized approach for dealing with new technology issues?
- Are interfaces and integration treated as important subprojects in technology implementation?
- Are lessons learned gathered from new technology implementation?
- Are missed technology opportunities reviewed?

Figure 3.12   New Technology Performance Measures

SUMMARY

Technology is at the heart of IT. Much of the IT management literature focuses on implementation management. With managers realizing the importance of systems and technology, technology selection and implementation have become more political. The entry of politics into technology evaluation and selection has always been present, but it has become more pervasive and important. The analysis tables in this chapter are aimed at helping you deal with the politics around the technology.

It is often assumed that IT managers are or should be proactive in technology selection. Yet, it is in fact the reverse that is true. Left to our own devices, we would prefer to make the current architecture work better as opposed to throwing more new technology on top of the architecture. Key words here are simplification and selectivity.

Chapter 4

Develop Your Strategic IT Plan

INTRODUCTION

In Chapter 2 you began some of the first steps in IT planning. There a series of tables and relationships were developed between business processes and business objectives, vision, strategy, and issues. The importance of relating IT to the business through business processes was also presented as a major successful method of not only building the IT strategic plan, but also the alignment between IT and the business.

Why create a strategic IT plan? Many organizations have developed plans that then sit on the shelf and are never used. So why go through the effort? There are several reasons, including:

- Without a strategic plan, IT is subject to external forces and technologies that can create disruption in the work.
- In the absence of a plan, management may begin to question the direction of IT. Then IT appears to management like a group just working on various projects without focus.
- A critical element today in IT is the successful alignment of IT with the business. It is very difficult to do without having a strategic IT plan.
- IT tends to be more reactive without a plan. That is, it tends to just respond to the next problem that arises.
- A strategic IT plan provides a vehicle for management and business units to understand IT and be more supportive of IT initiatives.
- It is difficult to gain support for infrastructure improvements since you have to show overall longer term impact. To get these approved without the plan, you would have to do a similar amount of planning.

In this chapter, we will build a strategic IT plan and then go through the work of developing a project slate. A *project slate* is a collection of projects and work to be done in the next period. The project slate is the roadmap for resource allocation of IT resources and emphasis.

There have been many efforts and methods for developing the strategic IT plan. Many of these fail and have problems. Some of the reasons behind the failure are the following.

• The planning process involves a great deal of specialized planning jargon and terminology. This makes the process more difficult to understand. In addition, it requires more training of people to be involved effectively in the planning process.

• The planning process takes too long and involves too many resources. We assume, in this book, that there are no additional resources available. You have to plan with what you have.

• The planning methods and techniques require specialized consultants to guide and do the work. This has several drawbacks. First, there is less ownership by IT after the plan has been developed. Second, it creates a dependence for IT upon outside help. This is not a good idea given the importance of IT planning.

• After the planning effort has been carried out one time, the effort to create updated plans rivals that of the initial planning effort. This is excessive given the limited resources and time available.

The planning method presented here has been employed successfully in over 60 organizations in 40 different industries and 20 countries. It has been used by IT groups ranging from less than 10 people to over 400 people. There is no jargon—only common sense.

Listed are some of the key ingredients of the planning process presented here.

• The IT plan is developed in a collaborative way with participation from IT staff and managers, general managers, and business units. In this way you will have more understanding, support, and ownership.

• The core of the plan rests on lists and tables. These can be easily maintained and updated.

• The planning process can be carried out without major full-time involvement. This limits the resource burden.

• There is no jargon. The method is common sense. There is no need for any extensive training.

• The plans results in detailed actions and projects. It does not end with fuzzy objectives and strategies.

How often should the strategic IT plan be developed? Most organizations do this once a year. This is in line with the business plan. However, there are many dynamic factors affecting IT. These include:

• New technology opportunities that appear.
• Management initiates a new direction and generates new projects.

- Specific business units make requests of resources.
- Projects are completed or are terminated, thereby releasing resources.

If you do the planning on an annual basis, then the above factors will disrupt and often destroy the plan. You will then find at the end of the year that many action items of the plan were not implemented.

From experience, it is recommended that the plan be updated more frequently. At least twice a year and preferably quarterly. This gives you more opportunity to handle changes and more dynamic factors that come along.

In planning, you should take a low key approach. Don't overpromise. This is likely to happen as some managers may think that because something is in the plan, it will automatically be carried out and implemented. Not giving it too much attention also takes some of the politics out of the planning process as well.

The planning process follows a series of steps. However, these steps can be initiated in parallel to reduce the overall time.

- Measure IT today. This step provides performance score cards for IT.
- Review the existing business plans and see where the business is going.
- Develop the initial version of the strategic IT plan.
- Get feedback and refine the plan.
- Map the plan down to key business units.

Wait, the work is not done. You have a plan with specific action items. However, you have no resources. Even the best action items from a plan have to compete for resources with current work, projects, and other items. There is competition. Thus, there is another part of the planning process—resource allocation. Unless you proactively allocate IT resources, very little will probably be done with the planning action items.

MEASURE CURRENT IT

Before you start developing the plan itself, you want to see how IT is doing. By doing performance measurement, you can identify potential areas of improvement. Through a collaborative approach, IT managers and staff can see why change is needed and some of the areas for change. After all, the purpose of the plan is to effect change and improvement in IT and systems and technology application. Return to Fig. 1.5. This gives a performance score card for IT. These elements provide a useful guide for existing problems and shortcomings.

Another action to take is to assess your current IT architecture. Here Figs 3.5–3.8 can be employed. These map the systems into the processes as well as business factors. They can assist you in determining which systems are causing the most negative impacts on the business processes. Additionally, they can aid in determining the technology gaps and holes as well as technology issues.

A different action is to review past plans generated within IT. Here you are looking for action items. Then you can assess what happened to these after the plan was approved. You can also review the existing planning process.

REVIEW THE EXISTING BUSINESS PLANS AND BUSINESS DIRECTION

The tables and figures in Chapter 2 are useful here. These provide specific mappings between business processes on the one hand and vision, mission, objectives, and issues on the other. Now this seems like a lot of work. However, if you look carefully at the tables in Chapter 2, you find that these will not change much over time. Indeed, the mission and vision are not likely to change. The processes remain the same. The business issues may need to be updated.

DEVELOP THE INITIAL IT STRATEGIC PLAN

Let's begin by making some definitions. These are the planning elements for which you will construct lists and then tables for the strategic IT plan.

• *Issues and opportunities.* These are items that should be addressed by the strategic IT plan. Issues are IT-related problems. Opportunities are potential new initiatives that can be undertaken. Figure 4.1 gives some examples of issues and opportunities.

• *Objectives.* These are long-term goals for IT. They cannot be satisfied or achieved in a 1-year period. Objectives provide direction for IT. Examples are given in Fig. 4.2.

• Many legacy systems require too much support and are too difficult to change
• Client-server systems offer opportunities, but require substantial learning curve
• What should we do—intranet or client-server?
• Should we employ object oriented tools and methods or continue to use languages such as COBOL?
• What is the systems role vis-à-vis reengineering?
• Should we acquire packages?

Figure 4.1   Sample IT Issues and Opportunities

• Focus systems resources on supporting only critical business processes
• Provide a full range of systems services to business units
• Support integrated access to company information and databases

Figure 4.2   Sample IT Objectives

• *Constraints.* Constraints are limitations on IT, its work, and resources. Unlike issues and opportunities, you cannot change constraints. They have to be accepted as is. Some common constraints appear in Fig. 4.3.

• *Strategies.* Strategies are general actions that can be taken to support the objectives. A strategy is more than an action item or specific thing that you can do. It is an umbrella for a number of action items. Figure 4.4 contains some examples of strategies.

• *Action items.* These are specific steps that can be taken in support of the strategies. Action items can include:

— policy changes,
— organization change,
— procedures and training,
— IT project ideas.

Note that action items are more than project ideas. Examples are given in Fig. 4.5.

Note there is a multi–multi relationship between these elements. That is, one strategy may support multiple objectives. One objective may require more than one strategy.

You put these together and show how they relate. This is done in Fig. 4.6. Here the heavy solid arrows indicate the objectives going around the constraints to address the issues and opportunities. The dashed lines represent the strategies. The dotted lines are for the action items.

- Technology gaps
- Limited funding
- Current staff lack modern skills
- Difficulty in getting new staff
- Current organization

Figure 4.3 Sample IT Constraints

- Implement wide area network
- Acquire or build new client-server systems to support certain key business processes
- Carry out all new development with reengineering

Figure 4.4 Sample IT Strategies

- Implement a steering committee approach for all systems projects
- Insist on tangible benefits for all funded projects
- Implement a prototype client-server system for department X
- Support limited Internet access within the organization
- Develop an intranet application first

Figure 4.5 Sample IT Action Items

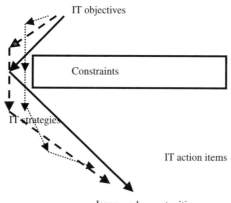

Figure 4.6   Diagram of IT Planning Elements

In general, there are usually many issues and opportunities. Not all will be addressed in the plan. There are typically only a few objectives since they are general. There are more strategies and even more action items.

It is useful to define objectives in specific categories. Experience has shown that the following list is valuable here. This will provide you with coverage to ensure completeness.

- Staffing in IT;
- IT architecture;
- Hardware;
- Network;
- External network;
- Business processes;
- Methods and tools;
- Software packages;
- Application software;
- User role.

There are also categories for action items. Here is a list drawn from past work.

- Application software;
- System software;
- Network management, operating, and utilities software;
- Wide area/local area networks;
- Extranet/intranet/Internet;
- Hardware and operating systems;
- Systems staff;
- Consultants and outsourcing;

- Controls;
- Measurement;
- Policies;
- User and management roles.

Having laid out the planning elements, let's discuss how to do the planning. You do not want to place an undue burden on people who have many other things to do. Thus, it makes sense to make lists of the planning elements. This is better than a blank piece of paper. Managers tend to respond better to examples. Show people the lists and get their feedback. Take note of their comments. If new items come up, you should ask yourself why you did not think of these yourself before. Answering this will help your future planning effort.

After obtaining feedback on the lists, you can now prepare sample planning tables. There are two sets of these. In Fig. 4.7 appears a list of the planning tables that relate to IT. Some comments on these are helpful.

- If you look at the number of combinations possible, there are ten potential tables. However, the ones listed here have proven to be the most useful.
- The table of IT objectives versus issues and opportunities reveals the extent to which the objectives handle the issues.
- However, just because there are complete objectives, this does not mean that the issues will be addressed. For this, you want to show and discuss the table of action items versus issues and opportunities.
- There is a chain of relationships linking IT objectives, IT strategies, and action items. This chain is supported by the two tables, IT objectives versus IT strategies and IT strategies versus action items.
- To show the impact of real life constraints, the table of IT objectives versus constraints can be employed.
- Management is often not interested in detailed actions, many of which may be technical. Thus, you want to use the table of IT strategies versus issues and opportunities to indicate that the IT objectives are supported.

The next step is to take the business factors discussed in Chapter 2 (business processes, business issues, business vision, business objectives, and business strategies) and relate these to the IT planning factors given above. You can now build the tables below based upon the business processes. These tables are very

- IT objectives versus IT strategies
- IT objectives versus constraints
- IT strategies versus action items
- IT objectives versus issues and opportunities
- Action items versus issues and opportunities
- IT objectives versus action items

Figure 4.7 IT-Related Planning Tables

important because they are the basis for the alignment of IT with the business. Here are some additional comments.

• IT issues and opportunities versus business processes. This table reveals the importance and effect of the issues and opportunities on business process performance.

• IT action items versus business processes. This table indicates the direct impact of completing the action items on the business work.

• IT objectives versus business processes. This table shows how reaching the IT objectives will benefit specific business processes.

What are the entries in the tables? It is a good idea to stick with something simple. We have found a rating of high, medium, and low to usually be sufficient. You can add comments at the bottom of the table to explain how some of the ratings were derived.

Now you have a collection of tables that relate IT planning elements to the business processes. These can now be combined with the business tables through what is equivalent to matrix multiplication and produce the tables in Fig. 4.8. For example, if a business objective is highly dependent on a specific business process and if that process is benefited by achieving an individual IT objective, then the relationship between the business objective and the IT objective is high. Comments in the figure indicate how the tables can be employed.

These tables are really the tangible evidence that IT and the strategic IT plan are aligned to the business. In a presentation or review, you would start with these end product tables. Then you could zoom down to the detail of two tables that involve the business processes on one hand and the business and IT factor on the other. This supports the basic facts that:

Business vision and objectives while fuzzy relate to the business processes.
The business processes are the heart of whether or not the
business is a success.
IT strategic planning elements can be related to the business processes.
Business planning elements are linked to IT planning elements
through the business processes.

There must be some words of caution here. IT action items and objectives, even if totally and instantly achieved successfully, will not likely solve the entire business issue or enable the company to reach its vision. You have to be more modest in what IT work can really achieve.

When you have finished these, you will then present them to management and key staff for review. Again, you will incorporate their comments. You might want to present the table without any entries. Then you can ask people to vote according to the criteria listed above.

At this point, you have developed the planning lists and a series of tables that relate business and IT factors. You are prepared now to draft the

- IT objectives versus business vision. This table is important to show the *high level alignment* of IT to the business
- IT objectives versus business objectives. Here there is a side-by-side *linkage* of objectives
- IT strategies versus business strategies. This table indicates the *support* of the IT strategic plan to the major initiatives of the business
- IT issues and opportunities versus business issues. This table reveals the *relevance* of the IT issues to the business
- IT action items versus business issues. Here the benefit of the completed actions is given in terms of helping to *solve* the business issues
- IT action items versus business objectives or strategies. These two tables can indicate how the action items provide some *fulfillment* of the business strategies and objectives

Figure 4.8   Business and IT Planning Tables

Executive Summary
1. Introduction
   - Why the plan and planning process are needed
   - How the plan is to be used
   - Approach employed to collect data
2. Issues and opportunities
   - Challenges faced in competition and industry
   - Internal issues
   - Business opportunities
   - Technology opportunities
3. Objectives
   - Objectives and constraints
   - How objectives meet issues
4. Strategies
   - Individual strategies
   - How the strategies support the objectives
5. Action items and project candidates
   - Action items and their impact and benefit
   - Strategies and action items
   - How the action items are related and interdependent
   - Action items versus issues and opportunities
6. Recommendations for action
   - Specific steps to be taken next
   - How these steps support the plan
   - Benefits from actions
7. Planning tables

Figure 4.9   Outline of the Strategic IT Plan Document

strategic IT planning document. Figure 4.9 gives a sample outline of the document.

The strategic IT planning document and any presentation should be simple to review by management since it is based upon the same lists and tables. You can see that the planning lists and tables are also easy to update later.

- Failure to link the plan to the real world
- Ignore how action items tie together
- Get too focused on one specific area
- Take too general a view
- Become overattentive to technology and not enough to business
- Allow one of the assessments to gain too much importance
- Fail to do marketing of the plan as you go
- Rely too much on formal presentations
- Insufficient communications with lower level people involved in business process
- Over reliance on consultants—loss of control
- Over reliance on exotic methods
- Unwillingness to adopt the scope and method to the business situation
- Over focus on formal presentations—focus on informal reviews
- Overfocus on formal approvals of plan—keep things low key
- Failure to link current activities to the plan
- Giving too much credit to the plan—the plan is only the result of logical thinking
- Changing the plan due to some new technology—the plan loses stability
- Failure to follow up after plan approval—this is a key cause of failure
- Failure to consider how action items will be funded
- Failure to address how resources will be diverted in organized way
- Overdependence on one person for planning
- Failure to align business department plans to their own planning process
- Over reliance on a planning tool or database
- Insufficient outside information
- Too much outside information
- Failure to make available information gained during the planning process

Figure 4.10   Potential Problems in IT Planning

In creating the plan, you may run into problems. A list of these has been given in Fig. 4.10. Note that some are very unlikely to occur. Nevertheless, these were included since they have been encountered in the past.

RELATE THE STRATEGIC IT PLAN TO THE BUSINESS UNITS

You have a strategic IT plan and have related it to the business. Are you finished? Not quite. You should move the strategic IT plan down to several key business units. Of course, there is insufficient time and resources to do this for all business units. So you have to select some of the most important business units. To help you select these, return to the table in Chapter 2 of the business units versus business processes. Based on the most critical business processes, you can then identify the related business units that support these processes.

You can begin with developing department objectives and issues related to the business processes. Here you can produce the following two tables in collaboration with the business unit.

- Business unit objectives versus business processes.
- Business unit issues versus business processes.

Next, you can use the planning tables that you have already developed to generate the following additional tables.

- Business unit issues versus issues and opportunities. This table can be used to reveal how the IT issues and opportunities contribute to the business unit issues.
- Business unit issues versus action items. This table shows the impact and benefit of the completed action items on the problems and issues of the business unit.
- Business unit objectives versus IT objectives. This gives alignment of IT to the business unit.
- Business unit objectives versus action items. This indicates the contribution of completing the action items on the business unit objectives.

Why would they want to participate in this effort? First, it is in their self-interest. Some of the action items will help their processes and should then benefit them. Second, this gives them an opportunity to have a role in the development of the plan. If possible, the plan should not be produced in final form until several of these business unit automation plans are developed.

If you have time and there is interest, you can create a small business unit automation plan. This plan has the following key elements.

- Discussion of involvement of the business unit in the processes.
- Business unit issues and their impact on process performance.
- Business unit objectives as they relate to the business processes.
- IT objectives mapped down and related to the business processes.
- IT action items mapped down to the business processes.
- Planning tables that have been listed above.

Politically, going this extra step can be very valuable in getting the plan approved. It will be difficult for higher level managers to dismiss some of the plan if the major business units are supportive of the plan and can envision the benefits of having the action items completed.

IT PLANNING GUIDELINES

There are a number of guidelines that will help you in using this planning approach.

- Develop a strawman plan as you go. This is a growing draft of the plan. It is very useful in case you have to show the results of the planning effort so far.

- If you find an action item that has benefit and can be implemented right away, then don't wait until the plan is completed.
- Build a list of issues, objectives, etc., as you go.
- Adopt software to support the tables. You can use a simple database or spreadsheet.
- Start small by defining lists from your own knowledge and experience.
- Start to market the benefits of the plan at the same time that you alert management to the infrastructure investment. This is critical since management will be expecting the results and will not be surprised.
- Keep addressing the dilemma that infrastructure investment is required before payoff from the technology, if this is an issue.
- Develop alternative approaches—keep things as they are; maximize the technology; stretch out the technology investment. Use this in your definition and development of objectives and strategies.
- Show how the infrastructure is interdependent on business processes.
- Show how the other systems activities (beyond the plan) must tie to the plan. You can do this by relating action items to current work.
- Determine what systems personnel resources are needed and which projects and work will be impacted by redirection. This will be useful later in resource allocation.
- As you define action items, begin to sketch out their overall schedule and cost.
- Start to build a scenario of how the business will be better if the plan results are achieved. When faced with skepticism, do not overpromise—indicate why the plan is needed.
- Keep the planning team and effort small.
- Create an implementation approach as you go.
- Be able to defend action items and how they link together in a mesh. Think about creating scenarios:
  - What will be the situation if there is no basic change for 2–3 years?
  - What would happen if money and resources were not issues?
  - Your plan is the middle ground.
- Allow managers to deal with politics.
- Align yourself with a group of managers—not one single manager.
- Press for getting more time if that is necessary—money is not the issue in developing the plan.
- Try to have some elements of the plan implemented prior to plan presentation.
- Be aware of sources of resistance:
  - Systems staff and managers who resist new technology;
  - Business units who fear loss of resources;
  - Business units who fear that their technology will not be included in the architecture;
  - People who want short-term benefits.

GET THE IT STRATEGIC PLAN AND ACTION ITEMS APPROVED

• *A major upgrade or replacement to the network.* If the current network is running fine, then most managers would not be supportive of this action item. You have to justify it by emphasizing the problems that will occur in the business if the network is not modernized.

• *Major new software.* While the current software system has problems, it is still perceived to be adequate. Here you would point out how the software is failing and then you would look at the business impact.

• *Process change or overhaul.* This can be very political. People wonder why this is an IT project. They might think that it should be a business one. As such, it does not belong in the plan.

Whether the action item is one of these or something else, experience shows that one of the best ways to sell the action item informally is based on fear of what happens if the action item is not undertaken. Why is this so? Because people have heard about IT benefits for years and then they see that they never materialize. People can better understand the negative impacts of what will happen if the action item is not undertaken.

Action items do not exist in isolation. Typically, there are multiple action items to support and implement an IT strategy. For example, modernization of a network may mean that there are four action items: (1) additions to staff; (2) the network modernization itself; (3) changes in facilities to support the network; (4) additional hardware upgrades. One of the worse things that can happen is that two or three out of four get approved, but the remainder do not. Big problem! To prevent this from happening, you should bundle the action items around the strategy.

Now that you have marketed the plan to some of the business units, you are prepared to do the same informal marketing to upper management. The marketing approach changes for this audience. You will be approaching individual managers with the plan. The two salient elements of the strategic IT plan are the alignment with the business vision and objectives, and the impact and benefit of the action items. Here, as opposed to the negative impacts of not carrying out the action items, you will focus on the positive benefits. Odds are in your favor since most business units, managers, and staff have long forgotten the vision and objectives. Management is typically very much aware of these because they spent a great deal of time and substantial amounts of money in developing and marketing these across the corporation. When they see that they are being involved in the strategic IT plan, they will tend to be more supportive.

Obviously, after all of this informal work, you are ready for formal presentations. You want to make as few formal presentations as possible. Each formal presentation creates risk for the approval of the plan since a manager can use the meeting as a forum to attack IT on some specific issue that may have nothing to do with the plan.

Should you present the strategic IT plan in an academic manner? That is, you would go through the planning process followed by the detailed elements. This will likely be too boring and ineffective. First, ask yourself what you want to achieve. Do you want to get the plan approved? That would be too easy.

The real goal of the presentation of the strategic IT plan is to get approval of the action items.

For without their approval, the plan will sit on the shelf and go nowhere. This goal is far more ambitious, but essential if you are to move ahead and implement the plan. Many people want to stop with the approval of the plan because that is easier.

• *Summary of business and IT issues and opportunities.* This gets attention and also puts the focus on the problems that have to be solved.

• *Business processes and issues.* This brings the issues down to tangible effects on the real work. This should get more attention.

• *IT strategies and business processes.* Here you are presenting the strategies and their impacts on the processes in terms of solving the problems and addressing the issues.

• *Alignment of IT with the business.* In this part of the presentation, you will present the relationship of IT objectives to the mission, vision, and business objectives.

• *Action items.* Here you will list the action items under each IT strategy. This links the action items to the strategies presented earlier in the presentation.

• *Scenario or model of how the processes will work when the action items are successfully completed.* This closes the loop and shows how the problems and issues that started the presentation are addressed.

RESOURCE MANAGEMENT AND ALLOCATION

Most planning books and articles end here. After all, you have the plan approved. Unfortunately, in the real world, you are not finished. Even with endorsement of the plan, there are no resources for the work in the action items. In reality, the action items now have to compete with existing work and other demands. This is a major challenge to IT and to the business. Business managers do not have the time to understand all of the current work. Thus, it falls upon IT to come up with an organized approach to allocate resources in a common sense, organized, and structured approach.

Let's begin with the competing demands for resources that are faced by the action items. These include the following:

• *Current projects.* These have not only been approved, but are underway.

- *Backlog of work.* Probably many of these items have been in the backlog for a long time.
- *Operations and support.* There is a wide range of activities that are included. Many of these are essential if the systems are even to function.
- *Maintenance and enhancement.* This includes fixes to software, improvements to performance, new reports, additional data elements, new interfaces, etc.
- *Emergency fixes and problem solving.* These are not easy to control and take selected key resources away from other work.
- *Targets of opportunity.* These things appear sometimes from nowhere. They might be triggered by a management idea. Difficult to predict.

There are formidable competitors to the action items. They are more pressing and immediate. In some IT groups, the mix of work prior to the plan is similar to:

- Current projects—30%
- Operations and support—35%
- Maintenance and enhancement—20%
- Emergency fixes and problem solving—10%
- Targets of opportunity—5%

Of these, the weakest competitor is targets of opportunity. These are items that have not been invented. Yet, they are competition because when they arise due to management desires, they are assigned a high priority. If you have a plan in place and the plan is updated quarterly, then you can push for these items to be put through the planning process. However, that would only give you 5%. The backlog of work can become a part of the planning process as well.

Current projects and emergency fixes are very difficult to effect unless there is some specific problem in a project, or if the action items in the plan will reduce the extent of emergency fixes. Thus, the next place to look for resources is in operations and support, and maintenance and enhancement. Experience has shown that this is often a fertile ground to make reductions. Many maintenance and enhancement requests are often things that are nice to have and not essential.

The basic lesson learned here is that since there will not be any new IT resources,

The resources for the action items in the plan have to come out of current work. Targets of opportunity, maintenance and enhancement, and operations and support are the best areas in which to make some reductions.

A tactical approach is to start addressing the resource allocation issue before the strategic IT plan is approved. You want to identify potential areas of change and reduction ahead of the approval of the plan.

Note that even if everything goes well, there will not be a "sea change" in the resource allocation. Experience shows that a reasonable reallocation will result in something like the following.

- Action items from the strategic IT plan—at most 10%
- Current projects—30%
- Operations and support—30%
- Maintenance and enhancement–15–20%
- Emergency fixes and problem solving—10%
- Targets of opportunity—0%

This does not seem like much. However, you must realize that like the federal budget, much of the IT budget tends to be committed in advance. There is not much room for movement.

UPDATE YOUR IT STRATEGIC PLAN

Now let's suppose that the plan has been approved and work on the action items begun. Three months later, you want to update the plan. Here are some steps to take.

- Review the status of the action items that were started. Are they likely to deliver the benefits that were promised in the plan?
- Review the issues and opportunities to determine which have been handled already, which will be addressed by the action items, and which are still unresolved.
- Briefly revisit the business elements of the plan as discussed in Chapter 2 to see if there is anything new. Key items to consider are the business issues.
- Update the lists generated in the planning process. Create the planning tables as was performed in the development of the original plan.
- Add new targets of opportunity and additional issues as identified.
- Conduct informal reviews with line managers and within IT.

At this point, you have developed the updated lists and tables for the plan. You have gotten feedback and reaction, and made some changes and revisions. So you should be ready to present to management, right? Almost. You want to gather some more evidence of the benefits and impacts of the completed action items. It would be useful to get one or two line managers or employees to give some anecdotes or examples of how their world has changed.

When you make a presentation to the management, you want to first list the action items from the previous planning effort. Then you will want to give some of the evidence of the benefits. This will not only make management feel better, but get them to be more supportive of the next version of the plan. The remainder of the presentation can follow that of the original plan except that the alignment part can probably be shortened.

Experience indicates that once an accepted strategic IT planning process is in place, there will be less concern or arguments about how IT is aligned to the business.

In short, the strategic IT plan updates help to reinforce the alignment of IT and the business.

ALIGNMENT OF IT AND THE BUSINESS

The major approach in this chapter has been to develop tables that relate business and IT factors through the business processes. This not only makes sense due to the importance of the business processes, but it also gives you a more stable plan. Technology can change along with organizations, but the underlying business processes will remain because they are part of the nature of the business.

To summarize, there are some key planning tables that help with alignment of IT to the business. These are:

- IT objectives versus business processes.
- Action items versus business processes.
- Business objectives versus business processes.
- Business issues versus business processes.
- Business objectives versus IT objectives.
- Business objectives versus IT strategies.

MANAGE RISK

There are some specific risks that you must be aware of in undertaking a planning effort. Some of these are listed below.

- Not developing the plan as you go. If you wait until the end to put the plan together, then you will be unprepared if management wants to see results. Many managers are not comfortable with planning; they like action. If they are not familiar with IT, then this raises more concerns.
- Failure to identify action items beyond project ideas. You have to consider the range of steps that are required to support a strategy. That is why policies and procedures were mentioned, for example.
- Lack of attention to resource allocation and competition for the action items. Many planning efforts were successful in developing the plan, but failures in delivering results through the action items. You have to garner

support for the review of the resources and the proactive approach to reallocate some resources toward the action items.

• Stopping with approval of the plan, but not initiation of the action items. We take a very pragmatic approach. The planning effort is not worth it if nothing changes. Thus, as much or more attention to the approval and start of the action items is needed as that of plan approval.

EXAMPLES

SUPREME OIL

Supreme Oil employed a very ponderous IT planning method that had many steps and contained much jargon. It took a day for a new person to learn and become knowledgeable in the terminology. The method was put in place by a vendor who had since disappeared. The result was that no one paid attention to the plan. It was presented to management and promptly ignored. There were no action items.

As a result, new project ideas were surfaced and everything was approved individually. Chaos reigned. Things finally changed when management saw the importance of IT. Then a more common sense approach was used—resembling the method in this chapter. The IT management resisted the method so it fell on business unit managers to develop the plan. In the end the plan worked and actions items finally began to flow from the planning process.

TUCKER COUNTY

Tucker County had tried twice to develop an IT strategic plan. Each time the resources were pulled off of the effort due to other pressing needs. The manager of the largest division decided on his own that he and his organization needed the plan. So they contracted for the development of the plan as well as the action items. These were approved by management based upon the plan. IT was plainly embarrassed for they had no plan. The planning method that was used in the business unit was then applied to IT with success.

SHAMROCK AGRICULTURE

Shamrock, as you recall, had a very small IT group. There were no resources to be dedicated to the planning effort. A shortcut method was needed. Using the approach in the chapter, sample lists and tables were created from past planning efforts at other organizations. These were then employed as checklists by managers at Shamrock to develop the plan. Not a very elegant approach, but it was effective.

LESSONS LEARNED

• Avoid generating a massive planning report. It is likely that very few people will read it. Concentrate instead on the lists and tables and then the presentation. Try to create the planning document as an enlargement from the presentations.

• Look over the literature, websites, and planning documents and start making lists of the planning elements that have been presented in this chapter. Do this at the very beginning of the planning effort. Experience has shown that this can save a great deal of time and help you to be more complete.

• Even though this is an IT strategic plan, make sure that there is little or no technical jargon or buzzwords in the tables, documents, or presentations. These will just turn people off. When you are discussing the plan with IT, then you can create a table in which the left-hand column lists the business terminology and the right-hand column the more technical words.

PERFORMANCE MEASURES FOR IT PLANNING

There are two parts to measuring IT planning. The first focuses on the planning process (Fig. 4.11). This figure consists of a series of questions to help you evaluate your current IT planning process and method.

The second measure is to assess the plan itself. Figure 4.12 gives a list of factors and questions to consider in assessing the value and effectiveness of your IT strategic plan.

• How long has the planning process been in place?
• Have there been any efforts to assess its effectiveness or improve the planning process? This should be ongoing.
• How many different IT managers and staff are involved in the planning process? The more that are involved, the better.
• How many business unit managers and senior staff are involved in the planning process? The same comment as the preceding item applies here.
• What is the elapsed time needed to develop the IT plan? If this consumes more than an 6–8 elapsed weeks, then it is taking too long.
• Is the planning method formal or informal?
• Does the planning method rely on specialized planning terminology?
• Is the planning process applied to develop automation plans for business units?
• Is alignment of IT to the business addressed through the planning process?
• What is the level of upper level management participation in the planning process?
• When new IT opportunities surface, are they considered as part of the planning process?
• How often is the strategic IT plan updated?

Figure 4.11 Evaluating Current IT Planning Process and Method

- Is the plan developed in a collaborative mode or by a few people for review?
- Does the plan contain specific action items?
- Do the action items go beyond project ideas and include policies and procedures?
- How many of the action items in the plan are approved?
- How many of the action items are funded?
- How many of the action items are provided with resources?
- Is there a proactive resource allocation process?
- How often is the plan referred to by management and IT management?
- What happens to project ideas that violate or are not included in the plan?
- Is there a formal review method to determine what the benefits were to the action items?
- What happens to the action items that were not approved?

Figure 4.12   Performance Measures for the Strategic IT Plan

SUMMARY

The actual IT work and results are the most important part of the alignment of the IT to the business. However, it is critical that management understands and agrees with the direction of IT and the projects and work that are undertaken. Unless you have developed an IT strategic plan similar to the approach in this chapter, you risk having management not being understanding or supportive of IT.

The basic purpose of the strategic IT plan is to: (1) develop the direction of IT for the future; (2) show how IT work is aligned to the business; (3) identify and justify specific actions that will support the business mission, vision, and processes.

Critical success factors in the planning process include:

- A common sense approach without jargon.
- Collaboration to gain consensus and support for the plan.
- An incremental approach where first lists and then planning tables are constructed.

Part II

Manage the People and the Work

.

Chapter 5

Manage Risk and the Project Portfolio

INTRODUCTION

In traditional project management, a user request comes in for work. If the work is substantial, if the funds and resources are available, and if there is support from the business for the project, then a project leader is identified to create a project plan. After some time, the plan is approved, a project team is formed, and work begins. It all seems so straightforward and standard. Yet, read between the lines and you can see why many IT projects are doomed to fail from the start and why others never achieve their expectations or goals.

Even with the high incidence of failure, people continue to use the same tired methods. Why? They are following standard project management. This fits for construction and other activities, but it fails often for IT projects. Why is this so? Because IT projects are different. Figure 5.1 gives four comparison areas. Let's examine each.

Area	Standard	IT
Focus	Single projects	Multiple projects
Resources	Dedicated to single projects	Shared among projects and regular work
Issues	Mostly technical	Management, process, political as well as technical
Project success	Completion on-time and within budget	Get process improvement to justify the project; completion on-time and within budget

Figure 5.1 Differences between Standard and IT Projects

• What is success in an IT project? In traditional projects such as construction, the benefits are self-evident. If you finish a bridge, people drive on it. This is not true with IT projects. You can finish a project under budget and ahead of schedule and yet find that people do not use the project end product. There are no benefits. Even though technically the project is a success, it is really a failure. Success in IT projects occurs after the system has been installed, the process has been changed to take advantage of the system, the old process has been destroyed, and the benefits of the new process have been measured. Therefore, the main criterion for success for an IT project is change and the resulting benefits. The secondary criteria for success are to finish the work on-time and within budget.

• The focus on standard projects is on a single project. In IT, people are shared between multiple projects and nonproject work. Often, a project needs a programmer or analyst for their knowledge of specific systems. Yet, this same knowledge is required to maintain the current system. The person's time will then be split between maintenance, support, and the new project. The overall focus in IT is on multiple projects and resource allocation among the projects and regular work.

• Issues and problems are mostly viewed as technical in standard project management. However, as we have seen, IT projects tend to change processes and realign the roles, responsibilities, and power of individuals within and between departments. Thus, it is not surprising that political, business, and management issues often tend to dominate IT projects. The methods and approaches for issues of these types are very different from that of technical issues.

WHERE AND HOW IT PROJECTS ORIGINATE

In many IT groups, IT waits until they receive a request from a business department. IT then works with the users to study the request and determine the appropriate action. This could range from doing nothing to implementing a new system. There are problems here—right at the start.

By waiting for user requests, IT is placed in a reactive mode. Opportunities are missed. Resources are wasted on marginal projects.

There are several things that have to be addressed here so that IT is not like a village fire department—waiting for the next fire. The first is to proactively seek out opportunities. The second is to change the approach to examine project opportunities that can be user requests. Let's examine each of these in sequence.

We begin with the results of the previous part of the book where we addressed alignment of IT and the business. There we looked at business and IT objectives, issues, and other factors. We discussed alignment in terms of business processes.

To implement what we did before, we begin with business objectives, issues, and processes. We assume that we have identified and reviewed lists for each of these.

Two tables can be prepared. The first is shown in Fig. 5.2 and consists of business objectives as rows and processes as columns. Now note that we are not including all processes. There are too many. You should restrict attention to processes that cross multiple departments or are viewed as critical to management. The table entry is the importance of the process to achieving the business objective. This is the positive side of the analysis in that you are focusing on processes that will help achieve strategic objectives. Work on these processes tends to be on a larger scale and over a longer time period.

The second table is given in Fig. 5.3 and consists of rows being business issues or problems or challenges. The columns are the same processes. The entry is the extent to which changing the process will help resolve the business issue. This is the negative side of the analysis—directing attention to processes that need work to address problems. These tend to be short and intermediate term efforts.

In both tables you see a small example from Shamrock Agriculture. There are three processes—sales, order processing, and general ledger. There are two objectives that are common to many firms relating to revenue and costs. There are issues related to the number and severity of customer complaints as well as timely financial data. In the example, the process that stands out for work is the sales process. Order processing is next and the general ledger is third.

This analysis so far helps to identify critical processes. You would develop these tables as you did those in the previous part of the book—through collaboration with management and employees. The next step is to write down the

Processes			
Objectives	**Sales**	**Order processing**	**General ledger**
Increase sales	Sales process is cumbersome; sales take too long	Little or no impact	No impact
Cut costs	Efficiency could reduce staff time	Supplier transactions are awkward and time consuming	No impact

Figure 5.2   Table of Business Objectives Versus Processes

Processes			
Issues	**Sales**	**Order processing**	**General ledger**
Customer complaints about service	Sales process is awkward	No impact	No impact
Timely financial data is needed	Contributes to financial data	Little impact	Much of general ledger work is manual

Figure 5.3   Table of Business Issues Versus Processes

IT projects

Processes	Implement new POS	New HR reports	E-Business with selected suppliers
Sales	Critical	No impact	Little impact
Order processing	Little impact	No impact	Critical
General ledger	No impact	No impact	No impact

Figure 5.4   Table of Processes Versus IT Projects

IT projects that are underway. You should include all projects of at least 1 month in duration. You can now create a new table of processes as rows and projects as columns. The entry is the effect of the specific project on the individual process. An example for Shamrock Agriculture is given in Fig. 5.4. There are three project ideas. One is to implement a new point-of-sale (POS) system and process. The second is to generate new human resource reports. The third is to implement E-Business with suppliers. The first and the third are critical to the processes. The second one, dealing with human resource reports, can be dropped. Ah, but can it? Remember that this book deals in the real political world where influence, power, and similar factors count for a lot. Experience has shown that this table can be used as a weapon with the Human Resource management to defer their request.

There are now two candidates for projects left—POS and E-Business. From the tables of business objectives versus processes and business issues versus processes, it is clear that POS is the winner among the new project ideas.

Now let's turn to the examination of any project opportunity. Traditionally, this is the user request form. We drop this phrase since it is reactive. In most user request forms, the items in Fig. 5.5 are provided to IT. IT then performs analysis with the user departments and adds this to the information in the request. In reviewing the items in Fig. 5.5, you can see that there are problems. First, the business people may not have the technical or overall business knowledge to define a solution. It can be argued that this should be the responsibility of IT with the business departments. Second, many of the items are subjective with no backup or explanation. Two examples are benefits and urgency or priority. This may be what one manager thinks without any backup.

The traditional user request form often has the following problems:

• Many items are subjective and are not backed up or explained.
• There is nothing to prevent frivolous or marginal requests from being submitted. After all, none of the items in Fig. 5.5 discuss the user role.
• There is no impact statement to indicate what will happen if the request cannot be satisfied.

Let's now consider a more modern and comprehensive opportunity form that deals with these and other political issues. Look at Fig. 5.6 and compare it with Fig. 5.5. Here are some of the differences.

- Date of request
- Requestor and department
- Title of request
- Purpose of request
- Description of current problem
- Discussion of solution
- Benefits to the solution
- Urgency and priority for work

Figure 5.5   List of Common Items in a User Request Form

- Date form completed
- Person and department completing form
- Title
- Purpose of the proposed work—business not technical
- Description of the current problem
- Impact to the department if the problem is not addressed
- Impact to the department if the solution to the problem is deferred
- Benefits of a solution to the business
- How the benefits will be verified and validated
- Roles and responsibilities that the generating department will play in the work if it is approved

Figure 5.6   List of Items in an Opportunity Form

- Purpose of the proposed work—this is business focused. There should be no technical purpose since that is part of the solution, not the problem.
- Description of the current problem—same.
- Impact to the department if the problem is not addressed. This and the next item address the urgency and priority of the work. The department must explain what they will do if there is no project. Will things just continue? Or, will things deteriorate?
- Impact to the department if the solution to the problem is deferred.
- Benefits of a solution to the business—same.
- How the benefits will be verified and validated. This is new and forces the department to indicate how they intend to make the benefits tangible and measurable.
- Roles and responsibilities that the generating department will play in the work if it is approved. The purpose of this item is to get the departments to commit to having a major role in the implementation of a solution. The department cannot be observers, but must be players. They must have "skin in the game."

ASSESS CURRENT PROJECTS

Given the problems with traditional IT projects, where do we start? Let's begin by analyzing the current IT projects. What are some of the potential issues and problems with the current projects? A list of potential problem areas appears in Fig. 5.7. Here are some comments on each of these.

• *Budget status.* Not only can you see what the current budget versus actual is, but also what expenditures lie ahead.

• *Schedule status.* This is the planned versus actual schedule. Here you want to get behind why there is slippage. You can see what unplanned work has been done and is planned.

• *Number and type of outstanding issues or problems.* This is key to understanding what is going on in a project. The mix of internally versus externally focused issues is important since the external issues tend to be much harder to resolve.

• *Available staffing for the project.* This looks at the demands for the time of the people on the team.

• *Validity of business need.* This is a test to see if the business situation, the organization, and department management are the same and still warrant the project. After all, you could be doing a project well, but the need for the work could have evaporated.

• *Technology change.* There could be new technology that has become available that makes the current technology used in the project obsolete. Alternatively, the new technology being used in the project is causing major problems.

Use the items in Fig. 5.7 as a checklist for all current projects. You can also use the items to create a new table—the format of which is shown in Fig. 5.8. Here

  • Budget status
  • Schedule status
  • Number and type of outstanding issues or problems
  • Available staffing for the project
  • Validity of business need
  • Technology change

Figure 5.7   Potential Problem Areas with Current Projects

	Current Projects			
Item				
Budget status				
Schedule status				
Number and type of outstanding issues or problems				
Available staffing for the project				
Validity of business need				
Technology change				

Figure 5.8   Table of Rating of Current Projects

the rows are the items in Fig. 5.7 and the columns are the projects. The table entry is a comment or a score (1–5, with 5 high) as to the rating of the individual project on the item.

You will use this evaluation in the next step where we consider project evaluation and selection.

PROJECT EVALUATION AND SELECTION

Sit back and review what you have so far. First, you have considered and evaluated on a preliminary basis new project ideas. You have also evaluated the current projects. Now you want to use the results of these to generate a project slate—a set of approved projects that can be worked on until they are completed or until the next project review occurs.

How often should you go through the project selection process? In many organizations, this is carried out on an annual basis. Experience shows that this is too long. There are also several specific problems, including:

- allocating resources on an annual basis tends to tie up resources for too long.
- people on the project teams may not feel under pressure to perform since the project was approved for the year.
- management and others may have new project ideas that deserve attention. These often will not wait until the next annual review. So they will be reviewed and those that are approved will proceed to rip off resources from the current projects—crippling and maiming these efforts.

As an alternative, it is recommended that projects be reviewed on a quarterly basis. This puts pressure on the teams to get results so that their projects can continue. It also supports more dynamic allocation of resources.

Given that frequency of selection has been reviewed, we can turn to the approach for selection. Traditionally, the following guidelines are used.

- Management may subjectively approve projects with little input. People are afraid to question management out of fear of losing their jobs. They, after all, will have the opportunity to sabotage the projects later when the projects do not have management attention (remember, this is a political as well as a management book).
- Return on investment (ROI) or internal rate of return. This is common and management can say that only projects that meet a specific numerical target will be approved. It sounds good on the surface. Look underneath and you find a can of worms. Who comes up with the estimates? Who has time to validate the numbers? Most importantly, in a survey that we did with over 400 firms, less than 10% validate the numbers after the completion of the project. Without validation, the numbers are a game.

• Cost versus benefits. The same comments for ROI and internal rate of return apply here.

Here is an improved approach that has proven to yield better results in many organizations. First, you want to get an overall view of the projects, both current and potential. The first step is to develop the table in Fig. 5.9 in which the rows are the processes and the columns are the better current and potential projects after the weeding out evaluation described above. The table entry is an "X" if the project gives benefit and supports the specific process. Otherwise, the entry is blank. For example, a network project to improve system performance will likely have many benefits. A project that supports only a few people in one department may have no X. You will develop this table in a collaborative way.

Here are the analysis steps to take with the table.

• Look at the current projects that have no Xs or only one or two Xs. These are candidates for elimination and cancellation.

• Look at the new potential projects that have a number of Xs. These are likely to be good candidates for work.

So are you done? No! You need to consider other criteria, including the impact of not doing the project or canceling the project, resource availability, the tangible benefits, support of business objectives, handling of business issues, and project risk. You can approach this by first creating these more detailed analysis tables.

• *Resources versus projects table*. The rows are resources and the columns are the projects. You place an "X" if the resource is needed by that project. This shows competing demands for resources.

• *Impacts versus projects table*. Here you would identify a series of potential impacts on the business if the project does not go ahead or is stopped. These might include: inability to handle certain business, increased costs, etc. These are rows. Columns are the projects. The entry is a rating (high, medium, low) in terms of the impact of project being stopped or not started.

• *Benefits versus projects table*. The areas of benefits might be revenue enhancement, cost savings, improved customer service, and others are the rows. The entry is a rating of high, medium, or low.

• *Business objectives versus projects table*. This table is the rating of how completing the project will affect the attainment of the business objective.

Current and potential projects

Processes			

Figure 5.9   Table of Processes Versus Projects

Current and potential projects

Evaluation area			
Support of major processes			
Importance to business issues			
Importance to business objectives			
Tangible benefits			
Potential project issues			
Impacts if not done			
Resources			

Figure 5.10   Summary Evaluation Table of Projects

• *Business issues versus projects table.* This table is the rating of how completing the project will help resolve the business issue.

• *Project risk areas versus projects table.* Risk areas include technical, management, cultural, team, project work, methods and tools, business departments, etc. The entry is an assessment based upon experience as to whether the project, if done, will be afflicted in a severe way by the type of issues.

Now that you have the six alternative ratings in different tables, you can now combine and summarize it all into one table. The layout appears in Fig. 5.10. Now managers and others can perform trade-offs to see what is most important.

How do you go about this work? Follow our approach from the previous part of the book. You will be employing a collaborative approach where you provide people with lists and then tables for review. You will then use the feedback to refine the tables and lists. Through this process, managers and key employees will buy into the analysis. This gives them a sense of ownership of the work. Otherwise, if you hand it to people completed, they will likely disown and be more critical of it.

Note that having done this one time, you make successive project reviews much easier. First, you can establish databases for past evaluations to show departments and employees how to go about their own analysis. This will help to streamline the evaluation and selection process. Second, you can use this to evaluate project results for completed work. Third, you can reuse the tables and information as you go.

COMPREHENSIVE RESOURCE ALLOCATION

In an academic, perfect world, you might be done. After all, you have the slate defined and management has supported it. But this is the real world. It is nasty

- Ongoing support
- Training, leave, vacation
- Emergency fixes
- Targets of opportunity
- Maintenance of systems
- Operations
- Enhancements
- Existing projects that are approved
- New projects that are approved

Figure 5.11   Types of Work that Competes for Project Resources

out there. There are many competing demands for resources. Figure 5.11 lists some of these. Here are some comments.

- *Ongoing support.* This is a major drain on IT resources. Obviously, it cannot be avoided, but it can be minimized.
- *Training, leave, vacation.* This is not easily controlled.
- *Emergency fixes.* These can be almost predicted based upon experience with past problems. However, the exact timing is not.
- *Targets of opportunity.* These may involve management ideas, new technology, etc. They can be controlled through quarterly evaluation and selection and forcing these things to be projects.
- *Maintenance of systems.* This is an area where you have to look to see what will happen if the maintenance work is not done. We have found that much of this is desirable, but not essential.
- *Operations.* This is similar to support.
- *Enhancements.* Similar comments from maintenance apply here.

In a reactive IT world in which there is little planning and selection, there will not be many projects. Most of the resources will be consumed by maintenance, operations, support, and enhancement. There is also a political factor at work. Many IT staff tend to favor regular, daily work over doing project work. It is less demanding and stressful. There are fewer, if any, deadlines.

One way of politically trying to control nonproject work is to create an allocation table for critical IT resources. An example is shown in Fig. 5.12. Here the resources are given as rows. The first column is the percentage of time in nonproject work for that resource. The second and up to the last columns are the winning projects in the project slate. The table entry is the percentage of work in that particular project. The last column is 100%.

This approach and table can be used before projects are chosen for inclusion in the slate or after the slate is determined. The political purpose is use the projects to put pressure to control, limit, and reduce nonproject work.

			Projects			
Resource	**Nonproject work**					**100%**

Figure 5.12 Resource Allocation Table for Critical IT Resources

SET UP A WINNING PROJECT

In traditional project management, you start with a work breakdown structure (WBS) that contains a complete list of tasks. You will then select the tasks and enter them into a project plan. This has substantial drawbacks for IT work. First, the WBS does not provide flexibility. Second, there is no sense of psychological ownership by the team or leader. People just pick tasks that appear close to what they will do.

You want a winning approach for project planning that has the following strengths:

• The approach improves on a cumulative basis over time.
• Team members can participate in project planning so that they assume more ownership and become more committed to the plan.
• The plan can be developed consistently and faster across a range of different project leaders from junior to senior.

There are three key ingredients to this new approach.

• *Templates*. A template consists of high level tasks, dependencies, and general resources being assigned.
• *Issues database*. There is a shared database in IT for all project issues that have surfaced.
• *Lessons learned database*. This is a repository to house the experience gained from doing project work.

As you can, over time you can improve the templates to improve accuracy and completeness. You gather more lessons learned to improve project performance. The issues stabilize so that you get better at solving the same issues again and again. These elements and the plan can be related as in Fig. 5.13. Here are some comments.

• *Templates and plans*. Each project plan must originate from a template. This reduces time to create the plan. As you complete a plan, you can use the experience to improve the template.
• *Plans and issues*. You look at the tasks in the plan and find those that have issues and risk. Then you look at the issues database to find the issues. This

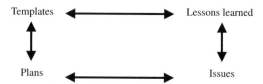

Figure 5.13   Templates, Issues, and Lessons Learned

helps you to create a complete list of issues since if the issue is not there, you add it. Next, you review the list of issues to see which apply to your project. Then you take each issue that applies and find the corresponding tasks. This may uncover missing tasks. In this way, you validate the tasks and issues.

• *Issues and lessons learned.* You apply the lessons learned to solve an issue. As you solve an issue, you gather experience and improve or refine the lessons learned.

• *Templates and lessons learned.* A book of lessons learned is worthless if you can't easily get to the relevant one that applies to your work. So you reference the lessons learned to the tasks and milestones in the template. In that way, you can quickly find the right lessons learned. Over time both the templates and lessons learned get better and more detailed.

Here are some additional guidelines for project planning.

• Templates can be viewed as objects. Each type of subproject such as testing, defining requirements, etc. is a class of objects. You define a template for each class. When you generate a subplan, then you create a new object in the class that inherits the properties of the class.

• The project leader(s) select the templates for subprojects that apply. This is a component approach for creating the project plan. The leader assigns areas of templates out to the project team members. The team members first define detailed tasks that are reviewed by the leaders.

• During the review of the detailed tasks, new issues may arise. This is good since it is better to identify issues earlier rather than later. After the review, detailed dependencies, specific resources, and durations and dates can be defined and reviewed.

At the end of this part, you have the first cut of the plan. It is likely that the schedule is too long and is not acceptable. What do you do? Do you start all over and put pressure on the team to get shorter, but unrealistic estimates? Not a good idea. A better approach is to split up tasks to create more parallel effort and so reduce elapsed time. Second, you can look at the issues behind the risky tasks. Figure 5.14 is a GANTT chart that has risky tasks labeled with hashed lines. We call paths in the project plan that include risky tasks the *management critical paths*. The tasks that have risk or issues are shown in vertical lines. Tasks on the

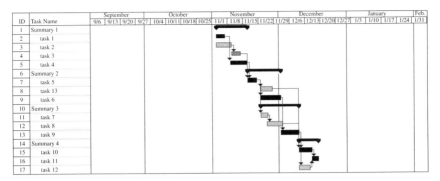

Figure 5.14   Sample GANTT Chart

critical path are shown in hash marks. Finally, if these steps do not do the job, look at the tasks on the critical path.

DEFINE THE ROLE OF MANAGEMENT

In traditional thinking, management should have an active role in successful projects. True, up to a point. Management needs to support the project at the start. But after that, extensive management involvement can interfere and slow down the project work. Thus, it is better if management is only involved in reviewing progress and in dealing with key issues. This is a more limited and feasible role. It also draws upon the managers' capabilities and power in resolving issues.

REPORT ON THE PROJECT

Project reporting should be standardized and deal with issues as well as progress. Listed below are items to include in a project report. This may be done on a monthly basis.

- Name of the project.
- Date of the report.
- Business purpose of the project. This keeps the focus on change in the processes.
- Business scope of the project. This ensures that the project is not viewed only in technical terms.
- Summary GANTT chart—shows planned versus actual.
- Cumulative budget versus actual—an "s" shaped curve.

- Milestones achieved in business terms.
- Upcoming milestones in business terms.
- Percentage of the project completed.
- Percentage of the risky tasks completed. This is the ratio of the tasks completed with issues to the total number of tasks with issues.
- Percentage of the work associated with risky tasks that is completed. This is the ratio of the total hours associated with completed risky tasks to the total number of hours in the project with issues.
- Percentage of the tasks ahead with issues. This is the ratio of the number of unstarted or in process tasks with risk to the total number of unstarted or in process tasks.
- Percentage of the future work with risk. This is the ratio of the total number of hours in the project left with issues to the total number of hours ahead in the project.

Some of these measures are good indicators of problems.

HOLD PROJECT MEETINGS

In many IT groups there are weekly project meetings. These are often used to collect status. Often, these meetings are worthless and there is no sharing of information. Each person on the team just recites what he or she is doing with the project leader taking notes. Another problem is that most people will not admit that they have problems in front of the group or team.

Another method is to gather status ahead of the meeting. Then in the meeting the status can be summarized. This leaves time to either discuss issues or handle lessons learned—much more valuable than status. You do not necessarily solve the issues in the meeting, but discussion can be helpful.

There are a number of subjects for lessons learned meetings, including:

- introducing new team members where they talk about what they learned and what issues they encountered in the past;
- reviewing milestones and work among team members;
- discussing how to go about the work in the next phase of the project;
- having users or vendors present what they have done to share knowledge;
- having key team members discuss their work to share knowledge.

Another change is to move away from weekly meetings. If the project is going fine, you can meet less often. If there are issues and problems, you may need to meet more often. Then what happens is that the urgency of the project is made clear to the team. After all, the project leader is really the equivalent of a director in a movie. The director controls timing so that the project leader can vary the frequency of meetings depending on urgency.

IMPLEMENT COLLABORATION IN PROJECTS

Projects imply and mean teamwork. Teamwork is not just having people attend project meetings together. In IT projects, people are often assigned individual tasks where there is in fact little teamwork. This can result in major problems. Team members can hide issues from the project leaders. A team member can leave the project, creating major hassles and impacts. Knowledge is not shared.

To ensure teamwork, a better approach is to assign most of the tasks to two people. Then someone may raise the issue of accountability. To address this, you can insist that one person is in charge. This approach supports more sharing of knowledge, backup, and earlier warning on problems.

Collaboration extends to the project leaders. If you have one project leader, you are at risk in the following areas.

- The project leader could leave with no backup.
- Junior project leaders may not have experience in handling issues.
- Junior project leaders have no one to talk to easily for peer-to-peer sharing of experience.
- If the project leader irritates or angers some manager, the price to the project can be high.

A more modern approach is to appoint two project leaders for every significant project. Each time one is in charge. This supports sharing of knowledge, backup, and provides an alternative person to deal with a manager. If one project leader has two projects and another has three projects, then the two have five projects.

TRACK PROJECTS

The method for tracking a single standard project begins with two comparisons.

- Budget versus actual—a comparison of costs.
- Planned versus actual schedule—comparison of the baseline schedule for the work and the actual results and status.

There are problems with this approach. First, neither of these is sensitive to issues or risk. In IT projects and work, the money is often spent at the front end on hardware, facilities, software, and networks. At the back end you have just labor hours. But most of the risk in an IT project are at the end of the project. Examples of risky areas include: data conversion, testing, integration, and user acceptance. The situation is often like that in Fig. 5.15. Here the solid line is the cost and the dotted line the risk. Notice the dark vertical line. At this point, the project is way over 60% complete. However, the risk is less than 50% covered. Not a good situation.

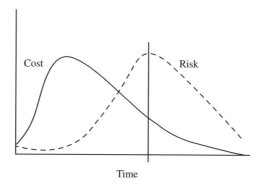

Figure 5.15   Cost and Risk in Projects

Let's consider a numerical example. Let's suppose that there are three tasks in sequence—A, B, and C as follows.

- Task A—40 hr, completed, no risk or issues.
- Task B—20 hr, 50% complete, issues are present.
- Task C—40 hr, not started, issues are present.

The percentage complete is 50%. However, the percentage of the risk that is complete is only 16.67%. We have seen projects like this. Looking at the percentage associated with risk is often a good predictor of problems or failure.

PERFORM MULTIPLE PROJECT ANALYSIS

There are some useful tools to analyze multiple projects. Here are some examples.

- Summary GANTT chart across all projects. This gives an overall view of the projects by showing planned versus actual schedules.
- Summary GANTT chart along with tasks that have issues and risk. This is an excellent tool for showing management how some of the issues are time urgent. This is probably the most effective objective way to show someone that a particular issue should be resolved soon.
- Table of issues versus projects. Here the table entry is the impact of the issue on the project. This table when used with the previous chart can indicate to the management how a specific issue is affecting several projects.

ALIGNMENT OF IT AND THE BUSINESS

In IT, projects are where the true alignment of IT and the business will come true. However, focusing on the technical part of the projects does not make sense. Instead, you have to test alignment by addressing the following questions.

- Were the most beneficial projects to the business selected?
- How much IT effort is going into marginal and not critical projects?
- Are support, maintenance, and operations work being controlled to maximize the effort in projects to support the business?
- Are the business staff involved in the project work?
- Do the business and its employees support the idea of change?
- Are processes and work changed after the projects are completed?
- Are benefits in projects being measured?
- Are significant business changes reflected in the related IT projects?

MANAGE RISK

Risk has been defined as being related to issues. Thus, managing risk in a project is tantamount to managing issues. Each issue may have different impacts. Some issues, such as those that are political, are more difficult and complex to solve. To get at risk, we employ the issues database. Tasks that have risk and issues can be flagged so that they can be pulled out for analysis. There are a number of graphs that can be created to consider risk and issues in projects. Here are some examples.

- *Total issues found in the project* (Fig. 5.16). In a good project, the total number of issues will taper off so that few new issues are found later in the project.
- *Total unresolved open issues* (Fig. 5.17). Here the number of open issues rises as more problems are found. Then issues are solved faster than found. There is often a bump toward implementation as more issues appear.
- *Average time to resolve an issue* (Fig. 5.18). The time should increase until the team and leader gather steam and skill at issues resolution and then decline.
- *Mix of open issues by type* (Fig. 5.19). There are two charts here for two different projects. If you were a project leader, which would you rather be in

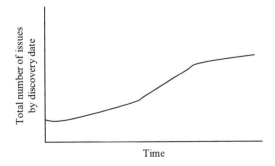

Figure 5.16 Total Issues

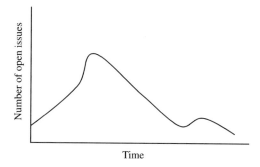

Figure 5.17   Total Unresolved Open Issues

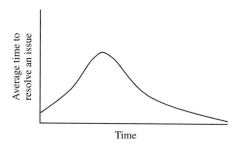

Figure 5.18   Average Time to Resolve an Issue

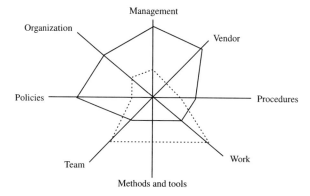

Figure 5.19   Mix of Open Issues by Type

charge of? The answer is the dashed one since the issues are more controlled within the team. For the solid one, the issues are uncontrolled.

• *Aging of open issues* (Fig. 5.20). Most of the recently discovered issues are not solved as would be expected. The bump on the left indicates that there are old, unresolved issues. These would indicate that the project is in trouble.

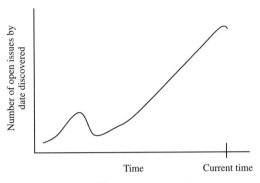

Figure 5.20   Aging of Open Issues

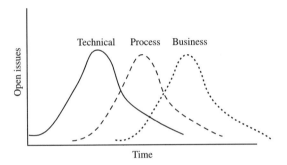

Figure 5.21   Issues by Type over Time

• *Handling of issues by type over time* (Fig. 5.21). This chart shows that typically technical issues appear and are dealt with first. Then come process issues where exceptions appear. Finally, business issues appear due to resistance to change and other factors.

For most of these you can also refine this by considering a type of issue. These graphs are easy to construct since they require only a few data elements that are readily at hand. The graphs can be produced on a spreadsheet.

The graphs are very useful in showing management and project leaders the state of the issues in one or more projects. You can also combine this with the discussion later in this chapter on Performance measures for projects.

EXAMPLES

SUPREME OIL

Supreme Oil IT had tried a number of different methodologies, but none seemed to work consistently. Yet, they did not want to adopt the methods in this chapter all at once. They started with issues and project meetings. This was later expanded with success into the lessons learned and templates. There was some resistance among IT managers and staff since they felt that each IT project was unique. Thus, templates would not be useful. However, templates are only general level tasks. The detailed work is flexible and can be defined in any way by the team.

TUCKER COUNTY

Tucker represented a very traditional IT group. After several failures, the IT group adopted controlled, traditional project management. The IT group went from under control to over control. Business units rebelled at the control since no projects were being completed. One large business unit was allowed to manage projects on its own and adopted the approach discussed here with success. Issues were identified, tracked, and placed in a database. When the number of issues reached about 150, it was discovered that there were few new issues. We would like to report that the success spread to the core IT group. But it did not happen. At the time of writing this chapter, they are still stuck in the control mode. Rumor has it that several IT managers will soon be sacked.

SHAMROCK AGRICULTURE

In Shamrock, IT work began on a small scale without the need for structure or organization. As the workload grew, the need for better and more structure in projects was evident. The managers of both the business and IT had seen the failure of traditional project management. The approach in this chapter was adopted early and yielded benefits from the start. The benefits included the following:

- less time involved in project management;
- earlier identification and resolution of issues;
- active gathering and use of lessons learned that improved software quality.

LESSONS LEARNED

- How do you estimate tasks? What if you have a task that cannot easily be estimated? First, you divide up the tasks to isolate the part that cannot be estimated. Next, you ask why you cannot estimate this part. This will surface more issues. Now by working on the issue, you can estimate.
- Do you pad tasks as contingencies? This is really not a good idea. If all tasks were padded, the project would take years to complete. Contingencies arise because of issues. If you identify and deal with issues, then you minimize

the contingencies. Here is a useful tip. Create contingent tasks in templates and put these at the bottom of the schedule. They appear and loom over the plan, but are not linked to the schedule. Then if management asks about issues, you can link in the contingent tasks to show the impact.

• Generally in IT projects you want to avoid PERT charts. These provide a sequential view of the project. Psychologically, we have found that this can slow down the project since people may not want to start tasks until predecessor tasks have been done. However, in IT projects, you can often start tasks earlier.

• The critical path has limited use in IT projects because it does not reflect the risks and issues in the project. As you know, the critical path is the longest path in the project such that if any of the tasks on the path are delayed, the project is delayed. This says nothing about risk or issues. Thus, the management critical paths that focus on risk is a better measure.

PERFORMANCE MEASURES FOR RISK AND PROJECT MANAGEMENT

Some specific performance measures have already been presented and can be reviewed here.

• Age of the oldest outstanding major issue. The longer a major issues remains unresolved, the more likely that the project will be in trouble.

• Mix of issues by type and degree of control. You want to have most of the open issues being capable of being addressed within the team.

• Percentage of the work remaining in the project that has issues. The higher this is, the more the project is in danger.

• GANTT chart of summary tasks and tasks with issues.

• Table of issues versus projects.

• Average time to resolve an issue. This is a good indicator of management, IT, vendor, and business unit performance.

SUMMARY

If you look on the surface, it appears that the approach proposed in this chapter is very different from traditional project management. Yet, it is really defining new, more modern methods to address IT projects and the project portfolio. Notice the emphasis on templates, collaboration, and lessons learned. These are some of the common themes through the other chapters. The methods in this chapter are also consistent with the Project Management Body of Knowledge (PMBOK).

Chapter 6

Manage the IT Staff

INTRODUCTION

The major factor in IT performance is personnel performance. If there is a lack of motivation, then the work suffers. Morale has received a great deal of attention and it will get some here. However, there is another problem at the heart of many IT problems—lack of teamwork. People in IT often work as individuals. Most project meetings deal with status so that teamwork is left for the people on their own. Since most work in IT is individually assigned, there is little encouragement for IT staff to work with others. While management in IT may preach teamwork, their actions of individual assignments and lack of providing a forum for teamwork speak far louder.

In IT management, to be successful, your actions must be matched up with your words.

In IT it is not getting people to do their work. If that was all there was to it, IT could be managed like a standard business department. There are some basic differences between the work that IT people do and many business employees. Unfortunately, business managers who take over IT groups learn this the hard way. Some examples of the differences are:

• a substantial part of IT requires creativity and is not routine. This includes problem solving, emergency fixes, and design;
• much of IT cannot be done in one or two days. IT work is job or project oriented whereas employees work on shorter tasks that can be performed in a few minutes to an hour or so;

- IT employees tend to work on a wider variety of work. During a typical week, an IT programmer may handle several systems problems, work on design, and participate in reviews. Many IT people have learned how to multitask their work. Many business employees work on one task at a time—single threading.

Each of these differences has an impact on how you manage IT staff. You are dependent on the problem-solving and creative abilities of the employees. This means that morale is a very important factor in IT—probably more so than in routine work.

EVALUATE THE CURRENT STAFF

An evaluation of the skills, knowledge, and interaction of the IT staff will give you a better understanding of the strengths and weaknesses of the group in terms of meeting demands for IT services. Some additional benefits are:

- Identification of where you have overdependence on specific people.
- Determination of gaps in skills and knowledge.
- The relationship between IT staff and business units.

Note that this goes beyond the standard human resources performance appraisal. However, the results of this evaluation can be of assistance in preparing and then backing up the appraisal. Often, an employee is given a general appraisal without specific directions for improvement. The information that you and supervisors will create can assist in guiding the employee toward improved skills and morale.

Following the method of all chapters, a number of tables can be constructed to provide structure.

- *People versus tools* (Fig. 6.1). What you would do is to divide the IT staff into groups (development and maintenance, networking, operations, etc.). For each area proceed to make a list of the relevant tools that are available and should be employed. Then you create a table for each group with their names as rows and tools as columns. The table entry is the rating of their skill in the tool (high, medium, low).

What is this table used for? First, if you have a column where there is only one high rating, then you know that you are heavily dependent upon a single individual for expertise in the tool—a single point of failure and risk. Second, if there is a column where there are no high ratings, then no one on the IT staff is an expert in the tool. You can surmise that the tool is not being employed to its potential. Third, if you have a row with only low ratings, this means that the individual needs to improve his or her skills and knowledge in the tools.

- *People versus business units* (Fig. 6.2). The purpose of this table is to ascertain the relationship between individuals in an IT group and the business unit.

Group: _____

Tools

Employee			

Figure 6.1   IT Staff Versus Tool Skills

Group: _____

Business units

Employee			

Figure 6.2   IT Employees Versus Business Unit Relationships

Employees

Employees			

Figure 6.3   IT Staff Versus IT Staff

The rows are the individuals in the group and the columns are the business units. The entry can be a rating of high, medium, or low. Or, alternatively, it can contain names of the most frequent contacts.

This table can be employed to determine if a business unit has a single point of contact. This could lead you and the supervisors to widen the contacts. If you have a row with little or no contact with business units, then this person is working entirely within IT. There is little knowledge within the business units of what this person does. This might be acceptable in a technical support role, but it would be unacceptable for analysts. If there is a column in which there is no rating above low, then there is little contact between IT and that unit. This could be an issue and might be the cause for any problems between IT and that unit.

• *IT staff versus IT staff* (Fig. 6.3). Here you and the supervisors identify key individuals across the IT organization. Their names become both the rows and the columns. The table entry indicates the nature of the contact. The diagonal is obviously blank. You could put down in the table the degree and nature of the contact.

This table is valuable because it gives the manager and supervisors insight into the relationships between employees. It might also reveal where there are communication problems as well. If there is no contact where there should be, then you can take actions to have these two people work together on specific tasks.

• *IT staff versus strengths* (Fig. 6.4). The rows are the IT staff or key staff. The columns are strengths that they possibly have. A list to help you get started appears in Fig. 6.5. The table entry consists of two elements: a rating of high, medium, or low, and importance (high, medium, or low).

This table can reveal the strengths of individuals. However, when taken together with the importance, you can get an overall assessment of the capabilities of the individual. If you have a row in which there are mainly low entries, then the supervisor can work with this person in improving their abilities. If you have a column in which all entries are low and that strength is important, then you have a problem across the IT staff.

• *IT staff versus weaknesses* (Fig. 6.6). A list of potential weaknesses is given in Fig. 6.7. Starting with this, you can construct the columns in the table. Then you can proceed to do the same rating of applicability and importance that was employed in Fig. 6.4.

Taken together, Figs. 6.4 and 6.6 provide an overall assessment of each person in IT. If you have a large IT group, you will have to restrict attention to a subset of the employees (perhaps, those that have been in IT for over a year).

If your experience follows ours, you will find that you have some question marks in the tables. This is a good thing because it shows that you don't have a good understanding of that person's specific abilities. It will encourage you to go out and make more contacts.

Strengths

Employees			

Figure 6.4   IT Staff Versus Strengths

• Problem-solving skills
• Capabilities in using methods
• Capabilities in using tools
• Shows initiative
• Communicates well with others
• Shows potential for project management
• Shows potential for IT management
• Relates well to users and business units
• Works well with vendors

Figure 6.5   Examples of Strengths

Potential weaknesses

Employees			

Figure 6.6   IT Staff Versus Potential Weaknesses

- Problems in getting along with others
- Lack of following direction
- Does not employ tools correctly
- Does not appear to learn from experience
- Lack of business knowledge

Figure 6.7   Potential Weaknesses

How do you develop some of these tables? Well, you could do it yourself. However, this defeats the purpose. A better technique is to involve the supervisors in filling out the tables. This effort will surface some disagreements that can then be examined. The effort should lead to a consensus. Another benefit is that the evaluation will force the supervisors to work together. In the heat of the work there is often not much contact among the supervisors.

RECRUIT AND HIRE NEW IT EMPLOYEES

Someone leaves IT. Do you try to replace them with someone of the same skill set? Not necessarily. You should use the tables in the preceding section to identify where you have gaps and holes. You also may want to introduce someone into the organization who has experience in a new set of tools. Hiring new employees for IT is one of the golden opportunities you get to upgrade the overall skills and capabilities of the IT organization. These opportunities are often wasted because there is a lack of importance given to the potential positive impact of bringing new blood into the organization.

In starting the hiring process, you often have to produce a job description for Human Resources. Most of the time this consists of filling out a standard form that is followed for all employees regardless of their responsibilities. These forms usually include the following.

- Job title;
- Description of duties;
- Skills and knowledge required;
- Education required;
- Reporting relationship;
- Evaluation criteria for candidates.

Experience suggests that you expand this list. Here are some useful items to consider adding:

- Characteristics of a successful candidate.
- What you hope the person will contribute or bring to improve the organization.
- After one year on the job, what would constitute success on the job.
- Potential promotion path.

Let's assume that Human Resources has now received a number of resumes. How should you evaluate the resumes? Everyone will generally put down the positions held and job responsibilities. Look for specific achievements. Also, try to see what they have learned from their previous work. Are they looking for a position with expanded responsibilities? Try to detect why they want to leave their current position. One thing to do is to see if they have been on the same project for a long time. This may be a sign that they are burned out. It could also mean that the project is in trouble and that they want to jump ship.

After winnowing down the list of candidates, you have a few that will be interviewed. Here are some interviewing guidelines.

- Go over their resume with them briefly.
- Pose several issues or problems that they are likely to encounter in the job with you. This will catch them off guard. You can see how they respond to potential problems. This can be very insightful.
- Ask them what lessons they have learned from their past and current work. If they have trouble coming up with anything, then this could be a sign of weakness.
- Try them out in formulating a project. Suggest a potential project idea and ask them how they would organize the work.

Have the leading candidates interview not only with supervisors, but also with employees that they might work with. There are several benefits in doing this. First, the existing employees gain a sense of participation in the selection process. Second, they can give you positive or negative feedback. What do the employees ask the candidates? Suggest to the employees that they pose several detailed issues. They can also probe their knowledge of tools and methods.

After the interviews, talk with each supervisor and employee with whom they interviewed. Get the feedback one on one. If you get people in a group, then employees may just agree with the supervisors. Ask the employees how they would feel working with them. Ask what additional training they would have to pick up.

Now let's suppose that you have hired someone. Many times the person is assigned to the supervisor. The supervisor hands them work to do and they start. This is not a good idea since it fails to socialize them into the IT organization. A preferred method is to assign them to work with an existing employee on some tasks. This will provide you with more insight into their abilities, strengths, and weaknesses based on the feedback you receive from the current employee.

ALLOCATE PERSONNEL RESOURCES

Personnel assignment in IT is often handed over to the IT supervisors. They are then responsible for assignments. This can create problems.

- The IT manager is remote from the assignments.
- An employee tends to be 100% dedicated to the work under the supervisor. There is little opportunity for individuals to work across IT groups.

While this method may be appropriate for some technical support groups, the problems suggest that an improved technique should be considered.

The IT manager can hold a meeting with supervisors on a periodic basis—say every 2 weeks or once a month. During this meeting they can discuss personnel assignments. A wider range of criteria for assignment can be employed using this forum. Here are some sample criteria.

- Where would the employee be of most value to the overall organization?
- On what tasks would the employee be most beneficial to IT?
- What work would help the individual improve his or her skills?
- On what work could the employee try to resolve some of his shortcomings?

You can use the personnel tables in the second section of this chapter here for assistance.

Even you will end up allocating the people to the tasks under their supervisor, since you and the supervisors have considered a broader range of alternative work assignments.

Should you send an employee to training? There are a myriad of training classes available within firms and from outside companies. From giving many seminars, we have developed several questions that will aid in your answering the question.

- Will the employee be able to use the methods and information learned right away? If there is a substantial time gap, then much of the knowledge may be lost.
- Are the methods and techniques in the training consistent with the practices followed in IT? Of course, you may want to send someone to training to bring in new ideas that challenge the status quo.

Before they go to the training, set expectations for them. Give them an idea of what you expect them to do when they return. This will help them become more serious about getting something out of the training. Also, encourage them to bring questions and issues about the topic to the training. This should become part of any preparation prior to the training sessions.

What happens when the person returns from the training? Normally, they just go back to work. It is no wonder that some employees treat the training as a break from their normal work then, is it? A better idea is to have them make a presentation to the IT staff that do work that is applicable to the training. Have them cover in the presentation the following topics.

- What did they hear that was new and surprising? That makes things more interesting.

- Who did they meet in the training that they could keep in contact with later? This is an important side benefit—helping them network.
- If they could bring someone else to the same training, would they do it? Why or why not?
- Do the methods and techniques presented in the training make sense? Are they consistent with internal methods? Why or why not?
- What can they implement and use right away?
- Would there be any resistance to implementation of the ideas?
- How would they suggest implementing the ideas?
- What would be the benefit of using the ideas?
- What ideas can be implemented later?
- What, if any, changes are needed to use the ideas?

BUILD A COLLABORATIVE IT CULTURE

This sounds like one of those dreams that is never achieved. However, you not only want to make the effort, but even modest success can pay off. Here are some ideas to promote collaboration in IT.

- Have team members present the results of their work in meetings.
- Assign tasks to two employees with one in charge.
- Hold some social functions to encourage the people to network.
- Hold lessons learned meetings to plan future work.
- Conduct lessons learned meetings regarding methods and tools.
- Allocate several days per year for the IT employees to work in pairs in user departments doing their work.

This last item is very valuable for several reasons. First, it gives IT employees a chance to work together on non-IT work. Second, it shows IT's commitment to support the business processes. Third, the IT employees learn the jargon and procedures of the work in the business process. In doing this we have also found that some useful ideas for improving the business processes have surfaced as well.

MOTIVATE IT EMPLOYEES

In the introduction, morale was cited as important. Motivation links to morale. Some organizations believe that giving bonuses in the form of additional compensation is a good motivator for IT staff. We urge you to consider this in-depth before you try it. In one systems company, the firm needed to get a software product out the door to stay in business and remain credible with customers. To push things along they gave bonuses to the programmers. However, management did not think things through. Several severe problems occurred. First, within the group of programmers, there was an almost immediate comparison of bonuses. Those who did not receive the highest bonus became dejected and demoralized. Their productivity dropped. It did not recover. To make matters worse, the testers and quality assurance staff did not receive a bonus. The programmers gloated to the testers. They became outraged. Not only did their morale crash, but they also did not do thorough testing. The end result was that the product was shipped with many bugs and errors that the management was not aware of. The product died in the market. The firm was sold just prior to going into bankruptcy.

What can you do in the way of rewards? Here is a list of things that have worked in many organizations.

- Give people time off for working hard. Don't count it as vacation.
- Distribute coupons and certificates for food.
- Take employees out to lunch or dinner. This will give you an opportunity to meet the families of the hard working employees to show your appreciation.
- Make available laptop computers for their use at home. Most employees may already have these. If this is the case, give out software.

DEAL WITH PERSONNEL ISSUES

One problem occurs quite often in IT groups. That is, that two individuals do not get along. They may disagree on technology or how to do some piece of work. As a result, they sometimes shun contact with each other. In a situation in which they need to share information on a common project, they still have little contact.

What does an IT manager do in this situation? You cannot leave it alone because the work and collaboration are too important. One approach is to assign them more joint work. Each one will probably come to you and ask why you are doing this when you know that they do not get along well together. Your response is that you understand this and that there will be more joint work if they do not work together. After all, you are the manager and you are in charge. If you give into this, you risk losing more power.

Some employees may use their technical knowledge to gain informal power. This is done at the expense of that of the managers and supervisors. This is something that you cannot allow to go on. In this situation, experience shows that a useful method is to talk and ask questions of them in common language without technical jargon. Eventually, this will force them to use the same language. You are saying in effect that "While technical knowledge is important, they are still part of a team."

A third situation involves someone who is a loner. He or she does his or her work and has little contact with anyone else. Other IT employees leave them alone. In the past when IT resources were totally dedicated to one area, this could have been left alone. Not any longer. Systems are more integrated today and there are many more interfaces. Consider creating joint task and work assignments

involving this person. Also, get them to participate more in meetings by presenting what they have done.

UPGRADE SKILLS OF JUNIOR EMPLOYEES

Junior IT employees are often intimidated by the senior people. The senior
IT staff have four advantages over the junior ones: (1) they have more experience;
(2) they know more technically in general; (3) they know the internal systems;
and (4) they are familiar with the political ropes and have made contacts with
each other and with end users. If you throw junior people in to work without
preparation, they might survive on technical skills, but will be slower due to lack
of knowledge of the applications and architecture. They also may run into more
problems with business units since they would need to be brought up to speed.
The same comments apply to new employees with substantial experience.

There must be a better way of bringing junior and new employees in IT along
faster so that they become more effective faster. Here are some guidelines:

- Assign the junior employee to work with a specific senior person.
- Before doing this, take the senior person aside and point out the
advantages of having someone to help them.
- When you do this, hold a meeting with both of them to indicate how you
expect the work to be allocated. State what your expectations are with respect to
knowledge transfer.
- Indicate that after some period, you will be asking the junior person to
lead some smaller tasks.

Senior staff may still resent this and feel that it is just extra. However, if you make
a general practice of this, then they can see that they are being fairly treated and
not being singled out. In addition, the junior person can help them with some of
the routine work.

You should follow this approach with junior project leaders as was discussed in
Chapter 5. There the advantages of two project leaders instead of one were covered.

ALIGNMENT OF IT AND THE BUSINESS

One technique for assessing the alignment of IT with the business is to track
the number of personnel hours that were dedicated to supporting specific
processes. Use the table in Fig. 6.8. The columns are the business processes. The
rows are the areas or groups within IT. How do you spread the hours of support
staff who handle the network and other similar work? You can proportionally
allocate this based upon the rough size of the process. An alternative is to do it on
the basis of process importance. However, this is more political.

Business processes

IT areas			

Figure 6.8   Personnel Hours Versus Business Processes

Business units

IT areas			

Figure 6.9   Personnel Hours Versus Business Units

You can use this table together with those in Chapters 2 and 4 to see how IT actual work is supporting the business objectives, mission, and vision. This can be valuable ammunition for you with management.

Another method is to determine the allocation of IT time spent in support of each major business unit. Use the table in Fig. 6.9. Follow the same guidelines as for Fig. 6.8.

What is of interest is that the two tables may not match up. That is, even though a process is "owned" by a specific business unit, the allocation of time to the process does not match that of the business unit. Why does this happen? One reason is that the process may span several departments.

What are some benefits from creating these two tables? One reason is to help explain what IT is doing in business terms to management. Another reason is to determine if you need to perform the allocation of effort differently to better support the business mission and objectives.

MANAGE RISK

Things appear to be going fine. However, no one is talking much. This is not generally right for IT people. At least, there should be some complaining. When two children are in the next room playing and suddenly there is silence, you can safely assume that there is a problem. Do the same for IT. Silence should be interpreted as there being some problem. Try to take people aside one at a time and draw them. Don't be confrontational. Ask how things are going and what they are working on. Listen carefully. They should begin to open up.

In most IT groups, IT management becomes overly dependent upon a few people. This is in the nature of the work due to the in-depth knowledge of both applications and tools. Limited resources also force managers to avoid having backup staff—not an affordable luxury. To deal with this, you should determine where you have the greatest risk in terms of the following:

- Age and stability of the person.
- The importance of the specific knowledge that they have.
- The importance of the processes that they are supporting.

Problems can easily grow and get out of hand through word of mouth. IT employees talk amongst themselves. Rumors get around quickly. You should keep listening for any rumors. In meetings you can share some rumors and put them to rest along with their fears.

Another risk involves the control of the time and work of the people in IT. Over time some IT supervisors or senior IT staff may develop working relationships with business unit supervisors and their senior employees. Nothing wrong so far. Sometimes, the business unit people take advantage of the relationship and make requests directly to the either the IT staff members or the supervisor. Some small work begins. You, as the IT manager, have no knowledge of this. Then the effort consumes over a week of someone's time. Keep track of the contacts and relationships to ensure that this does not happen.

EXAMPLES

SUPREME OIL

The IT organization had a project management group that was headed by someone who wanted to enforce project management rules on everyone. In essence, she was usurping the authority of the manager. While it worked for jobs that had been designated as projects, extending the bureaucratic approach that she followed did not. She and her staff of three proceeded to drive the IT staff crazy. They resorted to calling as much of their work as possible regular work and not projects. This surfaced to IT management when they were shown statistics that revealed that only 25% of the labor was going into projects—clearly not high enough. Then the truth came out and the project management area received some re-education.

TUCKER COUNTY

The IT group at Tucker had three king and queen bees. These individuals wielded a great deal of informal power and intimidated the IT manager. How did they do it? Through their technical knowledge. This had developed into a pattern of behavior over the years and could not be changed because the IT manager had accepted his position.

When the new IT manager assumed the position, he was aware of the problem. Instead of accepting it, he challenged them by taking a business approach. He asked them to talk in standard language and not in technical language. This paved the way for a better relationship in which the new manager had the power position.

SHAMROCK AGRICULTURE

One of the IT staff was promoted into a supervisory position in charge of the infrastructure. Now this was a small IT group. Logically, he would have just continued to participate in the work as before. This did not work out. He started to assume to take on the roles of a manager when he only had one junior employee. He basically stopped doing the hands-on work. A number of network problems occurred that were not addressed in a timely manner. He was finally demoted. The lesson learned is that you should approach promoting an IT staff member into supervision carefully—realizing that different skills are required.

LESSONS LEARNED

- Be proactive in measuring the allocation of IT resources. Without measurement, you are leaving much to the supervisor's and employee's discretion. That will tend to allocate time to the situation that is crying out the loudest. This may not be the wisest use of resources.
- Make sure that you involve both supervisors and staff in doing the evaluations and assessments. Doing it yourself denies you the value of collaboration.
- Present some of the measurements to business units as well as upper management. This will show them that you have a proactive allocation technique that attempts to satisfy the major needs of the business. This is also valuable in showing departments that were denied resources why this occurred.

PERFORMANCE MEASURES FOR IT STAFFING

If you are successful in managing IT staff, then this will be borne out in the performance measures in Fig. 6.10. These questions relate to each of the sections and topics of this chapter.

Since teamwork is important, a list of questions has been prepared and appears in Fig. 6.11 to assess the extent and depth of teamwork in IT. If you find that there

- What approach is employed to assess IT staff performance?
- What methods are used relative to analyzing IT staff skills?
- What structure and procedures are followed in hiring and recruitment?
- How is collaboration supported by IT management?
- What steps are taken to track morale and raise it?
- How are IT resources allocated across business processes?
- How are IT resources allocated across business units?
- What percentage of the IT work is done on proactive versus reactive work?

Figure 6.10   Performance Measurements for IT Staffing Management

- How many of the tasks are assigned jointly?
- Are resources shared between IT groups?
- Are new employees assigned to work together with current employees?
- Do employees present the results of their work?
- How is the sharing of knowledge of the business processes shared?
- How is information shared relative to methods and tools?
- Do employees present the results of the training classes and seminars that they attend?
- To what extent do supervisors and employees participate in the evaluation of IT?

Figure 6.11   Evaluation of Teamwork in IT

are some problems with the answers to these questions, then this gives you insight into ways of improving the extent of teamwork.

SUMMARY

Many managers assume that they have the skills and experience to manage people. IT employees are different to direct than others due to the nature of work and circumstances. From experience you find that managing each IT group is unique and presents its own challenges. These are some of the reasons why, although being an IT manager can be frustrating, it can also be a very interesting and rewarding experience.

Chapter 7

Manage the Work

INTRODUCTION

Here you are considering how to review and manage the IT work. This is wide ranging so we will concentrate on specific areas. An overriding concern is time and its importance. Whether you are the IT manager, a project leader, or IT supervisor, you only have so much time to direct, review, and manage the work of their staff. You can read all of the books on time management, but you are still left with this inescapable fact.

Allocation of time in managing the work is a critical success factor in IT management.

In IT, what makes matters worse is that a manager can give attention to topics about which they have knowledge, experience, or interest. What happens then? The work where there are problems and issues and where there is risk do not receive attention. Then they can blow up into major crises. Here the same definition of risk will be employed as in Chapter 5.

Work has risk if there are issues and problems associated with the work.

Detection of risk through issue identification will be a focus in most of the sections of this chapter.

CHECK ON WORK INFORMALLY

It is not enough to rely on formal meetings and reviews. People will often tell you what you want to hear. They fear that if they raise issues in meetings or presentations, they will get blamed based on the old saying, "Blame the messenger bringing bad news." For these reasons, you want to initiate informal contacts with IT staff and others. This is also recommended in Chapter 10.

Here are some guidelines for your informal communications.

• As you walk through the organization, you should stop by individual's offices or cubicles and ask "How are things going?" Or words to that effect. Then you have to listen. Don't just starting walking off as they answer.

• Make contacts before and after meetings, over breaks, and before and after work.

• When you are having a conversation, focus on listening and watching. What is their body language? Are they defensive? Do they look at you or down at the floor?

• Ask them if they need any help. Volunteer to get involved. This is safe because they will seldom take you up on your offer. But you demonstrated a good faith effort to help.

• Each day make a list of the people that you contacted. We use a table of employee names as rows and dates as columns and just place an "X" along with any comments.

• If someone mentions an issue, you have to be careful. If you approach the supervisor right away, they will think that you are trying to do their job. They might go to the employee to stifle or structure future contacts. Instead, casually start researching the issue with supervisors and others. Do not attribute the issue to the employee.

• Encourage informal meetings with several employees about a specific technical topic.

• Make sure that you visit everyone. People who do not get contacted may feel left out. This means that you may have to be at work during all three shifts.

There are a number of benefits to spending a limited amount of time doing this. First, you are finding out what is going on. For over 20 years, we have employed these techniques and they work. They appear to take time at first, but you get used to it as a pattern and learn to fit it in with your other work. In one instance, we kept in touch with over 150 employees.

The methods also pay off in terms of morale of the staff. They also serve as a model for the supervisors and project leaders in IT to use. Encourage them to do the same thing. If they do, then you can arrange a meeting with supervisors to go over issues surfaced by the employees.

These informal contacts are very important because in IT, people often work alone on specific tasks. They only have contact with others when there is a need for information, etc. This is different from a standard business department where there is more joint work and people are doing the same things.

There are specific areas in IT that you must manage. Let's create a list and then go into more depth.

- Assessing current methods and tools in IT;
- Organizing work efforts;
- Reviewing work;
- Dealing with issues;
- Gathering and using lessons learned;
- Addressing documentation;
- Selecting and implementing new methods and tools;
- Managing routine and project work;
- Address resource conflicts.

ASSESS YOUR METHODS AND TOOLS

Methods and tools are at the heart of IT as they are in other fields. A method is the general technique that you will use. An example might be object oriented programming.

This is a nice method, but it requires some tools to make the method easier to follow. That is why we have software libraries of objects, compilers, editors, and other software tools.

What are your goals relative to methods and tools? Here is an optimistic list.

- Using the method and tool, the work products should be of *higher quality* and have fewer errors.
- The work can be performed in *less time* using the method and tool.
- There is *easier transferability*. If one person uses the method and tool and leaves, another person can pick it up quickly.
- Work becomes more *interchangeable* since people are using the same methods and tools.
- There can be *one set of standards and guidelines* for the set of methods and tools.
- It will be possible to *better estimate* how long the work will take based upon the method and tool.
- *Easier maintenance and enhancement* is possible.
- *Operations support is more timely.*

In Fig. 7.1, a table is presented for your methods and tools. In this table you list the various activities in IT as rows. The columns consist of the methods, tools, whether there was an expert for the method and tool, whether there were guidelines for effective use, and the existence of management expectations for results using

Area	Methods	Tools	Expert	Guidelines	Management expectations

Figure 7.1   Table of Methods and Tools

the methods and tools. Here you should work with the employees and supervisors in IT to create this table.

The first step is to have people make a list of the areas of IT activities. Try to be complete and detailed. This should then be reviewed. After the review, assign groups of the items to individuals to fill in the columns. This will likely have some interesting results. Here are some from experience.

- Some people are not aware of what resources are available.
- The benefits and so expectations of the tools are not clear.
- There are gaps in the methods and tools.

Let's discuss the gaps. You can have an area such as developing requirements that has no method or tool. People then just use manual methods of their own based on their experience. This can be a problem because without any formal approach, each person is on their own. The results will be based upon each person's experience and knowledge. This will produce uneven results.

You can have a method such as project presentations following a specific outline, but without a tool except for graphics presentation software. This is OK since there may not be another tool available.

There might be a tool with no method. This occurs because someone brings in a tool, but has no organized approach for using the tool. This can result in a great deal of wasted effort.

If there are no guidelines for the use of the method and tool, then again everyone is on their own. Each person must learn how to use the tools from scratch. This is wasteful and unproductive. Moreover, different people learn different things. So it is uneven.

What is the role of an expert? An expert in a method or tool is someone who has a great deal of experience and expertise in the technology. You cannot afford or, probably, find experts for all methods or tools, but it is valuable to determine the areas where there is no expert available.

Why are management expectations important? People are often told that a specific method or tool will be used. This announcement is then followed by training classes. However, it is often unclear to some of the staff what the purpose of the tool is. Let's take an example. Suppose you acquire Microsoft Project and require it to be used. On what projects? If everyone uses this tool, what will the benefits be? The staff goes to the training and learns the tool. They start to use it. All of this time they are still not clear on the benefits of doing this. To some it just seems like more overhead work that is getting in the way of the real work. This is not good. That is why management expectations for methods and tools are important.

ORGANIZE IT WORK EFFORTS

Some new IT work is going to start. This can be a part of a project or an effort to fix a problem or do a system upgrade. Often, the approach is that the manager assigns the work to the employees and then steps back. The assumption is that the employees are qualified and know what to do. This is natural since the manager has confidence in the employees based upon past performance.

Is this the right approach? Shouldn't the work be better planned? Perhaps, not in all cases, but it is useful to have a planning session at the start of the work. Here are some key items that should be covered in this meeting.

- What are the business and technical purposes of the work?
- What is the scope of the work? What is not specifically included?
- What are the roles and responsibilities of the people involved in the work?
- How will the individuals interact during the work?
- What are potential problems and issues that may be faced in doing the work?
- What are lessons learned from previous work that might be helpful here?
- What do we as individuals hope to gain and learn from doing the work?
- What will be called success in the work?
- How should the work be organized?
- How will the end products be reviewed and used?
- What methods and tools will be used? How will they be used?

You should distribute and employ this checklist. It should be addressed with the kick-off of each substantial IT effort. Note the question related to success. This is important because it sets the standard for the people doing the work. You could also ask what constitutes failure, but this may be excessively negative. Another question relates to what the individuals will gain from the work. Some managers would say that they are getting paid and that is enough. It is not suffi cient if you want to create a first class IT group. A person should gain in terms of knowledge and experience as well as expertise in the use of methods and tools. That is why IT is interesting compared to some regular business work—each assignment is different. If you get the people to answer this question, then they see that doing a good job on the work is in their own self-interest.

REVIEW WORK AND PROJECT MILESTONES

You are aware of the work and project schedules. In IT, almost all work results in an end product or milestone. With even a small IT group, there are often too many end products to review. As was stated in the Introduction, you have to be selective.

What should you review? Without guidelines, some managers will review what they are familiar with because they feel that they can add more to the effort. The review of other work products might be given to others. This is a bad approach. It is totally insensitive to risks and issues.

What is a better approach? Make a list of upcoming work products. With other managers in IT, identify issues and potential problems as well as importance for each. You can use the table in Fig. 7.2. Here the rows are the end products. The second column is the importance of the end product (high, medium, low). The third column is for issues. The fourth column is a rating of risk (high, medium, low). Based on importance and risk, you list the review priority in the last column. Note that there is no one answer. There is subjectivity involved.

Is all of this effort necessary? Well, it provides an organized approach for your reviews. Also, it keeps you focused on risk and issues. If you were to place each end product in the grid in Fig. 7.3, then you would focus on the end products in the oval. The horizontal axis is for risk while the vertical axis is importance. In the example, you would focus on end products 1, 2, and 7.

Why not go after just the end products that are important both for risk and importance? Because the high risk but low importance end products could result in later problems. You do not consider either the end products that are low in both measures or those that are high in importance, but low in risk. Is this approach uneven and unfair? Yes. That is because you only have limited time.

Now that you have decided on a general rating of end products, you could, if you had time, develop a finer grained rating. Then you would rate each end product on a scale of 0–3 based upon the following:

- 0—no review;
- 1—evaluate for the existence of the end product;

End product	Importance	Issues	Risk	Review priority

Figure 7.2   Table for Assessing End Products

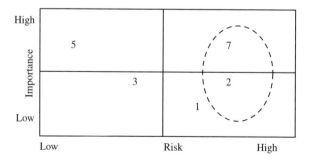

Figure 7.3   Grid for End Products

- 2—evaluate for the structure of the end product;
- 3—review the detailed content of the end product.

Each level brings a more detailed review. Most of the time, you will only have time to review those that are level 3.

Now let's turn to the review itself. A traditional approach is for managers to receive a document that represents the end product. Then you try to read through it. But what are you looking for? The documents are often long, ponderous, and detailed. Then you get together in a meeting. But the real issues or problems with the document are not addressed. Many such reviews are a joke.

In teaching we assign real world type projects. Students then hand in large papers. This resembles the same situation as above. Yet, we had limited time to spend on each paper. Surely, there must be a better way. We started to have students make presentations of their projects in class. From these we found that we could do a more thorough and accurate review.

Let's apply this approach to end products. You would have the individuals who produced the end product make a presentation. This presentation is different from that of a structured walkthrough. Here is an outline for the presentation.

- Purpose of the work;
- Issues faced in the work;
- Content summary of the end product;
- What could have been done better with more time;
- What lessons were learned from the work.

The issues faced in the work come from Chapter 5 and the identification of issues and association with tasks. You will want to do the same thing for substantive nonproject work. The last two topics are unusual. The first is to get people to look at how they could improve their work performance based on time and methods and tools. The second and last point allows them to state what they got out of doing the work. Why is this important? Because as an IT manager, you want to encourage lessons learned and career growth on the job. Not just send people to training classes.

As the presentation is going on, watch the body language. Listen to the tone of voice. Be attentive to where someone is very general or very detailed. These will give you signs of potential problem areas in the end product. After the presentation, you can now focus on these areas in the document.

DEAL WITH ISSUES

In the section on Organizing IT work, you defined and identified potential issues and problems in the work. During the work some of these or new issues are bound to surface. Figure 7.4 gives some examples of work issues.

- A person does not have enough time for the work
- Someone does not have expertise in a method or tool
- There are too many interruptions in the work
- There is an issue that they cannot address
- They are not getting the necessary information from someone else
- They are experiencing a hardware, network, or software problem

Figure 7.4   Examples of Issues in IT Work

How do you cope with these issues? First, from Chapter 5, you established an issues database that crosses all IT projects and regular, nonproject work. Now what you want to do is to employ the grid in Chapter 5 related to issues to determine those that have high impact and are time urgent. Focus your attention on these.

What do you do with an issue? Well, you first want to bundle several related issues. You must then avoid a "rush to judgment" to try and solve the issues. You want to try out several alternative actions, including:

- Do nothing about the issue. Wait for new information.
- Put more resources into the situation.
- Change the structure of the work to see if the issue disappears.
- Get outside resources to help with the issue.
- Determine if a method or tool would have any benefit.

Employ this as a checklist when you consider issues. In meetings feel free to discuss issues, but do not press for resolution. It is better to do that after the meeting.

USE LESSONS LEARNED EFFECTIVELY

In Chapter 5, the lessons learned databases were presented. For literally thousands of years writers and others have cited the importance of lessons learned and using experience. The Roman Empire extensively employed experience in carrying out engineering works—aqueducts, forums, temples, and other structures. They encouraged and enforced people to share ideas during and after work. People were rotated from site to site to share experiences and knowledge.

What hasn't this been successful in today's business and IT environments? In business, rather than share the information around the department, some find it easier to rely on king and queen bees. They are the repositories of knowledge. Earlier, some of the problems regarding politics and power for king and queen bees were discussed.

In IT, there is also the king and queen bee syndrome. Someone who knows a specific system is left with total maintenance and enhancement responsibility. Network troubleshooting is left in the hands of one person. One reason is the limited staffing in IT. Another reason is the time pressure to get work done—this doesn't provide the luxury of sharing information.

There is an additional IT problem. Many in IT view each assignment or piece of work as unique. Thus, since it is unique, logic says that what you learned from previous work may not be valuable in future or current work. An exception is the use of methods and tools. But at the higher levels of the work, many activities are the same; the difference is in the detail. That is why in Chapter 5, the use of templates for projects was emphasized.

Traditionally, you only gather lessons learned after the work is completed. There are several major problems with this. Some of the people have left for other things and are not available. If the work went on for some time, then some cannot remember what happened 6 months ago. They are caught up in immediate tasks.

A sound approach is to gather lessons learned from almost all IT on a regular basis. The knowledge is fresh and more accurate and complete. The resistance comes from managers who think that it interferes with the pace of the work. Staff may not see immediate value in lessons learned. This thinking is basically flawed. If you gather and employ lessons learned, experience reveals that you will reap these benefits:

- People will see more common patterns to their work.
- Morale will improve since employees see that management values their expertise, experience, and knowledge.
- Work in later and even current activities will improve.
- There will be a greater awareness of the need and value of learning from doing the work.

However, it is not enough to just write these lessons learned down. You must organize and structure them for later use. Lessons learned must be thought about and discussed. Through this effort, the lessons learned become more valuable, useful, and readily accessible.

What information would make a lesson learned more useful? Here is a list.

- To what situations does the lesson learned apply?
- What is the lesson learned?
- What are expected results and benefits from applying the lesson learned?
- What are guidelines to help you use the lesson learned effectively?

After you have answered these questions, you are left with the problem of how to organize these for later use. If you put them in a book or manual, then you can only find them through the table of contents or the index. Most people are unwilling to plow through 400 lessons learned to find the two that apply to their current or upcoming work.

To effectively organize lessons learned, you want to link them to something that is at hand. Here are some examples from business and IT.

- For IT, the best is to link the lesson learned to tasks in the project templates. What do you do with nonproject work? As much as possible, you should create templates for recurring regular work. You look at the task and then find the number of the lessons learned.

• In a transportation agency, lessons learned were gathered. The problem was how to use them. The lessons learned were connected to a GPS-based system in buses. Each lesson learned contained the latitude and longitude of the lesson learned.

• In a military organization, lessons learned were gathered to repair trucks. A three-dimensional schematic was employed so that when you clicked on the truck component, the lessons learned appeared.

From these examples, you can see that you want to link the lessons learned to the work.

Figure 7.5 gives a diagram for lessons learned. In this diagram, you can see the gathering, analyzing, and organizing of the lessons learned. Then they are applied. From their application, you gain more experience that can be employed to update the lessons learned.

In repeated use, you will find that there are the following outcomes:

• The existing lesson learned is valid and does not need updating.
• The lesson learned can be expanded upon or changed.
• The scope of the lesson learned has to be adjusted.

Programmers have employed this approach with modules of code. When we were COBOL programmers, we had about 75 modules that were used, reused, and refined. It saved a great deal of time.

With the issues database, the number of issues grows and then stabilizes. After awhile there are not many new issues. For lessons learned it is different. Overtime you can generate literally thousands of lessons learned. However, there must also be a weeding out so the number drops.

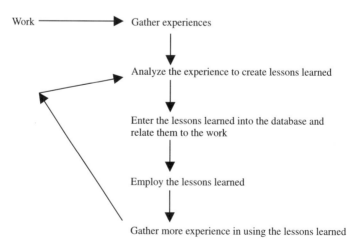

Figure 7.5   Lessons Learned

In this diagram, you can see the gathering, analyzing, and organizing of the lessons learned. Then they are applied. From their application, you gain more experience that can be employed to update the lessons learned.

The approach flows over into the business processes. If you employ lessons learned in doing business work, you increase quality and productivity. You also reduce the informal power of the king and queen bees. Morale may also be increased.

Generating lessons learned can be done with little cost. It just takes collaboration and time. For IT projects that extend over months, it is often a good idea to implement short-term changes that improve the work and contribute to an easier implementation of the system later. We call these short-term actions *Quick Hits*. Lessons learned have proven to be good Quick Hits.

DECIDE ON THE APPROACH FOR DOCUMENTATION

People in IT often complain about documentation and the effort that it requires. Many methods for system requirements, design, testing, etc., can dictate large amounts of documentation. In the real world, some critical questions are:

- What should be documented?
- How should documents be created?

Documentation has suffered from a number of criticisms. The wrong things are documented. Too much detailed documentation is generated about things that are obvious. Many documents are generated from blank paper or computer screens.

It should be emphasized that this is not just an IT issue. Many business processes have little or no written procedures. What is written down formally is often dated and not correct. People often rely on king and queen bees and on yellow "sticky" notes on the sides of cubicles.

The goal is to have a workable approach to documentation that will minimize the amount of documentation, reduce the effort in producing the documents, and still ensure that the most critical areas are addressed.

Let's address these one at a time. What should be documented? The answer depends on the specific topic. If there are few problems and hence little risk, then you might either minimize the document or not do it at all. In deciding whether to generate a document, you want to answer the following questions.

- Who will produce the document?
- Who will review the document?
- Who will use the document?
- Who will update and maintain the document?

- What alternative uses of the resources are there if the document is not produced?
- What is the risk if the document is not produced?

Let's take a simple example. Look at any manual for an automobile. These things have grown often into several hundred pages. They make uneven assumptions about the audience. On the one hand, they assume that you are stupid and cannot open a door. Yet, how did you get into the car? On the other hand, they might tell you how to do repairs yourself. Not a good idea for most people. The most useful part of the manual and where you have risk relates to failure of the vehicle. This means electrical, brake, tire, or other problems—mostly due to wear and tear. Where are these? Scattered around on pages 89, 126, 148, and 234. Not very useful is it? Thus, it is not surprising that many of the manuals are never read, lie alone, forlorn in the glove compartment.

Taking this example as our cue, you can see that a logical approach is based on positive answers to the above of questions. This will trigger you to do the documentation. Pay attention to the last two questions. The alternative use of resources pertains to the opportunity cost if the document is not done. In consulting, when a client asked us for mounds of documentation, we presented a trade-off. Do they want the documentation or would they like more work? All chose more work. No surprise there.

The last question gets to the core of the documentation. What will really happen if the document is not there when you need it? Many documents in IT are out of date and not maintained. Hence, they are not reliable so that they are not used. Many times there is no harm. If there is no manual in the car and you get a flat tire, then based on your past experience and observation, you probably can figure it out for yourself.

Another question is how to generate a document. In IT, there are only a limited number of types of documents. Some examples are listed in Fig. 7.6. The goal in

Document	Comment
Project concept	Good and will be referred to often
Concept for the new process	Can be used in procedures, benefits, and requirements
User requirements	Can come from the new process
System requirements	With standardized tools and packages, this can be abbreviated
Screen design	Can be done through the software
Database layout	Can be done through the dbms
Program documentation	Should be internal to the code
System integration	Very useful
User procedures for the new system	Can be part of operations procedures
Test scripts	There can be too many so you want to concentrate on areas of risk
Training materials	Can be linked to the operations manual

Figure 7.6   Examples of IT Documentation

doing the documentation is to reduce the amount of work while producing quality, usable results in a reasonable time. The table indicates areas of reuse.

INTRODUCE NEW METHODS OR TOOLS

In a previous section you assessed the current methods and tools and produced a table of these. Gaps were identified. Here you want to evaluate and select new methods or tools and then implement them.

New methods or tools do not magically appear. A vendor will develop some tool; a consulting firm or academic develops a new method. Common to all is that they want these things adopted and used. They gain financial rewards and recognition. They promote the new methods and tools in articles in the literature, at trade shows, and through other media. They may give away the first few uses to gain experience and to get references. Then direct marketing follows. You now receive information on these. You are placed in a reactive mode.

It is better to be proactive. From the lessons learned and the analysis of the current methods and tools, you discover where improvements are needed. Then you can look for methods and tools that fill these holes and can replace the ones you have that are not working well. This is a more proactive approach.

When you are considering a new method or tool, you want to have an organized approach for evaluation. Here are some critical questions to answer.

- How does the method or tool fit in with what you have? This is critical to avoid having methods that conflict or tools that require multiple data entry.
- What is the learning curve? How much effort, time, and cost are required to gain expertise? Learning requires that you take people from their existing work to learn as well.
- Does the new method or tool fit within your culture? This is not a trivial question. If the tool requires a great deal of discipline and enforcement and that is the not the style in your organization, it will likely fail or run into problems.
- How would you measure the success of employing the method or tool? If this is fuzzy or long term, people are likely to be discouraged and will drop it.
- Will there be resistance to the method or tool? If the method requires a new way of thinking such as object oriented programming, then there can be some resistance to change.
- How do you determine if people are using the method or tool? For every method or tool, you want to have some measurement and verification approach. You cannot assume that just because you mandate it and people go to training, it will be used.

Structured programming is a good example here. This came along as a method to generate more maintainable COBOL code. However, COBOL did not easily handle structured programming. As a result more code had to be written.

Moreover, it was almost impossible to verify whether every programmer was using structured programming. There were no automated tools for verification. Surprise! It largely failed.

Now let's turn our attention to implementation. One approach is to train most of the staff to whom the method or tool applies. This is fraught with peril. Many will not use the method or tool right away. So the training will be wasted. Here is a better approach.

- Train a few people who can use the method or tool right away.
- Have them use it and monitor the work.
- Gather lessons learned on how best to take advantage of the method or tool.

This will test the value and viability of the method or tool. Before expanding the training, you should hold a meeting in which the individuals who used the method or tool relate their experience. These topics should be covered.

- Overall, how effective was the method or tool?
- How did it compare with previous methods and tools?
- What tips and experience did they learn that they would apply to the next assignment?
- How should other employees learn the method or tool?

ALIGNMENT OF IT AND THE BUSINESS

While you can plan and measure alignment of IT with the business, it is the work itself where the "rubber meets the road" (Fig. 7.7). Note that these questions relate directly to the work. If there are problems with some of the answers or if the answer is sometimes negative, then there are likely problems with the work itself. These then impact IT performance and *impact* the actual alignment of IT.

- Did the methods and tools contribute to better quality work and improved schedules at lower cost?
- Is there collaboration and sharing of knowledge in the work?
- Are lessons learned gathered and used to improve the work?
- Are the skills of junior people raised during the work?
- Is most of the work managed as projects with greater higher level control?
- Is there a reasonable amount of documentation required?
- Is the documentation adequately reviewed and used?
- Is new work planned in advance in terms of how it will be accomplished?
- Are milestones and end products adequately reviewed in terms of risk?
- Are the end products related to value and contribution?

Figure 7.7   Alignment Assessment of IT Work

MANAGE RISK

There are many potential issues and sources of risk in IT work. Here are some common ones that can be addressed with a more structured and organized management of the IT work.

- People just get started on the assignments without any planning. Then they find that some or much of what was done had to be redone.
- There was insufficient attention to potential problems in the work. This often stems from poor reviews of end products and lack of planning and evaluating documentation.
- There is insufficient effort to increase efficiency and effectiveness. Things just go from day-to-day.
- There is an uneven use of methods and tools. Some use them well. Some fail or have major problems—affecting the schedule and cost of the work.
- There appears to be no learning. The same mistakes are made again and again.

EXAMPLES

SUPREME OIL

Supreme Oil IT had a standard policy and procedure manual. Much effort was expended in creating it, reviewing it, and training in its use. But then there was no follow up. No one was held accountable for not using the manual. There were many excuses for not using it.

The most common was that it would take too much time to do the extra work. Another excuse was that it produced a lot of documentation that was not used. After a year, management noticed that there were a number of project failures. These were all traceable to not following the manual.

To remedy the situation, several steps were taken. First, guidelines were produced for using the policies and procedures. Second, completed work products were placed on the network for people to copy and use as models. Third, there was a greater effort in work planning to determine how the guidelines would be followed. This was successful.

TUCKER COUNTY

Milestone and end product reviews were haphazard. It ended up being based upon the interests of the IT manager. After a number of poor end products were produced, business units pressed for change. The IT manager responded by instituting reviews of all work products. This was totally unreasonable. Nothing was getting done. Then the staff started to do more cursory reviews to get things out. The situation was not addressed until a new IT manager arrived.

SHAMROCK AGRICULTURE

At Shamrock, the IT manager reviewed most of the work personally. When the work was mostly maintenance with little development, this was no problem. However, the workload grew. Requests for new systems required more analysis. Then there were also many requests for enhancements. The backlog of work was growing and the manager was not coping well. Something had to give.

Fortunately, the manager recognized the problem before there was a crisis. He delegated more work. He hired a consultant to assist in the analysis. Some of the new development and analysis were outsourced. All of these actions definitely helped, but there was still too much. So he began to focus on the higher risk areas and the backlog disappeared.

LESSONS LEARNED

- In order to change how IT work is managed, you should pursue multiple initiatives in parallel. Otherwise, the time to carry out change may be too long.
- Measure where you are today and then measure again at 6-month intervals. Also, conduct informal measurements in terms of what people say.
- Assume that there will be resistance to change in IT. You want to address this by gaining acknowledgment of the current problems. Thus, for methods and tools you would want to have people agree that there are gaps and problems with those currently in use. To change your documentation approach, you want to get agreement that too much time is spent on generating documents that are not of significant value.

PERFORMANCE MEASURES FOR WORK MANAGEMENT

There are several possible performance measures to employ here. These include:

- General assessment of management of work (Fig. 7.8).
- Assessment of your review of work (Fig. 7.9).
- Evaluation of methods and tools (Fig. 7.10).

- Is the IT work measured beyond budget and schedule?
- Is there adequate emphasis on risk and issues?
- Is the use of methods and tools being measured and managed?
- Is there real teamwork in carrying out IT assignments?
- Has the overall quality of the IT work improved over time?
- Is there a structured approach for introducing new methods and tools?
- How do IT managers check on the work—formally or informally?
- How many surprises have there been in terms of the actual work?
- What is the general quality of the IT work?
- Is there substantial rework required after the work has been completed?

Figure 7.8 Performance Measures for Work Management

- How are end products selected for review?
- Have there been instances when an end product was approved, but later had to be revised due to problems?
- What is the approach for end product review? Does it focus on risk and issues?
- Do people give lessons learned from the review of the work?
- Is there any effort to see if people are doing later work better after a review?
- How many of the end products are reviewed in detail?
- How many end products are just accepted based on the word of the person(s) who performed the work?
- Are the results of the end product reviews captured in lessons learned?
- Are issues that surface during a review included in the issues database?

Figure 7.9 Performance Measures for Work Review

- Have you identified the gaps in your current methods and tools?
- How do you identify new methods and tools?
- How are new methods and tools evaluated?
- How are new methods and tools selected?
- How are methods and tools evaluated in terms of effectiveness?
- Are management expectations clearly spelled out?
- How do you get new employees up to speed on the methods and tools?
- How effective is the training in methods and tools?
- Do you make an effort to eliminate some of the older, less effective methods and tools?
- How do you verify that the methods and tools are employed effectively?
- Are guidelines produced for using the methods and tools more effectively?
- How do you measure the value of the methods and tools?

Figure 7.10 Performance Measures for Methods and Tools

SUMMARY

Managing IT work means managing your time effectively. IT work consists not only of the work itself and getting status on the work. Rather, it includes the methods and tools, reviews of end products, dealing with issues, and using experience. One general objective in managing the work is to improve morale and attitude toward the work. Another goal is to achieve cumulative improvement. This has been an elusive target for many IT groups. Yet, it is absolutely essential if we are to make IT more predictable and meet the increasing demands of the business.

Part III

Direct and Coordinate IT

Chapter 8

Coordinate Business Unit Activities

INTRODUCTION

Many business units are heavily involved in the operations of their systems. A business unit typically has a person who does on the spot, initial diagnosis of problems and answering questions. Managers and employees are using the systems for production, analysis of production, and handling of other supporting processes. Since they use systems everyday, it is natural for them to take IT support for granted.

Problems emerge when there are needs for additional IT work. Here, there is often a lack of coordination and planning. Some examples of the problems are:

• A business manager makes a request of IT without reviewing it with the employees. The IT manager may listen to the request and then treat it with high priority without a thorough investigation.

• Employees find problems that they then relate to middle management. A middle level manager then makes direct contact with an IT programmer and asks for some action. The programmer then drops whatever he or she was working on.

What are the impacts of these situations? The response will likely not be immediate. This may turn off the users. Working on ad hoc business requests can destroy the productivity of IT. In one IT group, the IT work was tracked for 2 weeks in detail. It was discovered that over 70% of the programming and networking staffs' time were consumed by such work. No real progress was made on several significant projects and upgrades.

At the heart of the problems are two factors. One, on the business side, is the presumption that IT should be ready and available to help them—almost at the drop of a hat. The other, on the IT side, is the desire to please users and business managers.

Having satisfied and happy users is a nice goal. However, satisfaction and happiness are very fleeting. There is sometimes the attitude, "What has IT done for us lately?" Why does this happen? Often, it is because there were no reasonable and articulated expectations and definitions of roles and responsibilities.

In this chapter, the following topics will be covered that relate to business units. First, the definition of the roles and responsibilities of business units with respect to IT needs to be defined jointly. The current state of business automation should be reviewed. To gain more stability in the relationship between business departments and IT, long-term plans should be developed for the major business processes that the department uses. With process plans defined, you can then proceed to develop an IT strategy for the business unit based upon the work in Chapter 4 related to strategic IT planning. Then attention will be turned to more detailed IT support and responding to user requests.

What are the benefits if you carry out these activities successfully?

• The business unit managers and employees will clearly know their roles and what constitutes acceptable behavior.
• IT becomes more knowledgeable about the business in terms of work, direction, and needs.
• IT can be more proactive in supporting the business as opposed to waiting for the next business request.
• The business unit can do more effective coordination of its IT effort.
• With many needs now defined, there will tend to be fewer ad hoc requests.

This may appear negative about business units. It is not intended to be. The business plays a key role in IT. The purpose of the above steps is to structure the activities and actions of the business units so that both the business and IT are more productive and effective.

COLLABORATE ON DEFINING THE ROLES OF BUSINESS UNITS IN IT

Let's start with an individual application system. Let's consider the operations of one system. In this situation, the traditional role of the business unit might include the following:

• Perform work using the system.
• Identify problems for the system to IT.
• Participate in testing changes to the application system.
• Determine any enhancements that are necessary and justify these.

There are a number of problems if the role is kept within these limits. Notice, for example, there is no real link between the process and the system. The system is treated separately. Another problem is that there is no strategy for the process and, hence, no direction for the system. Changes that are requested tend to be tactical, consume IT resources, and are often justified by the limited benefits received. In fact, experience shows that the changes typically are either to handle new business or to add features that are nice to have.

A more productive set of responsibilities consists of the following:

- Analyze the performance of the process that includes the system.
- Identify potential changes to the application that will substantially contribute to the performance of the business process.
- Perform work using the system.
- Identify problems in the process as well as the system.
- Participate in testing changes.
- Develop operations procedures for both the process and system.

This list is more encompassing than the first and is process focused. There are a number of benefits to this expanded role. Some of these are:

- The process and system are tightly linked.
- Any proposed change will be connected to real benefit in the process, not just in the use of the system.
- End users adopt more of a sense of ownership of both the process and the system.

Now suppose that you are going to carry out an IT project to support improvements to a business process. The traditional business role is:

- Provide information to support systems analysis and design for the new system.
- Participate in the development of user procedures for the system.
- Take part in the testing of the system
- Perform some of the data conversion work.
- Support training in the use of the system.

Let's add more to this given our orientation toward the business processes. Here are some additional items:

- Review the current process and work to identify problems.
- Collaborate in the definition of the new business processes.
- Determine the benefits of the new process and how they will be realized.
- Implement procedure, policy, and other near-term changes that support the implementation of the new process later.
- Develop operations procedures that include the user procedures.

- Build training materials.
- Train the employees.
- Train new employees.

A typical business response might be that they do not have sufficient resources. Everyone is tied up in the work. The next thing that you might encounter is that the project is an IT project so they should not have to do these things. The third response is that the end users are not qualified to do the work. Here is how you should respond.

- If everyone in the department is too busy, then the project should not be started. User participation is key to change and success.
- Unless the work is entirely in IT involving the infrastructure, there is no such thing as an IT project. It is a business project to improve or replace a business process of which IT is a major, but not the only, part.
- End users working jointly with IT staff can perform these activities.

Now let's move up to the IT involvement overall for a business unit. We all agree that the business processes are very important. They should be carefully planned and managed. There should be an overall process coordinator in the business unit. His duties include the following:

- Develop and update the process plans.
- Define with the employees the changes that will support the improvement of the business process.
- Measure the performance of the business processes and systems.
- Manage the flow of information between the business unit and IT.
- Provide feedback to IT on their performance.
- Identify potential improvements to the business processes.
- Review how employees are doing their work in the processes.

This is for a higher level person in the department. Note that these activities are not full time. Once they are established, the person can do his or her normal work.

Next, there should be a lower level coordinator who handles day-to-day problems with the business process and system as they arise. This person works through the process coordinator in communicating with IT management. They work directly with IT staff on specific issues.

There are several benefits of this method of two-tiered process coordination. First, the phrase is "process coordination" not system coordination. This is by intent. The process performance is the key. This approach provides a single point of contact for IT management (the process coordinator), the business employees (the lower level coordinator), and the IT staff (both).

Figure 8.1 gives a list of responsibilities and roles for the business unit that is consistent with the above discussion.

- General process coordination
- Detailed, day-to-day process coordination
- Training of all staff in the business process
- Ensuring that knowledge in doing the work is shared among employees
- Looking for and implementing process changes that do not involve IT
- Working to incorporate shadow systems into the overall system
- Eliminating exception work and workarounds wherever possible
- Controlling the informal power of the king and queen bees
- Developing and maintaining documentation and training materials on the business processes
- Measuring the performance of the business processes
- Working collaboratively with IT on changes and fixes to the software

Figure 8.1   Roles and Responsibilities of the Business Unit in IT

How do you market the new responsibilities to a business unit? A good method is to appeal to self-interest. That is, if IT has to do more of the work, then the business employees will not assume ownership. They will think that responsibility for benefits, etc., lie with IT. While this is ridiculous, you should bring this forward. Additionally, after the documentation has been completed, someone has to update it. Since the users are the owners of it, they should perform the development and maintenance. Now turn to training. IT does not really know when new employees show up to do work. The department does. So they should assume responsibility for both initial and ongoing training.

CREATE LONG-TERM PROCESS PLANS

What is a process plan? The process plan provides the long-term direction for the business process. As such, it provides the business and IT managers and staff with a better understanding of the following:

- The problems in the current work and their impacts.
- Potential changes that can be made in the short-term (Quick Hits) together with their benefits.
- A vision of the long-term process.
- The detailed long-term process and the benefits.

One benefit from doing this is that using collaboration, employees gain consensus on the problems and what is needed. This will make it easier for both IT and business management later. Another benefit is that the direction of the process is laid out clearly so that any requests for systems changes can be evaluated in terms of the process plan. The process plan also helps to identify to the management the extent to which improvements are possible. A fourth benefit is that the plan delineates Quick Hits that can be taken in the immediate future to improve the process. This alone can justify the process plan. In short, the process plan provides an umbrella for an organized approach to process improvement.

If this is such a good idea, why doesn't everyone do this? Well, it is overhead effort. Many people think their processes are OK so they do not require process plans. Others focus on the business and IT plans. This is faulty since the processes are what really count in business performance.

How do you start? Begin with applying the business process performance measurements in Chapter 2 (Fig. 2.16). This tells you how the process is performing today. Develop this score card in a collaborative way with the employees. Why do this? Can't you do it yourself? Of course, you can. That is neither the point nor the purpose. The goal in developing the score card is not just to get the evaluation, it is also to have employees bring up the problems in the current work. This is a good start, but there is more to do.

Go out into the business process and see how the work is being performed by different people. Is the work consistent? If not, then there are additional problems. Here are some additional steps for you to take.

• Another step is to ferret out the exception work. Remember that this is not only time consuming, but also taking up senior business employee's time since the exceptions require more knowledge.
• Find the shadow systems. In the long-term process, you will want to automate and standardize these.
• Identify the workarounds. These are getting in the way of productivity.
• Evaluate the quality, completeness, and currency of the training materials and operations procedures.

Now you are getting a grasp of the problems in the process as well as gaining an understanding of the process performance. Create a group within the department to look at the problems and issues. First, get them to determine the impacts of the problems on the performance of the work. This can be depressing, but it is valuable. Why? Because the employees are now realizing that problems in the business processes exist and that there are substantial impacts on process performance flowing from these problems. The next step is to rank the issues in terms of their importance and impact. Through discussions and voting, you should be able to gain a consensus ranking from those who have the greatest impact to the least.

To raise morale and in order to move to positive steps, have them find some potential actions and changes that can be made that can address each problem. Make sure that they consider more than system changes. Have them think about policies, procedures, staff assignments, training, documentation, and work layout. The results will be that some issues can be taken care of by simple changes or Quick Hits. Others will require a combination of system and business changes. Still others will not have any easy solution.

Problems (ranked)	Impacts	Solutions	Ease of implementation	Quick Hit or long-term change

Figure 8.2 Table in Support of Process Planning

With the ranking and the changes identified, it is time for the next round of voting. Here you want to have employees based upon their experience vote on how easy the changes will be to implement. They can take into account what they think the resistance to change will be along with time and money.

You can now summarize what you have so far in a table. Figure 8.2 provides the structure for the table. The rows are the problems. The first column indicates the impact of each problem. All but the last column come directly from the preceding steps. The last column labels the changes in terms of whether they are Quick Hits or require longer term change efforts.

You are now ready to develop the long-term process. Don't start this until you have undertaken the above steps. The long-term process should, after all, handle the issues and problems that have been detailed. Defining the long-term work at a general level is too vague. Experience shows that employees should concentrate on specific, common transactions. Don't even think about exceptions.

Make a list of transactions with the employees. Then assign these out to them. Here are some guidelines.

• Write down the individual steps in the transaction.
• The work performed in the step.
• For each step, associate any of the issues and problems that were identified above.
• Put down the impacts of the issue on the step and transaction.

Have the employees now match up the Quick Hits to the transactions. One Quick Hit may apply to several transactions. Since the employees do the work everyday, they are in the best position to determine how the process will work if the Quick Hits are implemented. This is best accomplished by documenting the following:

• The individual transaction steps.
• The modified work that is done after Quick Hits.
• The remaining issues that would not have been addressed by Quick Hits.
• The differences between this workflow and that of the current work.
• The benefits of the changes to the work.

If the employees perform this for the top 10 or so transactions, these generally account for over 60–70% of the volume of work. It will now be possible to estimate the total benefits of the Quick Hits.

- Introduction—purpose and scope, why the process plan was created
- Summary of the current process and system
- Issues in the current process and impacts
- Examples of common transactions as they are today
- Table of problems, impacts, and solutions
- Quick Hit changes and their benefits
- Long-term direction for the process
- Long-term specific transactions and the differences with the current and Quick Hits
- Specific actions that can be taken

Figure 8.3   Outline of the Process Plan

The employees have now worked out the effects of the Quick Hits. Using brainstorming and creativity, try to get people to think about how they would like the work to be done if there were no constraints on systems, technology, money, facilities, etc. Do not impose reality yet. If they are running into problems, take a simple example transaction. Here are the items to specify for the long-term transaction.

- The future transaction steps.
- The work that will be performed in each step.
- The difference between these steps and the work after the Quick Hits.
- The difference between these steps and the current work.
- The benefits of the changes to the work after the Quick Hits.
- The benefits of the changes from the current work.

As before, you can now estimate the benefits of the long-term process. You can now also generalize the transactions that you considered into a vision of the general process.

Figure 8.3 gives an outline of the process plan. After you develop it, circulate it among the employees to get feedback and validation. When you present to the business unit management, take care to involve several of the employees in the presentation. This will indicate commitment to change.

DEVELOP A BUSINESS UNIT IT STRATEGY

What is a business unit IT strategy? Well, it is really not a detailed strategy. Rather, it contains a number of elements that pertain to processes, mission, vision, and IT. The strategy includes the following elements:

- The importance of systems and technology to the business unit.
- The mission of the business unit and how it is related to the business processes.
- The relationship of the mission of the business unit to that of the company.
- The role of IT in supporting the mission of the business unit.

You can support this through a series of tables. The first table in Fig. 8.4 gives the mission elements versus the business processes. The entry details how each process supports the individual mission element. Using Chapter 2, you can prepare the table in Fig. 8.5 that gives the relationship between the business unit mission and the company mission. The entry is a "X" if the business unit mission element is important to the specific company mission element. To help you check for consistency, you can employ the table of mission versus business processes. Figure 8.6 gives the role of IT in supporting each business process. Listed as rows are the various activities that IT performs in helping out a process. The table entry indicates the type of support required. Finally, Fig. 8.7 can be created from the tables in Figs 8.4 and 8.6. The table in this figure relates IT support to the business unit mission.

One benefit of having management define and discuss these tables is that they learn how the business unit relates to the overall business in some detail. This replaces general perceptions. Next, the tables assist both IT and the business unit in determining the type of IT support required and what it means to the business. This definitely helps IT in setting priorities.

Processes

Mission element			

Figure 8.4 Mission Elements for a Business Unit Versus Processes

Company mission element

Business unit mission element			

Figure 8.5 Business Unit Mission Versus Company Mission

Business unit processes

IT support element			

Figure 8.6 IT Support Versus Business Processes

Business unit mission

IT support element			

Figure 8.7 IT support Versus Business Unit Mission

PROVIDE EFFECTIVE END USER SUPPORT

End user support is always provided by IT. The question here is the extent to which the support is effective. What does effective mean? Effective here means that

- The business processes work efficiently and effectively
- The business unit IT strategy is supported through IT effort
- The combined IT work on a process supports the attainment of the long-term view of the process

Don't most IT groups strive for these goals through their support? They try, but it is difficult to do if there is no process plan or business unit IT strategy. To measure your progress, the questions in Fig. 8.8 are provided.

ALIGNMENT OF IT AND THE BUSINESS

Since this chapter deals with business involvement in IT, alignment of IT to the business can be almost directly measured here. Figure 8.9 gives a list of questions that can help you appraise the degree of alignment with individual business units.

- What is the division of IT resources among the business processes operated by the business unit? Does this allocation fit with the importance of the processes?
- In reviewing support of a business unit, did the support promote the attainment of the business unit IT strategy?
- Did the IT support promote the process plan?
- When comparing the business process today and a year ago, did IT support contribute to positive change?
- What was the percentage of IT support resources in process improvement versus repairs and emergency fixes?

Figure 8.8 Questions Related to IT Support Effectiveness

- What is the extent of communications between the business unit and IT?
- If problems in the business process are identified, are non-IT solutions considered?
- Does the business unit have process plans? Are these updated?
- Do the process plans give a clear idea of the nature of the long-term future of the work?
- What is the allocation of IT resources across business units? Does this allocation match up with the key processes that support the business vision and mission?
- What important IT initiatives relative to business processes were not begun? Why did this occur?

Figure 8.9 Questions Related to IT and Business Unit Alignment

MANAGE RISK

There is substantial risk in the relationship between IT and the business units. A major risk is that substantial IT resources are devoted to minor enhancements that do not contribute to attaining the process plan or the business IT strategy.

Do the strategic IT plan and the IT resource allocation take into account the relative importance of the business processes and process plans? If not, there could be a major risk. IT can be criticized for not working on the projects that will make major contributions to the business. We have said that IT success can promote the success of the business. However, it is also true that:

Misallocated IT resources and work dedicated to marginal business activities can prevent the business from achieving its potential in terms of revenue, costs, and profitability.

EXAMPLES

SUPREME OIL

Supreme Oil is a multinational energy company. As systems and technology became more deployed and the business became more dependent upon IT, it became clear that there had to be greater structure to IT activities in the business units. The approach that was taken was to establish the two tiers of coordination. Larger business units had a lower level coordinator in each department.

An oversight committee was formed to share information and coordinate IT across the various business units. This was headed by the IT manager. The upper level coordinators in business units were the other members. The committee initially met quarterly to address the numerous IT issues. As these were addressed, the frequency became annual.

Later, IT was split up so that each major business unit had its own IT group. The oversight approach had worked well and so the members were replaced by their respective IT managers in each business unit.

TUCKER COUNTY

Tucker County had no oversight or planning for business departments. Everything was ad hoc and "catch as catch can." In response, some of the department supervisors had established personal relationships with individuals in IT. They used these relationships to get requests handled. At the end of 1 year, it was uncovered that IT had completed only 30% of its planned work. Working on these ad hoc requests was the reason. The IT manager blamed obsolete technology.

To both upper managers and business managers, this answer was not credible. With the aid of a consultant, an oversight committee was created. This committee was chaired by a business unit manager familiar with IT. The direction that the committee took was to take over the direction of IT from the manager. Department employees and supervisors were told by their managers to work through their own management with problems and not to contact IT. This worked.

SHAMROCK AGRICULTURE

Most of the business units in Shamrock worked in unique activities. There was only a limited number of processes that crossed departments. Process plans were developed for these cross-department processes. The coordination committee for IT consisted of members of the departments involved in these processes.

For the other business units, IT was subject to the style of the individual business management. In the case of one business unit, the manager wanted to have more modern systems even though the current systems worked. On his own he contacted several vendors and initiated contract negotiations. He did not inform either upper management or the IT manager. After negotiations, he presented the contracts to headquarters as a fait accompli. Senior managers became almost irate. The IT manager was sent in to review the situation. Other packages that were better than those selected by the business unit manager were identified. However, it was too late. The business manager stated that, "The new software was necessary and essential to meet his business goals and keep the operations going." IT and senior management decided that the best course of action was to let the installation proceed, expecting it to fail. Failure did result. The software was never completely installed or operational. The department employees did not like the new software and preferred the existing software. There was almost a rebellion.

Some good came from this disaster. First, the company implemented policies to prevent this situation from ever recurring. Second, IT was directed to work more closely with these "standalone" departments. Additional process plans were developed. Third, the business manager who initiated the problems was demoted and transferred.

LESSONS LEARNED

- From experience, it is important to start to work one business unit that is forward thinking and friendly to IT. Then you can use the experience and success from this unit to move to other business units.
- It is impossible to provide support to all business units in developing process plans and their IT strategies. You have to select which departments and business units are most important to the business. In the case of Shamrock Agriculture, the number of critical business units was three out of nine.

• You may encounter some resistance among IT staff in providing the planning type of support. Yet, as we have seen, this is critical for IT to become more proactive and productive in support of the business units. To bring some IT staff around, you should demonstrate how much support was really not of that much importance.

• Fairness is a bad idea. That is, allocating resources evenly across business units is not in line with the business process importance or the business mission. This means that in implementing the discussion in this chapter, you will find that, inevitably, support for some business units will be minimal. That is the price to be paid when you have limited IT resources.

PERFORMANCE MEASURES FOR USER RELATIONS

One set of performance measures can be defined for individual business units. This is given in Fig. 8.10. Here are some comments on these items.

• IT should develop individual performance measures with each major business unit. The items in the figure provide a starting point.

• Some companies use performance measures such as these as part of the evaluation of departments and business units. IT performance is then related to the rating of business performance.

Another group of performance measures relates to IT. Figure 8.11 provides a list of questions that IT can apply to assess its own performance over time.

• Does the department maintain up-to-date operations procedures?
• Are new employees formally trained in the processes and systems?
• How many business unit managers and staff have direct contact with IT employees?
• Is the business process measured and evaluated?
• Do business employees resist change? If so, how does their management react?

Figure 8.10 Performance Measures for Department Involvement in IT

• What is the turnover in IT staff in working with the business unit?
• Do IT staff provide a consistent or contradictory message to the business unit?
• What is the quality of the IT work? Do many problems appear after there are system changes?
• Do IT staff help guide business employees in analyzing the process, doing documentation, performing testing, and other tasks?
• Does IT do a thorough review of the benefit analysis performed by the business unit?
• Are the user and system requirements consistent?
• Do the changes to the system contribute to an improved business process?

Figure 8.11 Assessment of IT Performance from a Business Unit Perspective

- How many requests does a business unit make during a quarter?
- Does the business unit conduct analysis of the requests before they are turned over to IT?
- Is there widespread support for the changes that are generated by requests?
- Are department requests consistent?
- Are benefits measured after the changes to the system have been implemented?
- Is the process formally changed after the enhancements to the systems have been completed?
- To what extent do business employees participate in the testing of the changes to a system?
- To what extent do business units assume ownership of the operations procedures and training materials?

Figure 8.12   Overall Assessment of Business Involvement in IT

A third performance measure can be utilized by upper management to evaluate IT work from the standpoint of the business. This is given in Fig. 8.12.

SUMMARY

The role of the business units in IT has always been viewed as important. The problem has been that having said this, there was little structure imposed to make business unit participation in IT effective. The most successful processes in companies today owe at least some of their success to effective department involvement in IT. Many of the successful companies have implemented either the same or similar approaches to the ones discussed in this chapter. To see why structure is needed, go back to the Shamrock Agriculture example and you can see the impacts of lack of framework for IT involvement.

Chapter 9

Direct Outsourcing and Manage Vendors

INTRODUCTION

Outsourcing is the transferal of IT and/or business functions to an outside party—usually for an extended period of time. Why the extended time? Because it requires a great deal of effort to set up, establish, and then manage the outsourcing. For the vendor it means preparing for the outsourcing, negotiating for the contract, transitioning the work, doing the work, and managing the work. Outsourcing may not pay off for some time.

What are some of the advantages of outsourcing for you? Here are common benefits that are frequently cited.

- Economies of scale. The vendor is experienced in this work and can perform it at a lower cost since they are doing the same type of work for other firms.
- Concentration on core activities. If you outsource marginal activities, then you can direct your resources to these core activities. An example might be outsourcing the help desk in IT. However, there are costs in managing and coordinating outsourcing.
- Transfer of the problems to the vendor. If you are having problems in staffing or managing the work, then the vendor's expertise and experience can fill in the gap.
- Potentially lower cost. In some situations, you may save money by outsourcing. This is especially the case when you outsource overseas where the labor costs are 25% or less than your labor costs.

• Support for startup activities. If you are getting into a new business, then outsourcing may be the fastest way to get into business quickly. This has been the case for many e-commerce startup activities.

• Gain access to technical and/or business expertise that you do not have through the vendor personnel.

• Handling new work that the current staff cannot address.

• Obtain a fixed level of services for a fixed price.

• Fix problems in processes that the firm has been unable to address.

What are the disadvantages of outsourcing?

• Outsourcing creates dependencies for work with vendors.

• If the outsourcing doesn't work, then it may be difficult to get the work back or change vendors.

• Outsourcing vendors may make changes, institute policies, or use their software so as to lock you into their services.

• Every task or piece of work beyond that in the outsourcing contract will end up costing extra—perhaps, substantially escalating the costs.

• More issues are likely to surface as another, third party is involved.

Figure 9.1 gives several graphs relating to outsourcing. These graphs help to support a useful strategy for your outsourcing. In this figure, time is the horizontal axis. The vertical axis is cost. The cost of the work to be outsourced is shown as a solid horizontal line. However, what happens over time is that the process deteriorates. Costs increase as is shown by the solid line going up from the horizontal line. The outsourcing firm bids a price that is lower than the current cost. The savings to you are labeled A.

The problem is that many businesses or IT processes have problems and need work. You can either do it yourself or let the vendor do it. If you let the vendor clean up the process and streamline it, they get the benefits of it. You pay a higher

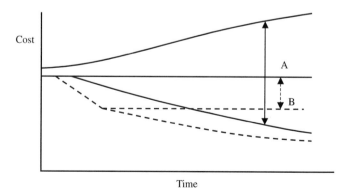

Figure 9.1   A Graphical View of Outsourcing

price than is needed. So if you clean up the work, then you drive the cost down as is shown by the dashed line that comes below the solid horizontal line. Now if you outsource the streamlined process, the vendor must propose a lower cost shown by the lower dashed line. The difference in the cost before and after cleanup is shown by B. The vendor now charges you a lower cost and you pocket the difference.

Why would you and the vendor want to have you clean up the work first? For you it is to get cost savings, better measurement, and a simpler process that will be more trouble-free if you decide to outsource. For the vendor, you have the most knowledge and control of the work. Therefore, you are in the best position to do the cleanup. The vendor may make less money, but there is reduced risk.

Is it better to consider outsourcing business or IT functions? Outsourcing IT functions has a history leading back to the 1960s with facilities management in which vendors managed computer centers for clients. Business outsourcing goes back thousands of years with the use of mercenary troops. Machiavelli in *The Prince* wrote the first guidelines on managing outsourcing—some of these are valid today for business.

Outsourcing overseas appears very attractive with much lower labor costs than either Europe, Japan, or the United States. Modern networks and communications support worldwide instantaneous contacts. The vendor may pay only 20–25% of the cost for the labor, but there are additional costs of management, transition, and operations. So the overall cost may be about 30% less. Experience shows that there are other problems with overseas outsourcing. Some of these are:

- While the people in the other country speak your language, the meaning and use of the words and terminology are different.
- The people overseas may require canned scripts to respond to specific questions. This is fine if you are outsourcing some activity that is highly structured.
- There are cultural differences that are often not considered in outsourcing. These range from religious and cultural holidays to attitudes toward work. They can affect the outsourcing work.
- The country where the work is being performed may have political unrest. The communications may not be up to par.
- Coordination with a group halfway around the world takes more coordination effort and time.

This is not to say that outsourcing is a bad idea. It just must be approved with eyes open and an organized approach. Outsourcing is a fact of life. It is now a part of business strategies to control costs. Most major firms now consider outsourcing for many, if not all, processes.

The major theme in this chapter is that you establish a win–win relationship with vendors in outsourcing. If you are getting the work too cheap, then the vendor suffers and you will eventually pay the price in lower levels of service, lower quality of work, or higher cost.

SOME EXAMPLES OF OUTSOURCING SUCCESS AND FAILURE

We helped a maker of furniture in Kalimantan (Borneo) in Indonesia establish an export trade for his wares. Everything had to be outsourced given the infrastructure, cost, available labor, and skill in his plant. After a great deal of study, the website and programming was performed in India. The goods were shipped to a warehouse in Mexico. The call center that was used was in Ireland. Why Ireland? Because many Irish do not speak English with an accent. The website was based on the Isle of Man for tax reasons. The final problem was where to establish a banking relationship. A bank on the island of Niue in the Pacific was setup. This has been very successful. Today over 40% of the goods from the plant are sent to Europe.

A major aerospace firm decided to outsource an engineering support area. Word leaked out to the employees in the group. They discussed it amongst themselves and decided that their jobs would be eliminated. There was a great deal of documentation that they employed. Their decision was to smuggle the documents home and then burn them in their fireplaces. This effort consumed several weeks. When management then showed up to announce their decision, they said "OK, but there is no documentation for what we do." Management then decided not to outsource the area. The people kept their jobs. This example reveals the need for planning and employee coordination in advance.

A major firm in the United States decided to outsource all of its IT work. They did not consider the legacy systems maintenance. Moreover, there was a unique systems architecture. This was a 3-year outsourcing arrangement. The company almost failed because the maintenance programmers quit along with the network support staff. There were many problems. The outsourcing contract was cancelled in 6 months. All work was brought back inside.

PURSUE AN ORGANIZED APPROACH TO OUTSOURCING

What is the approach that many firms use? Answer—none. They decide that some activity should be outsourced. Then they may or may not gather requirements that are complete. Most of the time they do not clean up the work. Then they prepare a Request for Proposal (RFP) or Request for Quotation (RFQ) and submit it to a number of vendors.

There is often a bidder's conference where vendors can ask questions. Proposals are then submitted and the lowest cost, qualified vendor is selected. The work is handed over and problems set in.

On the surface this appears to be normal. Why are there problems? Here is a list that has been gathered from experience relating to this usual approach.

- The activity is not selected carefully. Multiple business and IT activities interact and interface. There was no examination of alternatives for outsourcing. There is no outsourcing strategy.
- There is no detailed examination of the process and work to be outsourced. Requirements that are gathered are too general. There is no cleanup of the work.
- The RFP or RFQ is often flawed and incomplete. People who have not prepared either of these do the work. The vendors have to respond to incomplete requirements.
- The bidder's conference is the only opportunity to ask questions. Often, there is no tour or walkthrough of the area to be cleaned up.
- The employees involved in the activity to be outsourced are given too little information and so become apprehensive and fearful of their jobs. They can sabotage the outsourcing effort.
- There is no plan or detailed organized approach for the transition of the work. Problems arise.
- With all of these problems, the vendors sometime come back and raise issues that increase the cost.

Here are some specific steps to achieve greater outsourcing success.

- Develop an overall outsourcing strategy for process and IT outsourcing. This strategy should provide selection guidelines for processes and IT opportunities for outsourcing.
- Determine what is to be outsourced. This is the more in-depth assessment of the business and IT areas in line with the strategy.
- Prepare for outsourcing. This includes process measurement and possible cleanup.
- Prepare the RFP. This includes the requirements, the preparation and issuance of the RFP, and the bidder's conference.
- Select the vendor and negotiate the contract.
- Plan for the transition of the work to the vendor.
- Perform the transition of the work.
- Manage the vendor relationship and work.

DEVELOP AN OVERALL OUTSOURCING STRATEGY

The benefits of an outsourcing strategy have been discussed. The outsourcing strategy contains the following elements:

- How outsourcing will be planned. This gives the method for evaluating multiple processes in business and IT for outsourcing.

• Criteria for selection of work and processes for outsourcing. This includes how processes will be selected along with the general method for process measurement and cleanup.

• Roles and responsibilities of business units, support units (e.g., purchasing and legal), IT, and management.

• Approach for vendor evaluation and selection. This encompasses service level agreements (SLAs) and contracts.

• Method for planning and transitioning the work to the vendors.

• Management approach for overseeing the vendor work. How coordination of additional work and oversight of work will be done are covered here.

DETERMINE WHAT IS TO BE OUTSOURCED

There are many possibilities for business processes so attention will be centered on IT activities. Figure 9.2 gives a list of IT areas that can be potentially outsourced. Comments on specific areas are given below.

• Computer center operations is a standard operation. However, there are some risks. The vendor could go out of business. Moreover, there are security issues related to software and data. You will have to have an approach for overseeing the data center of the vendor. The vendor could install proprietary computer utilities or other software, making you dependent upon them.

- Operations of the computer center
- Major hardware support
- PC hardware: installation, maintenance, and upgrades
- Network planning and management
- Network installation and testing
- Network and systems security
- Internet links and operations
- Network operation and troubleshooting
- Help desk
- General IT-related training for software and networking
- Application system installation
- Application system training
- Application system customization, support, and maintenance
- Systems planning
- Technology assessment and architecture
- Systems analysis and design
- System development
- System integration
- System testing
- Data conversion and testing
- Evaluation and selection of software packages

Figure 9.2   Potential IT Outsourcing Areas

- PC support. This is very standard. However, it is a good idea to have two firms under contract. This will tend to keep each on their toes in terms of performance.
- Network planning and management is difficult to outsource because it is an ongoing need and important in determining both costs of operation and performance.
- Network operations, installation, and testing are more routine and are typical candidates for outsourcing.
- The help desk may be an issue. If the help desk handles many technical calls, then it might be too expensive to establish outsourcing. You could end up with a high percentage of the calls just being referred back to you—not much savings or benefit there. However, it is a suitable candidate if most of the calls are routine.
- Software training, installation support, and related activities are suitable for outsourcing since you will be drawing upon the expertise and experience of the vendor.
- Systems planning can be contracted out the first time. However, you should be able to do the updates to the plan on your own.
- Technology assessment firms such as the Gartner Group, Yankee Group, and other technology watch organizations can save you time and provide useful information more rapidly than when you do the research yourself. The same comments apply to software evaluation and selection.

Perhaps, the most difficult decision to make relates to software maintenance. If you are using standard software packages that have not been extensively customized, then this makes it a reasonable candidate. However, if the software consists of legacy systems, then the vendor would have to hire the same people to do the same work. No savings are likely here.

How do you select which activities are most suitable for outsourcing? Here are some criteria.

- Exposure if the vendor goes out of business.
- The likelihood that a vendor has the requisite skills and capabilities to perform the work.
- The extent to which you are dependent upon internal employees so that their knowledge is not easily transferred.
- The interrelationship between different activities. Interdependencies lead to considering several processes as a group.
- Whether the work involves critical business knowledge or sensitive information.
- Potential exposure if the employees leave or fail to work as hard.

The general process of evaluation should be based upon elimination. Anything you remove will be kept internal. Why not proactive selection? Because in today's environment, you want to consider the widest possible variety of work.

PREPARE FOR OUTSOURCING

Even before the selection is made, you should begin to work with the Human Resources group. You should assume that once the selection is made, word will leak out to the employees. You want to get ahead of this.

Now let's turn to the activity to be outsourced. You will first want to measure it using the process measurement list in Chapter 2. After the measurement, you will have identified actions that must be taken for cleanup. Keep in mind the following:

- There is only a limited time for cleanup. Usually, this is at most several months.
- You do not have time or money to embark on any major automation project. Anything you do will likely be replaced when the activity is outsourced.
- You have to be careful in making any promises to people involved in the activity because they might be part of the outsourced. Keep consulting with the Human Resource group. Obviously, they are going to have to be told what is going on and what will happen to them and their jobs.

These are substantial constraints in time, resources, and money. From experience, here are some potential areas of action:

- *Policies.* You may be able to simplify or streamline policies affecting the activity. If the activity is to be outsourced, you will certainly want to install new controls over the incoming work.
- *Procedures and workflow.* This is the nuts and bolts of who does what and how they do it. Making procedures simpler will likely reduce costs later.
- *Training.* You can update the training of the staff in the activity. This will ensure that there is greater consistency in the work.
- *Documentation.* The procedures and methods must be documented for turnover to the vendor.
- *Minor systems and technology work.* Although you cannot do wholesale replacement or changes, you can consider minor enhancements in the software.
- *Work layout.* It might be possible to improve the work layout for more efficient work without cost.

After you have performed these actions, then you can measure the process again to see the effects of the actions. A second impact is that the activity is now better understood, documented, and measured. This will become valuable when you are negotiating with an outsourcing vendor. The vendor cannot then claim that the first thing that they have to do is to cleanup the work.

What have you accomplished with this limited effort? First, you have lowered some costs and increased efficiency in the short term. It is possible that the changes have been so dramatic that there is no need to consider outsourcing.

Overall, by making the work more efficient, you are in a better position to perform the following:

- Negotiate on price and other terms.
- Measure and control the vendor effort.
- Support a faster turnover of work to the vendor.

PREPARE THE REQUEST FOR PROPOSAL

You should first identify the evaluation criteria. This depends upon the specific activity, but some general criteria can be given. These include:

- Performance improvement that the vendor could make in the activity in terms of performance or service.
- Potential economies of scale through outsourcing.
- Feasibility in doing the work without outsourcing; although negative, this criterion fits the situation where your outsourcing need is focused.
- Interdependencies of the activity with other activities that will be retained.
- Qualifications of the vendor to do the work.

Another action is to identify potential vendors. You can find vendors through the web, magazines, and literature. Draw up a list of questions that can be posed to the vendors to narrow the field. Start gathering information from the vendors.

In preparing the RFP, you want to include the following items.

- Goals of the outsourcing.
- Description of the requirements for outsourcing work in the form of lists.
- Skills and knowledge required of the outsourcing vendor.
- Technology and systems employed in the performance of the activity.
- Measurements of the current activity.
- Transition approach that will be employed after a vendor is selected and the contract is signed.
- Project plan for the transition.
- Ongoing measurement and management control approach for the work.
- Evaluation criteria that will be employed in the evaluation.
- Evaluation and selection method that will be used.
- References of current customers of the vendor.

After the RFP is issued, you will be holding a bidder's conference. This is an opportunity for you to present the objectives and additional information. It is a chance for vendors to ask questions. Here are some common sample questions that vendors may pose.

- What is the term of the outsourcing engagement?
- Of the objectives stated, how do these rank in importance?
- What do you envision happening to the internal staff?

- What restrictions and methods will be used to evaluate the current staff involved in the work?
- What documentation exists that relates to the activity?

SELECT THE RIGHT VENDORS

In doing the evaluation of proposals, you can use the criteria in the previous section. You can contact customers cited by the vendors. Some of the questions that you should consider are the following.

- How long have you had the outsourcing arrangement?
- What was the timeline of events from initial evaluation until today?
- What were the original goals for outsourcing?
- Were these goals achieved? If so, how? If not, why not?
- How do they manage the outsourcing vendor?
- How do they handle additional work requests?
- What is the quality of the people and work provided?
- Has their staffing and management been stable? What is the turnover?
- If they had to do it all over again, what would they do?
- Would they employ the same vendor for additional work?
- What benefits did they expect and achieve with respect to outsourcing?
- What were the difficulties and challenges that they encountered?

Answers to these questions not only assist you in the evaluation, they may also provide insight into how you can improve your outsourcing management techniques.

After you have narrowed down the number of vendors to about three or four, it is time to move on to finalist evaluation. You will probably have the vendors come in and make a presentation and answer questions. While you can ask general questions about the firm and past experience, it is recommended that you pose questions in the following areas:

- State several issues that you think are likely to arise in the work. Ask them to respond as to their approach. This will help you in determining their capabilities.
- Ask them to summarize some of their lessons learned from past similar work. This will not only indicate their experience, but the extent to which they have improved since their last work.

You have to establish both a contract and SLA. You can have the legal department work on these, but it may not be very useful. From experience, it is probably a good idea to start with the standard vendor documents. Note that we do not say that you will accept these as is.

The vendor documents are the starting points for negotiation.

Space does not permit a detailed discussion of contract negotiations or an SLA. However, here are some key conditions that must be part of the contract.

- *Dispute resolution process.* How will problems be addressed?
- *Additional unplanned work.* New opportunities for work will inevitably arise. When this occurs, what is the method for having these opportunities negotiated?
- *Management.* How will the outsourcing relationship be managed and coordinated?
- *Measurement.* How will vendor performance and the work results be measured?

The firm also needs to identify who will be the internal project leader for the transition and the individuals and their roles for ongoing management.

PLAN AND EXECUTE THE TRANSITION OF WORK

From a management perspective, you will want to establish the following:

- Common project plan with the vendor for transition. This will ensure that both sides are working from the same schedule.
- Common issues database and issue escalation and resolution method.
- How knowledge will be transferred to the vendor staff now.
- How knowledge will be transferred later back from the vendor to internal employees.
- The major elements of transition.
- How the transition will be monitored and the work tracked after the transition.

It would be best if the vendor staff "lived" in the department which will be outsourced. If they can be trained in the activity, that would be useful.

MANAGE THE OUTSOURCING

In managing the outsourcing after transition, you want to focus on the SLA. This provides an umbrella for measurement. However, there are also several other elements of monitoring and tracking. These are:

- Unannounced or announced visits to the vendor location to spot check what is going on.
- Regular reviews of performance.
- Regular reviews and handling of issues that have arisen.
- Analysis and review of additional work requests.

You will also want to employ the performance measurements that are presented later in this chapter.

What if you have major problems and have to terminate the relationship? You must then create a new transition plan to get the work back. Some of the questions to be answered are:

- What documentation will be required by the internal staff or another vendor?
- Can the vendor staff be considered for employment? After all, they have the knowledge. Getting them is the quickest way to get up and running.
- How will internal staff learn about the activity and get training?
- How will the knowledge and expertise that was gained by the vendor staff be transferred?
- How will the transition be managed?
- How will the activity be phased down in preparation for transfer?

MANAGE MULTIPLE VENDORS

How do you manage multiple vendors? If you are transitioning work to several vendors at the same time, then you should establish a joint transition effort. You also want to have a common issues database across all vendors.

During operations after outsourcing transition, many problems can arise. One vendor may tend to blame another one. You should anticipate this and prepare for it by telling this to the vendors. It is too much to hold vendor meetings with all vendors present. So you should set aside specific meetings where joint problems are discussed. In the investigation of problems, insist that the vendors work together in this troubleshooting effort. This will probably provide a better solution than having the vendors work sequentially, one at a time on a problem.

ALIGNMENT OF IT AND THE BUSINESS

In Chapters 2 and 4, basic tables were developed for the alignment of business and IT. Critical processes were identified that were important to the mission, vision, and business goals. It is probable that you will not consider outsourcing these. Thus, the alignment analysis helps you to eliminate candidates for possible outsourcing. You can use the tables in Chapter 4 to relate the application systems to the important processes. This will help you narrow the opportunities further in IT.

There is a basic question to ask about an activity that you are considering for outsourcing.

If the outsourcing vendor fails to perform and the work suffers, then what is the impact on the business?

Answering this will help ensure that the outsourcing effort is aligned with the business.

Early in this chapter, a number of potential benefits of outsourcing were listed. Assuming that some of these come true, it should be possible to see what happened to the remaining IT and business work. How were the business objectives, mission, and vision helped? How were some business issues addressed?

MANAGE RISK

Here are some things that can go wrong in outsourcing.

• *You fail to develop an outsourcing strategy.* The roles of business units are not clear and they start dealing directly with the vendor—raising costs and problems.

• *You fail to clean up or measure the activity prior to outsourcing.* This can happen if there is severe time pressure. This can raise the cost. If this occurs, then you and the vendor will have to develop a cleanup approach.

• *The vendor fails to perform adequately.* There can be misunderstandings and communications problems. Vendors may blame problems on internal staff for not making information available. They may state that employees are trying to sabotage the effort.

• *The vendor in working with you and the employees works to expand the scope of the outsourcing.* This should not be unexpected. The vendor would naturally like to make more money from the relationship. Without saying no to all of this, set rules at the start of the relationship for how new work will be evaluated. Define limits on contacts and their marketing effort.

• *There are differences about the performance in the SLA.* This should be anticipated at the start and an escalation method defined for dealing with this.

EXAMPLES

SUPREME OIL

The management at Supreme Oil took a negative view of outsourcing due to bad experiences with several other energy firms. However, the workload in IT was building up and the internal staff could not cope. Rather than hire more staff, the decision was made to use contract programmers who worked under the direction of internal managers. This was successful.

As time went on, internally developed software was replaced by software packages. The reliance on internal programmers diminished and the maintenance of the software packages was outsourced. Separately, the network operations were also outsourced. Today, about 60% of the IT work is outsourced—about 1/3 of this overseas.

TUCKER COUNTY

Tucker County wanted to outsource a call center that handled telephone calls from the public. The old center had 45 full-time staff. They worked with manual methods and an old computer system. It was very inefficient. People complained to the county about service. Management wanted to get rid of it because they did not have faith in the line management to improve it.

An analysis was conducted of the area. It was found that there would be too much cleanup required for a vendor. Moreover, the vendor would be forced to use the same manual and old computer systems. Thus, an effort was made to clean up the process and systems. A new system was installed that supported Geographic Information Systems (GIS) along with a number of county databases. New procedures and policies were implemented. A new telephone system was installed that linked to the system.

Why do all of this expensive cleanup when you are going to outsource it? Well, the county would have incurred the same expense with the vendor. As a result of the changes, the staffing level was reduced to 30. Service levels improved to acceptable levels. Turnover was no longer a problem.

So why not stop the outsourcing effort? Management did not see this as a core activity. The outsourcing went smoothly. Today, the staffing levels are down to 22 and service has improved even more.

SHAMROCK AGRICULTURE

A systematic analysis was performed for both business and IT activities. In the end three business areas were identified for outsourcing along with four for IT. Two of the IT areas linked together—network management and support, and PC support. These were outsourced together. Software packages were acquired from three different vendors. The packages from two vendors had to be interfaced so a separate project was established to interface these. The approach was successful in part because: (1) there were measurements conducted before and after outsourcing; (2) several areas were cleaned up prior to outsourcing; (3) employees were prepared for the outsourcing. Several were transferred to the outsourcing vendor.

LESSONS LEARNED

• Carry out identification and initial evaluation of vendors in parallel with the activity cleanup.

• Prepare documents and line up employees to participate in the transition while you are in contract negotiations.

• When the vendor has been selected, get the transition approach and planning ironed out during contract negotiation. These things can take some time and result in delays.

• Continue as long as you can with the cleanup of the process—until the issuance of the RFP. The better you make the process, the smoother the transition.

• Don't overpromise management on the cost savings. A substantial part of the savings will be consumed in the transition, dealing with transition problems, and in additional cost items later.

PERFORMANCE MEASURES FOR OUTSOURCING

There are several performance measures that are useful here. One is to assist in assessing your outsourcing process. This is given in Fig. 9.3. The second is to evaluate the vendor performance (Fig. 9.4). The third is to evaluate the business unit and IT performance during the outsourcing work. This appears in Fig. 9.5. The last one is important because outsourcing is a two-way street. When there are problems in an outsourcing arrangement, a substantial number of the problems can be traced back to the company management, IT, and business units.

- Do you have an outsourcing strategy?
- Do you regularly measure the performance of outsourcing vendors?
- How did the transition of work to the vendor do?
- Are lessons learned from past and current outsourcing efforts?
- Generally, is your firm performing better in outsourcing now than several years ago?
- What personnel problems surfaced in the outsourcing?
- Do you have a regular approach for identifying and evaluating new opportunities for outsourcing?
- Are you prepared to take back work that has been outsourced?
- Do you have a method for cleaning up processes and work prior to outsourcing?
- What have been the benefits of outsourcing?
- Has the firm been able to take advantage of the resources freed up from the outsourcing?

Figure 9.3 Performance Measures for Your Outsourcing Process

- What is the extent of contact with the vendor?
- Does the vendor readily assume ownership of problems and issues?
- What is the number of outstanding issues that the vendor is working on? Has this changed from their past performance?
- How is the vendor performing vis-à-vis the Service Level Agreement?
- What is the average elapsed time required to solve an issue by the vendor?
- What is the turnover of the vendor staff in doing your work?
- What additional work requests have surfaced?
- What is the actual versus planned cost of outsourcing?
- How has the vendor performed on the additional work requests?
- What information regarding the work is being transferred back to internal staff?
- What is the number of communication problems with the vendor?
- If you had to do it all over again, what would you do differently?

Figure 9.4   Performance Measures for Vendor Performance

- What is the role of upper level management in outsourcing? Are they too involved?
- Are business and IT employees helpful in providing information to the vendor?
- Do they just answer the vendor questions, or do they try to be more helpful.
- Do the business units and IT staff channel problems and additional requests through the outsourcing coordinator?
- What happens to the measurement results of the vendor work?
- What happens to the information transferred back from the vendor?
- Are employees made available to handle vendor questions and problems?
- What is the general attitude of internal employees toward the vendor? Do they see them as an adversary or a partner?
- What are the employee participation and attitude toward the cleanup and measurement of the process?

Figure 9.5   Performance Measures for IT, Management, and Business Unit Performance in Outsourcing

SUMMARY

There are two major themes in this chapter. First, outsourcing is inevitable for many firms. It just makes economic sense and the advantages outweigh the disadvantages. Second, if you want to achieve outsourcing success, you must pursue an organized approach. The step-by-step approach to outsourcing is really an expansion of some of the guidelines proposed by Machiavelli over 400 years ago. Many things change over time, but much at a general level remains the same. Again, the key idea is to create winning lasting relationships between you and the vendors.

Chapter 10

Communicate with Management

INTRODUCTION

In the previous chapters, specific elements of management communications were addressed. Here you will develop a framework for more effective communications with both upper level managers as well as business unit managers. Experience shows that many problems that IT encounters have their source in some problem or failure of communications with management.

What are some of the most common problems in management communications?

• IT managers make assumptions about what other managers know or are aware of. Then they do not inform them. Miscommunication occurs.
• The IT manager does not initiate contacts with upper level managers. Rather, he waits until he or she is called. Or, alternatively, waits until the next formal presentation. This may occur because the IT manager is intimidated by management. He may not feel comfortable. The impact of this situation is that ad hoc, unplanned contacts are driven by upper management. Normally, they will not make contact unless there is a problem. Thus, the communications always is around IT problems, rather than IT results and progress.
• The IT manager lacks an organized and planned approach for communications. Ad hoc communications tend to lead to problems. The manager sometimes gets too tied up in issues or routine work and neglects communications.

Overall, these tend to happen because there is a lack of organization. Communications is not taken seriously by some managers. Even when problems arise, some managers fail to sit down and trace the source of the issues—which is often communications.

When you communicate with someone, there are some basic decisions that you make.

- *The medium.* You have a number of choices here—in person, telephone, voice mail, e-mail, and fax. Selection here is important if you are trying to get your message across.
- *Audience.* You have to consider who the audience will be. Will you present information to several people? This can be a problem in that each person may have their own concerns. In a group meeting, these things will not come out into the open. You are likely to get a false impression of how the meeting went.
- *Length.* How long do you want to communicate? The problem observed with a number of IT managers is that they often talk too long and tend to repeat their message. The impact may be that the message is lost. The audience becomes bored.
- *The message.* What are you really trying to convey? If you don't think about it, there is a substantial likelihood that the message will be garbled, only part of the message will be transferred, or the message will be misunderstood.
- *The tone.* Especially in IT, you have to pay attention to the tone of your voice. If you are giving out good news in a monotonic, deadpan voice, some people may think that there is a real problem.

There are many more elements but you should at least think about these five.

IMPLEMENT COLLABORATION IN MANAGEMENT COMMUNICATIONS

Given that an organized approach is desirable, what should you do? The general communications strategy for IT managers is to employ collaborative communications. Here you want to have regular communications in which the audience participates in the discussion. Some managers communicate, but often it is only one way. They talk to another manager and provide information. The manager thanks them and the IT manager departs. This is not very effective.

There are levels of decisions that you must make in communications. At a higher level you have to choose between informal and formal communications. You then need to develop a schedule and plan of attack for each important manager for a week at a time. If you don't plan, then you fall back into ad hoc communications. At the tactical level, you have to make the decisions about the communications discussed in the previous section.

How do you know how you are doing? In the performance measurement section at the end of this chapter, a checklist is provided to help you evaluate the state and condition of your communications.

What if you detect miscommunications? Whose fault is that? Some tend to blame the audience since they are assuming that they conveyed the message properly. This is not true.

When there is a communication problem, you should take the responsibility.

There are some good reasons for doing this. First, it will help you work on future communications in more detail. Second, you will be more careful and think more when you communicate.

USE INFORMAL COMMUNICATIONS

In IT, informal communications are the most important type. They include telephone calls, in-person casual contacts, and office meetings. Informal communications have a number of advantages, including:

• There is no written record kept. This tends to make individuals more open in their comments.

• There are no written materials handed out. Thus, there is less structure and more give and take.

Don't kid yourself into believing that these "informal communications" do not have to be planned. They still do. Otherwise, you risk making the mistakes identified earlier.

There are a number of opportunities for informal communications. The obvious one is to schedule a meeting with a manager. However, most managers are very busy and do not have blocks of time available. One of us learned this the hard way. The situation was that one of us was an IT manager reporting to the CEO. The CEO had over 20 direct reports. Now you can say that this is excessive and a bad idea, but it was reality. Every time we wanted to schedule a meeting, the calendar was filled for weeks in advance. Thus, we had to resort to more informal methods.

Here are some successful methods of informal communications.

• Get to the manager early in the morning when they have just arrived for work. Give them only a few minute update and then leave. This does not disturb their day and you are not giving them bad news.

• Approach a manager in a parking lot or when they are walking in the hallway. This can appear as casual and as long as the information is not sensitive, there is no problem.

• See the manager when they are about to leave for the day or when they are in the parking lot. Also, if you are the same sex as the manager, don't pass up the bathroom as an opportunity for communications.

What do you communicate informally? You obviously do not discuss a major issue and give a lot of numbers. Here are some things to provide.

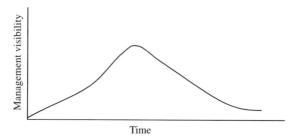

Figure 10.1   Visibility of an Issue to Management

- An overall update on multiple projects.
- An update on an issue.
- The general status of a specific project.

Always be ready to mention several issues. However, always indicate that there is no action required. You are just mentioning issues that you are working on. When you are communicating on issues, you should gradually mention the issue. Figure 10.1 gives a chart of how you can escalate an issue in terms of management visibility. You start with mentioning an issue, but it is not pressing and there is no action required. As the issue continues to grow, then you can point out alternatives. Still there is no immediate need for action or a decision. Then you can ask for a decision. After the decision you can take the actions required that flow from the decision. Later you can inform them of the results of the actions. This is a healthy way to get issues identified, discussed, and resolved.

Another item to present is a story from a business process, a project, or some other area of IT. This can serve to make IT more interesting to a manager. It also shows to them that you have both perspective and a sense of humor.

What will be their likely reaction? They will like it and look forward to seeing you. You are providing useful information that is sometimes entertaining. Most of the time when people come to the manager, it is with a problem or issue. This results in giving them more work. Now and then you will have to give them an issue. But there will be no surprise. That is a key to successful communications.

> **You should keep the manager sufficiently informed that there is never an IT surprise.**

MAKE FORMAL PRESENTATIONS

Regardless of informal communications, you will have to give formal presentations. Guidelines for specific presentations are given below.

• Create a standardized outline for each type of document and presentation given below. The sections below discuss the most common types of formal communications.

• Create a directory where you can store copies of all documents and presentations. Make access to this read only.

• Insist that all IT managers and staff who prepare documents or presentations place copies in the above directory.

• Enforce the rule that wherever possible, everyone is to review what has already been presented in the directory to ensure that there is consistency and reuse of materials to reduce the preparation time.

Before you disseminate a document or give a presentation, try to get to some of the key managers first. Label the document or presentation as a draft. Walk through the paper and get their feedback. After doing this, make some changes to reflect this feedback. This will have several decided advantages to the success of your communication. First, they will not be surprised when they read or hear the materials. Second, by giving them to have some feedback, they participate in the development of the materials and have some sense of ownership. Third, doing a one-on-one presentation with them allows you to give a relational view of the materials slanted toward their interests. You will not have a chance to do this in a presentation.

Before a presentation identify who might want to raise questions and issues during the presentation. Some managers do this to show how IT smart they are, or to make a good impression on upper level management. Make a list of the top five questions that can be asked. Be ready. Next, try out your presentation through a dry run with some of the IT managers and staff to get their reactions. This will help you in another way. They will be ready if someone in the audience of the presentation asks them questions. If they are caught off guard and then improvise an answer, there could be some serious miscommunications.

If questions arise during a presentation, address these directly. If you don't have the answer, say so. If you have to guess, don't do it. You could make an expensive mistake. After the presentation or the delivery of the document, follow up with visits to answer any questions.

With this background, attention can be turned to specific presentations.

• Overall status of IT.
• The status of a specific project.
• The status of an issue.
• A new project idea.
• A budget for IT work.

PRESENT THE OVERALL STATUS OF IT

This is a presentation on how IT is doing. What are you trying to get across? Normally, you are just providing information. You are not asking them for help on individual problems. Therefore, the presentation and material can be more laid back. Here are some sample topics that might be covered. The exact choice and order will obviously depend upon the situation.

- General IT planned versus actual budget—no surprises here.
- Status of multiple projects—here you can provide a combined summary GANTT chart that summarizes each major project.
- Split of work in IT—here you can show a pie chart that gives the percentage of IT staff hours in support, development, projects, etc.
- Division of work among processes—the percentage of work that was provided to support or improve each major business process is given. This should be shown first before that for organizations.
- Division of work among business units—this gives the percentage of work in support of each business unit.
- A table of issues versus projects—the rows are issues and the columns are projects; the table entry is an "X" if the specific issue affects the individual project and blank otherwise.
- Benefits from recently completed IT projects—this is a list of business benefits and impacts from IT work. You would also credit the business unit for supporting change.

In cases where there are infrastructure projects or work such as network upgrades, then the effort can be spread across multiple processes or business units based upon the number of users, for example.

REPORT TO MANAGEMENT ON STATUS

Here you are presenting to the management the status of IT work. Let's first consider the purpose. You want to convey the status of the project and that things are under control. However, you also want to make management aware of the risks and potential problems. Here are the elements in either your written or verbal presentation.

- *Review of the purpose and scope of the work from a business perspective.* This is important because it gets the audience on the same page.
- *Overall planned versus actual schedule.* Here you will employ a GANTT chart to compare the planned and actual schedule. You will also highlight any events that caused the actual schedule to slip.
- *Cumulative planned versus actual budget.* Here you indicate where the budget stands. You should use cumulative to show the overall trend in the budget. For example, if the actual budget is now higher than the planned budget, you can show when the actual will come into alignment with the planned. Alternatively, you can indicate the reasons why the actual budget exceeds or underruns the planned budget.

• *Work products finished*. This should be given in business terms—without technical jargon. You should also provide a list of upcoming work results.

• *Outstanding issues*. Here you should give a table of some of the key issues as rows. The columns are: the age of the issue since found, the importance of the issues, and the actions that are being taken on the issue.

• *Percentage of the total work and total work with risk that remains*. Remember from Chapter 5 that these are very different. In Chapter 5 we associated tasks with issues as having risk. You would indicate, for example, that 60% of the work remains to be done. You would also show that 75% of the work with issues and risk remain to be addressed.

Notice here that if you provide this information, you are giving both the good and bad news. The status, hopefully, is the good news and the issues are the bad news. You are also raising the level of awareness to management about specific problems through the status report. Often, we have seen this trigger actions to either investigate an issue or resolve it.

ADDRESS A SPECIFIC ISSUE

Normally, you will want to bundle several related issues here. What is your objective in this presentation? You want to get management action on the issue(s). However, you are also using this presentation politically to raise awareness of the issue(s). Here is an outline of the presentation.

• Introduction—what are the issue(s) from a business view;
• Impacts if the issues are not addressed soon—what happens if no action is taken;
• Table of the issues versus the business processes or business units—shows the specific impacts on the business;
• Benefits from solving the issues and how they will be realized;
• Potential actions that can be taken;
• Recommended actions.

Note that the issues are given not from an IT perspective, but from a business view. This makes the issues more understandable. The impacts raise the dread if the problems are not solved. However, these are general. So the next item of the table allows you to give specific impacts. This is all negative. You want to now turn to the positive. The fourth item is that of benefits and how they will be realized through addressing the issues. Realization of benefits is very important, because many IT presentations have given benefits, but many do not come true. Thus, the above outline mitigates any concerns about the benefits. The potential actions are provided to show that you considered a range of alternative actions. These could include: throwing money at the issues (this doesn't generally work), or throwing resources at the issues (this takes resources from other, necessary work).

Who should give this presentation? Not the IT manager alone. The business unit managers who are involved and impacted by the issues should be included and present the issues and their impacts as well as benefits. The IT manager can go into the potential actions. Both can give the recommended actions.

This technique of presentation shows management that the issues are important to the business—not just IT. It also shows that there was a great deal of thought and discussion regarding the issues before the presentation. Thus, you are more likely to get action.

PROPOSE NEW WORK

When you want to propose new IT work or projects, you are seeking the approval of the idea first. In the real world, you often do not get the idea approved, the budget provided, and the resources at the same time. In a democracy, legislators first vote on the concepts or ideas. Then, separately, they approve the funding for the ideas. This gives them protection against approving things in too much of a rush. Here the attention will be on the idea.

Let's suppose that you have been working with a business unit on a new idea. There has been initial research performed to estimate the benefits of the idea as well as what changes are necessary in the business to make the benefits come true. You have also estimated the schedule and funding needed.

If you followed a standard approach in your presentation, you might have an outline like this.

- Introduction—gives a summary of the business problem.
- Technical approach to the business problem.
- Costs of the solution.
- Schedule for the solution.
- Benefits for the solution.

This is truly a bad outline. Look at it again. There are no action items. If someone wants to investigate it further, what do they do? Undefined. How do we know that the benefits will come true? We don't. What are the issues or problems to overcome to get the change and the benefits? No idea. If you were to employ this outline, none of these would likely arise because they would be turned off by the technical approach.

Here is a better, more business-like outline. It should be familiar to you since it resembles standard radio or television 30-s commercials.

- Introduction—the problems in the business process and the impact of the problems on the business.
- New business process—how the business would work with completion of the work and changes.
- Benefits from the new business process and how they will be realized.

- Costs and schedule for the work.
- Potential issues and problems to be overcome.
- Actions that are needed right away.

Do you see how much better this second outline is? First, there is no technical discussion. Second, the problems in the process are immediately accompanied by the impacts. Third, there are specific actions that are proposed. These actions should not be to spend money. Rather, they should address issues, do a further, more detailed investigation, and similar actions. Both of you will later return for approval of the funding since you will have more detail in the work, the schedule, and the costs. By taking this direction, you will start to build momentum for the new work.

Who would give this presentation? Not the IT manager alone. The business unit manager would give the first three items because they are business oriented. The IT manager is not qualified or credible in giving this. The IT manager can give the costs, schedule, and potential problems. The business manager would close the presentation with the actions.

At Tucker County, this method was followed repeatedly. No new project was ever presented without a business manager accompanying us and giving part of the presentation. Another guideline was always followed. That is, when the impacts of the problems were given at the start of the presentation, the business manager would indicate in rather graphical terms what would happen in the process and to the business unit if the problems continued and were not addressed by the work. This is a very sound method because it notifies upper management ahead of time of the consequences of not going ahead. Moreover, it instills an element to get management support—*fear*. They see through the eyes of the business manager the effects of inaction.

Why is this a good approach? First, management sees that there is business support for the work. Second, they see that the business unit and IT worked *together* on the approach. They can see that there will potentially be less resistance to change so that it is *more likely* that the benefits will actually be achieved. Third, specific actions are outlined that the management can approve.

PRESENT AN IT BUDGET

There are several possibilities here. You could be presenting the IT budget overall. Alternatively, you may be presenting the budget for new work. Let's examine each of these.

For the overall IT budget, you not only want to give the summary budget and breakdown by area. You should also present the following items.

- Introduction—summary of past accomplishments and work results.
- New budget items and what will be accomplished by spending the money—the benefits.

- The direction of the budget and how the mission and vision of the business are supported.
  - How this budget is different from the current budget.
  - Some of the current activities that will be dropped along with new work that was rejected.
  - Near-term actions that will be taken regarding the new work.

Note that this is a political presentation. You are not just delivering the budget. You are providing information on what was accomplished with the money they gave you last time around. This shows that the IT investment was not misspent. You are showing the alignment of the budget for IT with the goals of the business. You are also indicating that many potential ideas were dropped. This shows selectivity. Next, you are indicating some of the current activities that will be either dropped or curtailed. This shows that you are taking a hard-line on the budget—valuable politically. Finally, by giving near-term actions, you provide management with a sense of urgency to move ahead.

For the budget for new work, you want to provide the following information.

- Introduction—summary of the project idea and the investigation—business unit manager.
- Examples of detailed transactions and work—before and after change—business unit employee.
  - Benefits from the change—business unit manager and employee.
  - Cost and schedule—IT manager.
  - Problems and issues—both resolved and unsolved—business unit manager.
  - Next actions—business unit manager.

Who should give this presentation? Now there should be three presenters. The business unit manager gives the introduction. The IT manager gives the budget and schedule. The new player is a business unit employee involved in the work. The role of this person is to give the details of the change, the benefit, and how the change can be carried. This technique will provide greater credibility to the new work. It will be very difficult for management to deny the new work. There is now a groundswell of support for the work at different levels in the business unit. If the work is not approved, word will get back to the employees in the business unit and morale will take a heavy blow. Is this a political presentation then? Of course, it is!

COMMUNICATE WITH BUSINESS UNIT MANAGERS

You communicate with business unit managers more often than upper management. Any communications problems here can lead to communications issues with upper management. Here are some guidelines for more effective communications with business unit managers.

• Assume that anything you say to a business manager will be conveyed to their employees and to upper management. This will make you more careful of what you say. It will also force you to plan communications more.
• There is a tendency for IT people to want to please people. When a business manager mentions a problem or makes a request, you naturally want to please them by indicating that you will take action. Resist this until you have investigated the issue or the request.
• Assume that there may be a hidden agenda in meetings with business managers. They have their own self-interest along with problems and needs of which you are unaware. In anticipation of this, you want to look behind what they say to you.
• Understand the style and viewpoint of individual business managers. Adopt your communications to accommodate this. For example, if a manager is more technical, then you can discuss topics in technical terms. If a manager does not like to deal with IT because it makes him uneasy, then you can make the meetings brief and to the point.
• Make an effort to visit three or four business managers each week. What do you cover in these meetings? Bring them up-to-date on progress on work that impacts them. Give credit to their employees who are participating in the work. Alert them to potential problems. This gives them an early warning system without forcing them to take action.

ALIGNMENT OF IT AND THE BUSINESS

While you can develop tables and relationship between business and IT factors, and IT can perform excellent work that benefits the business, you cannot assume that management will understand and see what happened. Effective communications with the business managers is a critical success factor in proving that there is alignment between business and IT.

Figure 10.2 gives a list of questions to help you assess your effectiveness in alignment to the business. Here are some amplifying comments.

• In presentations, do you always relate IT work to business impact?
• For every proposed idea, do you provide information on how the benefits will be realized?
• Do you explain how IT work supports the business vision and mission?
• Do managers raise questions about the benefits about some IT work and whether
• it will help the business? This indicates that some managers are questioning alignment
• After presentations, do managers still question the value of IT work?

Figure 10.2 Assessment of Business and IT Alignment through Communications

- You always want to talk to business people in business terms. If you resort to too much technical terms, then they may view you as a technical person and not as a manager. You are not a peer.
- IT has often promised many benefits that were not delivered. Often, it was not the fault of IT. To counteract this, you should stress how the benefits will be achieved and the role of the business units in achieving the benefits.
- Alignment must be explained and reinforced by relating IT projects and work to the mission and vision. This should be carried out as often as possible.

MANAGE RISK

The major risk is that a communications problem occurs first. Then the problem is either not detected or identified; the problem then grows. The problem typically then changes from being a communications problem to being issue based. Thus, out of seemingly nothing, an issue was created. It should not have been there in the first place. Suppose that you, as an IT manager, indicate to a business unit that things are tight and there may not be resources to support their desired work. This gets misconstrued into IT is not supportive. You have heard about the problem second-hand through the manager to whom you report. He tells you, "Do something for this guy?" What started out as a rather innocent and honest statement now results in a resource change.

In order to manage communications risk, you should take the following actions:

- Plan your communications carefully along the lines discussed above.
- When you are conveying a message, look for feedback and signs that the message got through in the way in which it was intended.
- Revisit individuals after meetings and presentations to get an impression of how they interpreted your message.
- Evaluate your communications on a regular basis. Make a note of the individuals that you seem to have problems communicating with.

EXAMPLES

SUPREME OIL

Supreme Oil had long established policies and procedures. These provided for regular progress reports, standard budget presentations, and all formal communications. All of this worked. As time went on and the pace of IT activity increased, there were more issues and decisions to make related to IT.

The communications approach that was based on formal communications was not working well in this new business environment. There needed to be more informal communications. Individual managers took the initiative and began to do more informally. Decisions were made based on informal communications and then summarized and related through the formal communications. It took 2 years for the policies and procedures to change to reflect the new reality.

TUCKER COUNTY

The IT manager had some poor relations with several key line managers. Upper management tended to leave IT alone. The IT manager communicated through control. That is, individual managers only were contacted when they had submitted requests or raised problems. Then the IT manager would exert control and dictate a solution. Morale in IT was not good. Business was starting to pursue its own IT solutions. The temporary communications solution was to build links between the supervisors in IT and the line managers—effectively bypassing the IT manager. The IT manager noticed this, but then chose to ignore it. The IT manager got more out of touch with what was going on. Eventually, he resigned—in large measure because of communications problems.

SHAMROCK AGRICULTURE

A new general manager was named to head the organization. The IT manager committed several communications blunders. First, he did not approach the new manager to update him on IT activities. The first contact happened when a line manager indicated an IT issue to the general manager. The general manager then called in the IT manager. The sight and scene were not pleasant. The general manager asked why he had not been informed of issues. Then he asked about the problem. The IT manager was not prepared and fumbled around for an answer. This left a horrible first impression.

The second mistake made by the IT manager was to attempt to recover the relationship through a formal presentation. The general manager asked several line managers to participate in the presentation without informing the IT manager. The IT manager showed up for the presentation and then was surprised to see such a large audience. He was caught off-guard the second time. Wait! There is more. The presentation contained a substantial amount of technical jargon. The general manager was clueless so had to ask about each slide.

Communications then moved into a frozen, formal state. There was mutual distrust. All of this was due to poor communications. The IT manager blamed the general manager for the problems since he gotten along well with the previous general manager. This was another mistake.

It took some time and work for the IT manager to realize that he had created the problems himself. He then tried a new tact. He began to have informal, 5–10 min contacts with the general manager. He would bring him up-to-date on some of the key projects. Then he would identify one or two issues and indicate what he was doing about them.

The situation did not turn around overnight. It took time, but it was successful. The informal contacts continue to this day. Four times a year there are brief formal presentations that are business oriented. There is no technical material.

LESSONS LEARNED

- You should use e-mail only for routine items. Never use e-mail as a medium for sensitive issues or even for most issues. There are several reasons for this. First, everyone uses e-mail so your message can be lost in the e-mail flood. Second, you create a paper trail and record that can be later abused. Third, when you write things down, you tend to take a position. People often will say one thing, but when they commit it in writing, it tends to be watered down.
- When you are talking to someone on the telephone, smile into the telephone. This sounds stupid, but try out this experiment. Call your own voice mail and give the same message twice—one time with a smile and the other time without a smile. Now compare the two. Do you see the difference?
- When you are going to be giving a formal presentation, do this exercise before the meeting. Lie down on a desk, floor, or couch and practice deep breathing using your chest. This will help you project your voice in a better tone. It will not be squeaky.
- Find out if a manager smokes. If this is the case, then go out to the smoking area. Many people tend to talk more and be more open when they are smoking.
- During a presentation do not fix your attention on one or two key managers. Look around the room and even look toward the audience seated in the rear of the room. Try to establish eye contact with each member of the audience.
- Include complete thoughts on your slides for your presentations. Don't just give a few words. This is counter to the standard presentation guidelines. However, taking this action will ensure that people will not later misconstrue what you presented. If you have topics instead of thoughts, then there is a great deal of room for misinterpretation when the presentation is passed on to others from people in the audience.
- During a presentation watch the body language of the audience. At the start some will sit there with their arms crossed. They are more reserved. If you succeed in getting your message across, their body language will change and their arms will open.

PERFORMANCE MEASURES FOR MANAGEMENT COMMUNICATIONS

You should evaluate how you are doing in communicating on a weekly basis. Figure 10.3 provides a checklist for assessing your own performance. Here are some comments about the checklist.

- You can test if you have a planned approach by considering what you do when preparing for meetings.
- There is a tendency to just go ahead from the meeting. You don't have the desire to review anything unpleasant.
- If business managers approach you with problems, then you failed. You should have gotten to them first. Your goal is zero.
- If you have to return to people to repeat what was covered, then you failed in doing presentations.
- You should spend a considerable time in management communications. This should be just behind problem solving and direct management.
- By measuring the number of communications problems, you can detect trends.
- Your method of communicating to each manager should be dependent on style and experience with past communications.
- In looking at corrective actions, you want to keep a log of these. Here is what we do. We keep a note in Microsoft Outlook of the problems in each month. Then we review these. Writing the problem down increases awareness.

There is another checklist to employ. After you have had a formal meeting or presentation, use the checklist in Fig. 10.4 to evaluate your performance. Do not wait for several hours or days to do this. Do it right away while the impression of the meeting is fresh on your mind.

- Do you have a planned and scheduled method for communicating with upper management?
- Do you evaluate your own communications performance?
- How often do business managers come to you with issues or problems?
- How many times do you have occasion to have to repeat presentations?
- How often do you have to go back and explain what was indicated in a memo or an e-mail?
- What percentage of your time is spent in communicating with management?
- How many communication problems have you experienced in the past month?
- Did you make the effort to trace the cause of communication problems?
- Do you take different steps in communicating with managers with whom you have had communications problems in the past?
- Have you taken corrective action after noticing a communication problem?

Figure 10.3   Measures for Assessing Your Communications Performance

- Who attended the meeting or presentation?
- Who was not there?
- Did any manager send subordinates? Is this a pattern?
- What questions were raised during the meeting?
- How effective did you respond to the questions?
- What was the follow up from the meeting?
- Was the follow up what was originally planned?
- How long did the meeting take?
- Did the meeting deviate from the planned agenda?
- What surprises came up during the meeting?
- How did you handle the surprises?
- Did the attitude of the audience change as the meeting progressed?

Figure 10.4   Checklist for Evaluating Your Performance After a Meeting or Presentation

- It is important to make some mental or written notes on each key member of the audience. This will assist you in future communications with them.
- The meeting duration should often be shorter than what was planned.
- If additional, unplanned items arise during the meeting, then there was a problem. This should not have occurred. With better planning and communications before the meeting, you should have been able to head off these items.
- If there is additional or unplanned follow up from the meeting, then you failed in the preparation for the meeting.

Do these things and others in this chapter appear too negative? The word "failure" appears a number of times on purpose. You must become more aware of the importance of communications.

SUMMARY

Management communications is right up there in the top qualifications for being an effective IT manager along with being able to address and solve issues. Many excellent problem-solving IT managers eventually run afoul of their own communications. They tend to take relationships for granted and assume that messages are getting across correctly. Never, ever make this assumption. Always assume that there will be miscommunications. It will make you more careful and give more attention to communications.

Chapter 11

Software Packages and System Development

INTRODUCTION

Application software is the main reason for the IT investment. Yes, software tools and e-mail are critical too. However, the support for productivity in doing transactions and work provides the greatest value to the business processes.

Years ago, there were no software packages. Everything had to be developed. One reason for this was the state of information technology. It was primitive compared to the state today. Another reason was that it was felt by some that each process in each organization was unique and so required individual software solutions.

Time went by and more companies began using computers. There was also a shortage of computer professionals to meet the demand. Not every firm could afford to have its own IT department. Some companies began using software at service bureaus that were in effect shared among many firms. With the exception of reports there was little customization to meet individual needs except for changing reports.

With further improvements in software development and the underlying system software and hardware, some firms started to develop software packages. Initially, the idea was to use the software package as the basis for further development to customize the software to meet the requirements of an individual company. Turnkey systems were developed and delivered through minicomputers. This triggered the development of software packages that operated on mainframe computers.

Today, you can see the results of the history. First, there are many more tools to develop, test, and help implement software. These satisfy the needs of those that seek development. The two most recent families of software development tools are wizards and object and component development tools. Wizards using database management systems (dbms) help less experienced users, and even professional staff develop small and limited applications as well as prototypes. Object oriented methods provide more structure for the development process and have been carried out in various languages, including Java and C#.

Second, the software packages became more sophisticated as well. The latest version of software packages consists of Enterprise Resource Planning (ERP) software packages. These can meet the needs of a wide variety of firms through customization not of the code, but through extensive tables and controls. By establishing parameters and business rules, you can meet many diverse requirements.

The situation today is that many firms rely on software packages for their basic application software. They may then in addition develop some software separate from or as an adjunct to the software packages. Internet software tends to be developed, for example. Much of the Internet software then interfaces to software packages.

Yet, the situation is not perfect. Most software packages are not component or object oriented based. Instead, they employ customization through tables. However, there are many situations where this limited flexibility is not sufficient. Since they cannot make major changes to the software package, they resort to other developed systems, to shadow systems, and to workarounds to the package. Some continue to run their old software.

These old software applications are commonly termed legacy systems. Legacy systems may have been initially developed 10 or even 20 years ago. They were programmed in COBOL and are still maintained and supported by internal IT staff. A common way of thinking is that legacy systems are bad. This is not true because they are old and difficult to maintain. This is not necessarily bad. You have to look at the situation in relative terms. While a car may be old, it may be able to do the job (getting you from A to B) just fine. One of us drives a 1985 Chevrolet. It still works fine. Replacement of a legacy system most often occurs because the old software no longer meets the current requirements of the business process. In addition, making changes to the legacy system may be too complex and time consuming. In addition, when you patch or change a legacy system, you may introduce new errors and bugs due to the complexity of the code.

Software packages are neither magic solutions nor silver bullets. Many software packages are also quite old. They have gone through many versions. Being based upon the tables discussed earlier, they have limited flexibility.

So the decision of whether to use a software package or do development is typically a major IT and business decision. Sometimes, you have the third option of just putting in more changes to the old, existing systems. This important decision should be addressed after the requirements. In some cases, however, the decision has already been made by management. Upper management, for example, may dictate that a specific software package will be implemented. Does this mean that you can drop the requirements analysis? No. It remains important for several reasons. First, you have to have the requirements to enter the business rules into the package.

Second, you want to measure the current process to see if there is improvement after the package has been installed. Third, you want to get the employees to acknowledge that problems exist in the current process as well as their impacts. You want the employees to support change.

EVALUATE THE PROCESS AND SYSTEM AND DETERMINE REQUIREMENTS

Having provided some background, let's turn our attention to how things get started. Either through a request or a plan, you feel that the existing software situation for a business process must be analyzed. Your key criteria in making this judgment should not only be the software, but also the business process. You should use the process performance measures in Chapter 2 to evaluate your business process condition.

Assuming that there is a need for investigation, you will go out and determine the business requirements along with how the current systems meet these. The traditional approach is to contact business unit managers and staff to see how the work is performed and to gather the current and potential future needs that they have. Many times this work is flawed. Here are some of the things that you will get as answers.

- If you ask people what is wrong with the current work, you will likely hear that everything is OK. Alternatively, you will get a few problems.
- Some people will indicate some minor changes.

What is wrong with this picture? People are engaged day-to-day in doing the work. They have not had the opportunity, desire, or time to consider change.

The problems get worse if you resort to interviewing. When you show to interview them, middle managers will often tell you what you want to hear. They will indicate some things that support their political agenda. Much of their information will be old and dated since they have not been involved in the process for some time. If you do interviews with supervisors and king and queen bees, you will receive a similar response. Moreover, these people are more likely to feel that there is no basic change. Now move down to the employee level. Some people do not know the process, but give information as if they do. Other people tell the IT staff what they want to hear. There is little or no validation of the interview findings in the work. IT staff rely too much on information provided by supervisors and a few key employees.

There are also problems with the IT staff response. IT staff often accept what people state at face value. They assume that:

- Users understand their problems;
- Users have an idea of what they need in terms of a new system;
- Users are willing to make changes to accommodate the new system.

As a result, requirements are often focused on what users stated that they needed or wanted. The system solution was framed in terms of the technical requirements. The new system would be the silver bullet. Little thought was given to policy changes, facilities modifications, and procedure alterations.

Another problem with traditional systems analysis was that it covered in scope all of the work. This encompasses common transactions as well as exceptions.

In retrospect, it is not surprising that even today many projects deliver results that are not beneficial to organizations or processes. There are some basic lessons learned that can be gathered from 40 years of IT work.

• Requirements can only be gathered when you know where you are going. Without a firm vision of the future process, it is very difficult to determine the road to travel to get there.

• While upper management and some middle managers may want change and a new system, employees who have been doing the work in the same way for many years do not see the need for any change. IT often did not take into account the resistance to change—another common ingredient for system failure.

• The scope of the solutions to business problems was far too narrow—being focused on delivering a new or modified system.

• Looking at all transactions is not only wasteful, but impossible. In most business processes, there are just too many exceptions to address.

The general approach is given in Fig. 11.1. Here you first evaluate the process and determine the issues and their impacts. Doing these things garners more support

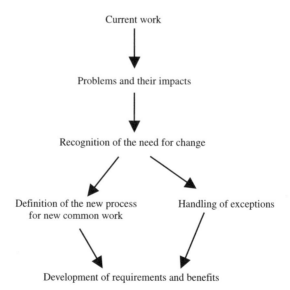

Figure 11.1   Overall View of the Requirements Approach

for change. Then you define the new process for the common work. In parallel, you address exception transactions. Then you can work on benefits and requirements. Here are more detailed guidelines.

• Gather information to evaluate the process first—not to gather requirements. This is more open and does not assume or commit you to major change. Involve lower level employees in assessing process performance and to identify problems and issues with the current work. Examples of problems are given in Fig. 11.2. This can be done through one-on-one contacts as well as small focus groups. Avoid interviewing.

• While you are conducting the evaluation, you should also sort out normal and common transactions from exception work. Exception work consists of transactions that are infrequent, require involvement of king and queen bees, and/or need special knowledge or expertise. Make two lists of these. Create the table in Fig. 11.3 that gives characteristics of the transactions. In this table, you will indicate your assessment of the skills required for the work.

• After you have identified some issues, then you can organize these in terms of which transactions they affect. Since you have divided the work into common and exceptions, the issues can be sorted out in the same way. Working with the employees you can determine the impacts of the problems and develop the table in Fig. 11.4. Some typical impacts are listed in Fig. 11.5.

• You can now combine the information in Figs 11.3 and 11.4 to determine the overall impact of the problems on the work. Get feedback comments from the employees. This is what you have been building up for from the preceding steps. You want the employees to recognize the need for change.

• The system will not handle a specific piece of work. So it must be performed manually, using a shadow system, or with workarounds
• Different people do the same type of work in different ways—leading to inconsistency and inefficiency
• An additional report is needed from the system. Without this there is additional manual work
• Some of the data from the system is keyed into a spreadsheet for later analysis
• There are several additional missing fields that need to be added to the system
• It takes too long to perform a transaction. There are too many steps
• The system needs to handle a specific transaction that it does not do now
• The network sometimes fails and we lose data
• We maintain manual files as well as those on the system

Figure 11.2 Examples of Problems with An Existing Process and System

Transaction	Common or exception	Volume per week	Frequency	Skills needed to do work

Figure 11.3 Characteristics of the Transactions

Transaction	Issues	Impacts	Comments

Figure 11.4   Table for Existing Transactions

- The work takes longer to do
- There are errors in some of the work so it must be rechecked and redone
- You have to go to a senior person to get directions on how to do the work
- There are no written procedures for the work
- The policies for handling the work are not clear
- The shadow system is needed and only one person can use it

Figure 11.5   List of Potential Impacts on the Work

Do you now gather requirements? Not yet. First, you have to work with employees to define the new process and how it will work. You will also separately work to address the exceptions. For defining the new process, you will consider only common transactions. These are the most frequently performed and have the greatest volume. Usually, they are much fewer in number than those of the exceptions. This follows the 80:20 rule where 20% of the transactions generate 80% of the volume of work. Use the table in Fig. 11.6 to document new transactions. This table contains the new business rules as well as the differences between the new and old at the transaction step level. Remember that you are defining with the employees the practical ideal work—not the impractical or what can be achieved with short-term changes.

Now you can build the table in Fig. 11.7 that gives the differences, how the issues are addressed, and benefits for the new work at the transaction level. This is a useful end product because it will become the basis for the requirements as well as the justification for going ahead with the change.

Next, proceed to define requirements for the transactions using Fig. 11.8. Here requirements are entered into the columns. The columns are categories of requirements. You can later summarize this at the process level. Note that these are processes not just system requirements.

The analysis is not finished. Turn now to the exceptions. Answer the following questions for each one.

- What gave rise to the exception? A policy? Practices?
- What if the work was not done?
- Can the work be eliminated or combined through policy or procedure change?
- Is there a way to restructure the exception to make it normal work?
- Can the exception be done in the same way it is now?

Any exception that survives these tests then must be treated as common. Requirements and benefits will be defined after the new version of the exception has been determined. This appears like much more work than just gathering

Transaction: _____

Step	Who	What	Rules	Differences with current

Figure 11.6   Definition of the New Common Transaction

Transaction	Issues	Differences	How issues are addressed	Benefits

Figure 11.7   New Transaction Analysis

Transaction	Policy	Procedure	Business rule	System	Work layout	Staffing/ training

Figure 11.8   Requirements for the New Process

requirements. Is the extra effort worth it? Yes. Here are some reasons from experience.

- It is not much more effort.
- You gain support for change.
- You determine much more tangible benefits and requirements.
- You eliminate work by weeding out some of the exceptions.
- You will have included the shadow systems in the requirements.
- You can use the data to gain management support for eliminating the exceptions and simplifying the work.
- The work results can be employed later to generate Quick Hits (short-term changes), operations procedures, and training materials

MAKE THE BUY OR BUILD DECISION

If you have made it this far, then you are ready to consider the decision of buy or build. There are really three options: change the current process and system but leave the basic work in tact; buy a package; develop software.

Here are some of the factors to consider in the decision.

- Available resources to do development.
- Development and test environment.
- Available time to support new development.

- Availability of software that has capabilities to meet the requirements.
- Budget that is available.
- Risk that you are willing to take with new development.

The decision is easier because you have cut down the number of transactions by eliminating exceptions. It will also be easier to consider software packages because there are typically fewer requirements by considering this approach.

EVALUATE AND SELECT SOFTWARE PACKAGES

Software selection is often based upon the features offered by different packages. Using this method you would draw up a list of features that you want and that are available. You would then create a table of features versus the individual software packages. There are problems with this approach. You really want a system that will perform the common and exception transactions that survived the analysis. Therefore, your attention should be on functions to do the work rather than features. Your feature list should be much smaller because there are often many software features that are nice to have, but are not essential. Figure 11.9 shows the difference. In this figure, there are two diagrams. In the first, Package A has more features than B. However, in the second diagram, B covers more of the functions than A. You should select B over A. The key idea with package evaluation is:

> **It is not the features that you get with the package that is important. Rather, it is the capabilities that you did not get from the packages that really count.**

Why is this? Because you will have to either customize the software, add new software, or do some other significant work to make up for the missing functions.

There are additional factors to consider in the software evaluation and selection work. These include:

- Cost of the software;
- Cost of supporting software (dbms, utilities, libraries, additional modules);

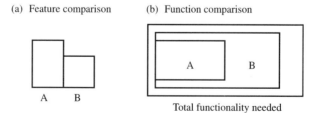

Figure 11.9   Two Diagrams in Software Evaluation

- Training cost;
- Time to install;
- Adaptation of the package;
- Experience of others with the software;
- Viability of the vendor;
- Stability of the software; reported problems;
- Availability of vendor staff to support installation;
- Availability and cost of consulting support for the software implementation.

These are all general evaluation criteria and steps. You want to get down to the detail to validate what you have done. Select two or three common, but different transactions. Compare how different packages handle the transaction. You will be comparing this in four ways.

- The current transaction.
- The current transaction after you have carried out short-term changes.
- The new transaction.
- The transaction as it would be performed with the specific software package.

This will be very interesting. First, the gap between the current and the package is the benefit if you do not carry out the Quick Hit changes. The gap between the current after short-term changes and the package is the residual benefit after Quick Hit changes. This shows you whether (1) it is worth doing the Quick Hits, and (2) whether the package will give benefits sufficient to justify the cost.

There is another gap. That is the difference between the new transaction and the transaction using the software package. This is difference between your realistic ideal way of performing the work and that of the software package. If there is not much difference, then you may want to question if the package is worth the cost, effort, and risk.

What happens if you select the wrong package? What are the risks? Here are some from past experience.

- The package does not fit most of the common transactions. Big surprise—very unpleasant.
- The vendor does not support any changes to the package. You may not get future support.
- It takes too much effort to implement the package.

IMPLEMENT THE SOFTWARE PACKAGE

You want to establish a common project plan with the vendor. Also, identify potential issues as was done in Chapter 5. In parallel to the installation of the package, you will want to undertake Quick Hit, short-term changes. These help to pave the way for greater acceptance of the package later and create a pro-change environment.

Nonetheless, you have to manage the implementation to ensure that end users do not give new requirements to the vendors. No new requirements should surface if you and the employees did your jobs well. So then why are new requirements coming up? There are several commonly encountered reasons. One is that king and queen bees are trying to keep exceptions alive. The second is that some people may be trying to warp the new system back to the way the old system functions. Not a good idea—no benefits. Vendors will cooperate since they want to make people happy and it generates more money and work. Head this off.

PERFORM SOFTWARE DEVELOPMENT

You will still do the analysis and Quick Hits as discussed above. Space does not permit a detailed discussion of system development so we will focus on some highlights. After getting the development team together, there are some useful actions to take.

- Use the approach in Chapter 5 to develop the project plan on a collaborative basis.
- Discuss and agree on all methods and tools that will be employed in development.
- Examine how the interfaces and integration will work with the current software (this step applies to software packages as well).
- Determine how testing and data conversion will be performed.

There are several problems that recur again and again in software development that should be identified.

- Using the best IT staff is dangerous. Some of these people are difficult to get along with. Some are loners. They are often pulled off of your project to work on emergency problems.
- Employing new technology, methods, or tools can be very dangerous. The time to learn, test, and gain expertise is not built into the plan. The project inevitably slips.

It is desirable to develop a prototype. However, this is different from the past since most people know what a GUI is. Keep the prototype for the user interface simple. Concentrate instead on the business rules and interfaces. That is where many issues and problems arise.

CARRY OUT DATA CONVERSION

Data conversion has sometimes been a real disaster and "can of worms." IT often assumes that since the data has been used by the employees for a long time, it is accurate and complete. Don't be misled. It is probably not true; they were using only selected fields.

The new system will have more data elements as well as expanded fields. You must not only map the fields between the old and new, but also determine the comparative meaning of the data elements between the old and new.

There are several approaches to data conversion. Convert the data as is and clean it up later. Have users enter the data into the new system. Then you have a partial conversion of the data. The questions that have to be addressed are:

- What exact data will be converted?
- How will testing of the data be done?
- What and how will additional data be entered?
- What is the timing of the conversion?

PRODUCE OPERATIONS PROCEDURES AND TRAINING MATERIALS

In the past, IT was tasked with developing user procedures for the new system. These were then turned over to the users. This sometimes failed because the users did not assume ownership of the procedures and training materials. Moreover, the user procedures only addressed the system aspects of the process.

A better approach is to have end users who were involved in the definition of the new process, testing, and data conversion do the operations procedures and training materials for the new process. Notice the emphasis on process. IT can help provide some of the user procedures, but the responsibility lies with the employees since they will be doing the work in the process. They will maintain and use both the operations procedures and training materials on a recurring basis.

CONDUCT THE TRAINING

Training should not be done by IT. IT can help train several users and supervisors. They can then do the training of the remainder of the employees. This is a more credible training approach since the training should be on the process, not just the system. In addition, many questions that employees will raise relate to the process and not the system. These can only be answered by the supervisors and trained users. Does IT have a role? Yes, they can participate and support the training on a limited scale.

Here is a useful training method.

- Begin the training with a summary of the current process and the problems today. Have the audience participate with "war stories" about their problems. This gains support for change.

- Give an overview of the new process and highlight with a few transactions how the new process is different from the old. It is here that you will show how the issues were solved.
  - Do the detailed training.
  - Have the audience discuss the benefits of the new process after training. This will reinforce the change.

GAIN USER ACCEPTANCE

In the real world, some users are reluctant to accept the new system. You may wonder why, given that, they participated in the steps so far. Here are some reasons from experience.

- They will be held accountable for benefits if they accept it.
- They still do not want to change.
- They fear that things will fail and they will be blamed.

Beyond training you can do a pilot implementation. This not only shakes down the new system and process, but it also gives the employees confidence in the new process. The employees who participate in the pilot can also do some of the training and help during implementation.

There is another way to gain user acceptance. Make the current process worse. That is, if you are moving to a new process, then you will stop making changes to the old system since it will be replaced. Take this and other steps to deteriorate the old process. This will get people more supportive of the new process. In one case, the response time of the old system worsened. People complained. The IT response was that since the new process was being implemented soon, there were no resources to fix the old system. This really helped acceptance of the new process.

ALIGNMENT OF IT AND THE BUSINESS

Much of the value and contribution of IT to the business lies in the perform-ance of the application software, whether developed or purchased. Alignment of IT partially rests upon how IT does its job in meeting the process requirements. Notice that the word "process" appears and not the terms "department" or "business unit." Managers and business employees may desire many things of the software, but some of these items are really just nice to have and are desirable. They are not essential to the business.

Let's give an example. In every recent car or truck one of us has had, a standard feature was cruise control. This allows you to set the speed of the vehicle without having to place your foot on the accelerator. If you believe in having positive con-trol over the car, then cruise control is not for you as you cede over control of the speed to the car. We don't use it and never have. We don't even know if it works or not. The same occurs with office productivity software and other items. Most of us employ about 5–10% of the features of the software.

In terms of overall alignment, you can use the work performed in the requirements analysis along with the tables in Chapters 2 and 4 to estimate the impact of improved processes on the business objectives, mission, and vision. This is a useful step when you go to management to gain approval for the new process.

MANAGE RISK

A major risk is that management commits to implementing a new process when it is not really needed. This happens because people want some major change. Instead, they find out later that they could have gotten the same or similar benefits with Quick Hit changes.

Another risk is that the software is installed, but the benefits are not realized. There was insufficient change to the business processes impacted by the new systems. This occurs all too frequently. That is why you must center your attention on change and benefits as much as on requirements.

EXAMPLES

SUPREME OIL

Supreme Oil used a traditional development approach. After several new systems were installed, it was found that there were missing requirements and that no one had thought of the new process. Thus, a hybrid inefficient new process was nailed on top of the new system. Major changes then had to be made to the systems.

TUCKER COUNTY

Tucker management was process focused. Thus, all new development efforts had to be justified in terms of changes to the business processes. It took the IT staff some time to move from traditional requirements analysis to the approach in this chapter. There had been several failures due to implementing the right new system, but not handling the resistance to change by lower level employees.

SHAMROCK AGRICULTURE

At Shamrock, a new financial system was installed. It replaced several systems that were working and fit the organization needs of Shamrock. No matter what the vendor and IT did, the new system could not perform what the old systems did. The end result was that the expensive, new financial system only replaced one of four of the old systems. The other three then had to be modified to feed the new system. Much more work and expense with little benefit.

LESSONS LEARNED

- The approach is this chapter represents a modernization and tuning of gathering requirements. The approach here is intended to address the politics of change. The lesson learned is that this can be as important as the requirements.
- Mention was made several times of Quick Hits. These are short-term changes that can eliminate exceptions and streamline work. Sometimes, these are more important than the new system because they promote an atmosphere of change as well as yielding tangible benefits.

PERFORMANCE MEASURES FOR PACKAGES AND DEVELOPMENT

One measure for application software is the approach that was followed in decision-making, evaluation, selection, implementation, and maintenance of the software. A number of items are listed in Fig. 11.10 the answers to which can help you evaluate your current methods.

Another critical measure of software packages and developed software is the extent to which the software meets the demands of the business process. Figure 11.11 gives a list of related questions to answer.

- How many employees were involved in the requirements analysis and assessment of the current process?
- Did the employees assume ownership of the new process?
- Did resistance to change diminish after the analysis and Quick Hits?
- How many users participated in training?
- What was the extent of user participation in developing training materials and operations procedures?
- What was user involvement in testing and data conversion?
- What happened to the old process?
- How were exceptions handled?
- Were the benefits of the new process measured?
- What changes had to be made to the software after it was turned over into production?
- What changes in user roles occurred with the new process?

Figure 11.10   Performance Questions Related to Software Activities

- What shadow systems are still in place? Existence of shadow systems indicates the gaps with the software
- How frequently and to what level of detail are processes measured?
- Are exception transactions identified?
- What percent of the work is in exceptions?
- What efforts have been taken to eliminate exceptions?
- Are shadow systems incorporated into the new systems?
- What new needs have surfaced since the new process has been live?

Figure 11.11 Performance Measures Related to Software Capabilities

SUMMARY

Application software is a core area of IT. Yet, many of the analysis and support methods have not been modernized for some time. Attention has instead been focused on the software itself and the methods and tools. In this chapter, a modified approach that focused on greater user involvement was discussed. The key to success of any application software lies in the performance of the business processes it supports. When you turn your attention to the process, then you can consider Quick Hits and exceptions. You can also carry out more change management activities.

Chapter 12

Implementing Change in IT Management

INTRODUCTION

This is the chapter where the major ideas and guidelines are organized and structured so that you can take action after reading this book to improve IT management. We will begin with summarizing some of the general themes that are stressed in the previous chapters. Specific actions in various areas are then addressed. Important to consider is resistance to change. When you attempt to change management style or focus, you will inevitably encounter some resistance. This topic is important to explore so that you can either head the resistance off or deal with it.

IMPLEMENT NEW ROLES AND RESPONSIBILITIES FOR IT

Traditionally, IT focused on the following activities.

- IT projects.
- Systems analysis in support of the business.
- Development and maintenance of software.
- Computer and network operations.
- Limited systems planning and control.

With the emphasis on business processes and the fact that many processes span multiple departments, there is no single owner of a process except for the CEO. There are some missing roles in relation to business processes.

Within IT there are also new roles with project management, process improvement, and change management. These arise in part because of the need for IT work not just to be completed, but also to result in significant and measurable benefits.

Taken together, you can see that there is an expanded role for IT. The new role includes the following:

- Measurement of business processes and IT;
- Collaboration and support of the business units for process improvement and change management;
- Development and maintenance of software;
- Computer and network operations as well as technology assessment;
- Support for issues and lessons learned databases as well as project templates;
- IT strategic planning and alignment with the business;
- Coordination and support in the management of outsourcing;
- IT projects.

This new role has become a fact in some companies and organizations today. It will expand in others for several reasons. First, the logical home for the role is IT. IT is the only group that has knowledge of many business processes, supports the entire organization, and is the home of systems and technology. Forming separate or new groups that would perform the new roles would just create conflicts and problems with IT. Is the IT of today suitable to undertake these new responsibilities? In some organizations, probably not. However, this does not mean that the IT organization cannot be changed. The changes are not of tidal wave proportions, but instead are a natural extensive of how IT and its roles and responsibilities have changed over the past 40 years.

INSTILL GREATER COLLABORATION

Collaboration and joint work have been stressed throughout. This should be natural, but in IT it is not. Often, while people pay lip service to teamwork, the actual situation is one individual effort. Individual effort is still important, but times have changed in IT. IT work has become too important and too complex for just individual efforts alone.

There are a number of benefits to you and the organization from greater collaboration. First, people are more aware of what IT is doing and the direction IT is taking. This leads to greater stability in IT work. Second, collaboration brings shared dependence. That is, IT becomes less dependent upon a few managers or employees. Third, there will be less questioning about the purpose, scope, and nature of IT work.

Let's see how teamwork and collaboration pay off in some of the key IT activities covered.

• *Strategic IT planning.* In many instances, the plan is developed by a few people, often in IT and some consultants. Then the plan is presented and what happens? Surprise, the plan runs into immediate resistance. People don't understand the thinking that went into the plan.

A better approach is to involve not just several more IT staff and managers, but also business managers and their employees. There is a trade-off in the number of people to involve. The more people you involve, the longer the elapsed time for the planning. However, the more people you involve, the greater understanding and support for the plan. The method that was developed in Chapter 4 is based upon incrementally developing lists and then planning tables.

• *Alignment between IT and the business.* Much has been discussed about alignment. Since IT is a support organization, you have to probe as to what is being supported. Traditional IT supported business departments. Modern IT is focused on supporting the major important processes in the business that are responsible for revenue, costs, and profitability. When you adopt this view, you can see that responding to small requests from individuals that have very few benefits results in resource waste and lost opportunities.

Alignment of business and IT comes through IT constantly centering its efforts on processes and then relating the work to the business vision, mission, objectives, and issues. Thus, IT has a business orientation, rather than a technical orientation. The systems and technology are only means to an end, not the end itself.

• *Governance and oversight of IT.* In Chapter 2, a framework for IT governance was discussed in terms of several IT overseeing or steering committees. While steering committees have been around for a long time and their benefits known, there has been a lack of specific guidelines for how to do the overseeing. Chapter 2 provided specific guidelines for the role of IT and business managers. In all of this, collaboration was the key.

If you add up the previous paragraph with the discussion under the preceding bullet, you find that the steering committees are overseeing more than IT. They are overseeing the business processes of which systems and technology are but a part. The steering committees present a forum for collaboration on business processes and the real work of the business.

• *Process improvement and change management.* Why carry out an IT project? Why improve or replace the IT infrastructure? Because these things support the business. However, if you finish all of this work on time and within budget, there are no benefits. There must be process change and change in attitudes. This requires substantial collaboration and joint work between IT and the business employees. There should be no such thing as an IT only project. All significant work in IT should be business related and involve substantial collaboration with the business employees.

- *Communications.* In Chapter 10, communications with upper management and business unit management was covered. There were many guidelines given that all emphasize collaboration and knowledge sharing. Successful collaboration in management communications means you are talking and communicating in business terms. Collaboration for IT managers is best carried out through extensive, regular informal communications.

- *Project management.* Chapter 5 dealt with IT projects. It was demonstrated that many of the techniques that work in traditional project management have to be modernized for IT and the business today.

From the start of the project, the emphasis is on teamwork, rather than a project team that consists of a collection of individual efforts. Shared tasks and shared project management were stressed. The benefits of a collaborative approach are important in that they pave the way for cumulative improvement of IT work.

- *New IT initiatives.* New concepts that include systems and technology should be business focused. You want to ensure that there is in-depth business involvement in formulating the purpose and scope of the proposed effort. In general, there should be four purposes to any new effort that involves IT: business, technical, political, and cultural. For as we have seen, this involvement and participation is the key to getting successful improvement in the business as well as lasting and sustainable results.

- *System development and operations.* Chapters 11 and 12 centered on development, software packages, and operations. These are at the core of what IT does. Traditionally, these were viewed as the technical domain of IT. Things are changing. To be successful, there must be a wider business role. This new business role was discussed in Chapter 8. Business must collaborate in the successful implementation of any IT-related effort. While people have paid lip service to this idea, it has never been more important as today. The importance of the business role will grow as IT work becomes more embedded in business activities.

- *Vendor management and outsourcing.* A new approach for collaborative effort with vendors was presented in Chapter 9. Often, vendor–client relations deal with the problems. However, successful outsourcing requires that the vendors and company managers and staff work together. When outsourcing was very limited, this was not viewed as all that important. Times have changed. There is too great a dependence on many organizations for them not to have extensive collaboration.

MEASURE WHAT YOU HAVE, DO, AND WHERE YOU ARE GOING

The significance of structured measurement cannot be understated. If you don't employ an organized approach, you will tend to move from event to event without gathering lessons learned to improve your performance. Measurement can be undertaken in two forms. One is collaborative where you measure to get support and joint ownership. The results of this type of measurement are to generate momentum for improvements.

- *Measurement of business processes.* This is critical to determine where things stand, where the best opportunities for IT work are, and what IT projects and work were accomplished. If the processes are not measured, then you really do not know where you stand in terms of the work and what should be done and what has been achieved.
- *Measurement of IT.* Early in the book, a scorecard for IT assessment was given. This provides the basis of a regular evaluation of IT that goes beyond budget and schedule performance. Without a more comprehensive measurement approach, IT tends to be evaluated on these two, mostly reactive measures.
- *Measurement of business unit involvement.* Business units sometimes treat involvement in projects and systems as routine and do not give them sufficient improvement. Then when problems arise, the business often blames IT. Measurement helps to show to upper management the comparative performance of different business departments.
- *Measurement of outsourcing.* Without measurement, outsourcing is often managed on a case-by-case basis. Lessons are not learned and applied to other situations. Measurement, on the other hand, raises the bar for the vendor in terms of the standards of performance. It also supports IT and the business in overseeing outsourcing and vendor performance.
- *Measurement of the IT planning process.* These measurements included not only how the plan was created and updated, but also how the resources were allocated to support the action items of the strategic IT plan. Without this measurement, the planning process might not be improved.
- *Measurement of alignment of IT to the business.* This measurement, through the business processes, helps to steer and direct IT. It also provides a general determination of the value of IT to the organization. Without this measurement, there is almost always doubt about what IT is contributing.
- *Measurement of the IT architecture.* Here you are assessing the current IT architecture and determining issues and opportunities for improvement that will benefit the business processes and work. Without this measurement, it is more difficult to gain management approval for updating the IT infrastructure since the need is not perceived by management.

The second type of measurement is self-assessment. Some of the measurements that have been developed include the following:

- *Measurement of communications.* Several checklists were provided related to your communications. Measurement helps by making you aware of the importance of communications as well as highlighting the problems that arise. Without this measurement, you tend to just plunge ahead and not learn from your mistakes.

• *Measurement in addressing issues and problems.* Your effectiveness in understanding, analyzing, and addressing problems is a major measure of whether you succeed or fail as a manager. How long an issue remains unresolved can be an indicator of a problem. If you don't measure, then you tend to address problems individually and in a vacuum.

• *Measurement of collaboration.* Here you measure how well you support collaboration and how you involve others in decision-making. Often, if you don't pay this much attention, you will revert back to isolated analysis and decision-making.

BECOME ISSUES FOCUSED

This is not negative. It is a positive approach to deal with risk. Risk in IT arises because of underlying problems or issues. You can talk all day long about risk, but if you fail to deal with the issues that gave rise to the risk, then you fail.

Each chapter has dealt on a section titled Manage risk. Let's highlight some of the potential failures and risks in IT management.

• *Failure to show the alignment with the business.* If alignment is not shown, then management begins to question what IT is doing and the direction it is taking. Management of IT is called into question.

• *Failure to manage new and existing technology.* If the wrong technology is selected, then much effort is expended on work to implement something that will not be used, will not result in tangible benefit, and will require substantial operational support. The same remarks apply to obsolete existing technology.

• *Failure in IT planning.* If the planning effort for IT fails or if the plan is produced and then not employed, the price that may be incurred is high. First, the credibility of IT suffers. Second, the resources dedicated to the planning effort were wasted. Third, without a plan, business managers and even IT managers will improvise solutions and projects. IT descends into a maintenance and reactive group.

• *Failure in IT work and projects.* As we saw, failure can occur in many ways. It is not just that the project went over budget or behind schedule. It is also that the benefits and change resulting from the IT work were never carried out or achieved. Confidence in IT to deliver meaningful results declines.

• *Failure in dealing effectively with business units.* IT must encourage a wider business role in IT than was traditionally the case. Process improvement and change management go hand-in-hand with the IT work. The business has a role throughout an IT project.

• *Failure in outsourcing.* While there have been some notable successes in outsourcing, there have also been failures. If you are outsourcing a business process, then the risk is that the entire process may collapse. If outsourcing is restricted to an IT activity, then the risk is that IT performance will suffer. The effectiveness of the business process is then affected.

• *Failure in communications.* The risk is that miscommunications affect IT work and direction. If relations with management sour due to communications problems, then IT management itself is at risk.

• *Failure in development, maintenance, and support.* While there can be a major failure in a project, the overall risk is that many problems and issues arise in these activities that are not addressed consistently or completely. Problems within IT grow and IT becomes less responsive to the business.

IMPLEMENT MORE DYNAMIC RESOURCE ALLOCATION

In times past, people would be allocated in IT to specific projects or to maintenance, operations, and support. Today, the business is more dynamic. Requirements and needs can arise quickly and change. The old method of allocation which was done ad hoc or on a quarterly basis no longer works.

IT management with some collaboration from business units must more dynamically address resource allocation for both IT and business employees. Key to this allocation is that between nonproject work and IT projects. If you do not implement this approach, the nonproject will tend to dominate what happens. IT flexibility is greatly reduced as the resources are bled off.

BECOME PROCESS ORIENTED

A great deal of attention has been paid to business processes and their importance. Traditionally, the management of the business process was left to the line manager in a department. However, this traditional approach does not fit the modern business.

• Single processes often cross multiple departments.
• Processes are much more intertwined and interdependent.
• Business employees are consumed by doing the work and do not have the time or skill to examine the process overall.
• Many business processes are being automated through E-Business.

The basic purpose of IT projects is to effect change in the business process. Thus, IT is becoming more process focused. This has already happened in many IT groups where the knowledge of the business rules and procedures is programmed into the software. In such cases, it is the IT staff that is knowledgeable about these rules and procedures.

ALIGN IT AND THE BUSINESS

Like managing risk, this has been discussed in each chapter. Alignment assessment is best performed with each major IT activity and project as well as in planning analysis. Successful business alignment occurs when:

- Key business processes are made efficient through systems and technology.
- The strategic IT plan is mapped against business objectives, vision, mission, and issues.
- Issues and opportunities that relate to IT are addressed from the perspective of alignment.
- Business profitability, revenue, and costs can be traced first to the business processes and then to the contribution and role of IT.

REDIRECT IT RESOURCES

IT resources must be redirected to work that provides greater value to the business. While operations, maintenance, and support are important, these activities just maintain what you have already.

You have limited IT resources. It is unlikely that you will get anymore. If you want to improve IT performance with existing resources, you have to redirect the existing resources away from operations and maintenance and toward new initiatives and projects. A two-pronged approach is to strategically do the allocation. Then every week you review and update the allocation and adjust to the situation. If this is not done, then there can be a tendency to revert to maintenance and operations.

Another part of getting more out of IT resources is to be more selective on what new IT projects are started. The IT manager in general should be indifferent to most new projects because they do not yield benefits that help IT. Indeed, all new system implementations result in more maintenance. Upper management should see the IT manager as a gatekeeper who can help discourage or restructure new project ideas.

You can also improve IT performance by getting more involvement in IT projects from business employees. This can help spread the limited IT resources across more work.

IMPLEMENT MORE EFFECTIVE PROJECT MANAGEMENT

IT projects are often addressed separately. Each one is different from the others. This attitude is very negative in terms of improving IT project performance. In general, IT projects fall into groups of similar projects. Similar projects such as the installation of two software packages are different at the detailed level but very similar at a high level. In order to achieve cumulative improvement, a number of steps were identified. These include:

- Establishing an issues database for all IT projects and work. You employ this on a regular basis so that after awhile few new issues appear.
- Building a lessons learned database in which you capture and reuse both good and bad experience for successive projects and work.
- Creating and updating project templates for all project work.

Another problem in IT project management is that many small projects are not treated as projects. Instead, they become regular, nonproject work. This results in the problem that they are not managed closely. All projects and as much nonproject work as possible should be treated as projects. This will give them closer scrutiny and management. Using the approach of templates, issues, and lessons learned, making something into a project does not create extra work.

DEAL EFFECTIVELY WITH RESISTANCE TO CHANGE

Resistance to change can come from upper management, within IT, and from the business units. Several causes of resistance include the following:

- IT supervisor and staff who feel comfortable with the status quo;
- Business unit managers and staff who resent IT interference and who do not want to relinquish control;
- Business managers and staff who do not want to assume any more responsibilities;
- Upper level managers who do not want to change their style.

What do you do when you encounter resistance? Here are some specific steps to take.

- Assume that you will get some resistance ahead of time. Thus, you should propose new ideas casually.
- Indicate that there are some opportunities for improving the current situation by pointing to the problems with the current approach.
- Indicate that if the current situation continues, there might be more substantial problems. This highlights the need for change.
- Propose several steps to take so that people can pick and choose. For the ones not chosen, you can revisit these later.
- After you have tried something new or a change, sit down with people and give them credit for participating. They will begin to be more accepting of the change.
- Do not take the resisters head on. This will just force them underground.

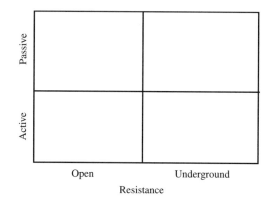

Figure 12.1 Types of Resistance

In Fig. 12.1, there is a diagram of resistance and whether it is open or not as well as passive versus active. Here are some comments.

• Active and open resistance is probably the easier to deal with. You can use logic and take your time in dealing with this. The resistance here is more logical.

• Open and passive resistance is evident when people do not challenge the change. Instead, they just keep raising questions. Address each of these as it arises.

• Active and covert resistance is one of the most difficult. Here a manager may endorse what you are proposing, but will then attempt to undermine it. You must take steps to detect that this is occurring from the statements of other people. Then you can start to address it.

• Covert and passive resistance is difficult to detect. These individuals may be very sullen and somber. They will not say much, but if things go wrong, they will possibly jump in and criticize. While you can try to win these people over, it may be best to deal with the other three types first. If you succeed there, then this group will likely come around.

Here are several examples. If you want to change the meetings from status to issues and lessons learned, point out that some people think that these meetings are very boring and dry. Much of what is discussed does not involve them. Then suggest that maybe we could all talk about other topics. They probably will ask "What?" You can respond with discussing but not resolving some of the issues.

Figure 12.2 gives some of the factors behind why people resist change. Only a few of these will apply to a situation. However, reviewing this list will make you more aware of people's concerns about change.

In another case, suppose that you want a vendor to share your project plan, issues, and provide knowledge. Here you might sit down with the vendor and

- Fear of change is contagious
- Cost savings is emphasized over job satisfaction
- In some situations, people were not properly trained in their current jobs so that they have more resistance to change
- Previous attempts at change in their business unit failed
- Change in another department resulted in job cutbacks. Fear of demotion or loss of position
- There has been a history of problems with management so that there is a lack of trust and faith
- People are unwilling to participate in change because management views the additional work as part of the job and does not value it
- Employees receive different signals and messages from management and various members of the change team
- Employees participate and volunteer information at the start of the change effort, but they see that other people take credit for their work
- The employees are not told what is expected of them. There is a lack of planning with them
- Resistance worked before in the past, it might work again
- There is substantial management change and turnover
- The change is not addressing major needs
- People are being pulled away from their work, but are still held accountable for the same performance. Management does not address issues raised by the employees
- There are major work pressures, such as year-end closing, right at the time when change is being attempted
- After the change has been defined, middle managers and the change team tinker with the details of the change
- No one makes it clear in detail how the new procedures are to work
- In carrying out the change, management does not value the knowledge and experience of the employees.

Figure 12.2   Some Factors behind Resistance to Change

share some war stories from past outsourcing work. Indicate that it is in both of your interests to not have these problems arise.

Notice the common thread in both examples—softness and casual. You are not imposing anything. You are having a discussion in which you identify some problems to avoid or some things that are wrong with the current situation. Then you are mentioning some ideas for change. Nothing is forced on anyone. Once you try out these approaches and they work, then people will accept more of the same. Again, nothing was either mandated or imposed.

Another part of resistance arises because managers have gotten impressions of you and IT over the years. These impressions may be difficult to change. What should you do then?

- Work in detailed and small changes. For example, in management communications, you could begin with more casual contacts. That is how the IT manager turned things around at Shamrock Agriculture.

- Don't expect a change in attitude overnight. It will come gradually and through body language and other signs.
- If a manager behaves in a traditional way, just take it in stride.

EXAMPLES

SUPREME OIL

For a number of years, the IT organization worked along in a traditional mode. No one in IT noticed what was going on in other energy firms or with the technology. Issues arose and grew, but were treated as just normal work.

The crisis occurred when upper management realized that there was a major problem. The basic processes were not being supported. The IT plan was out of touch with reality. IT resources were consumed in maintenance.

There was a major IT management shakeup. The new management was faced with so many problems that it was difficult to figure out where to begin. They started with communications, issues, and the focus on the business processes. After these were understood and improved, a new, modern IT strategic plan was established. Alignment was addressed in the plan. The plan was accompanied by a new governance structure. This provided the roadmap for a number of new initiatives to address and improve the business processes. All of these new projects were undertaken in the context of process improvement and change management. It took over a year to turn the situation around, but it worked.

TUCKER COUNTY

Some of the problems in Tucker County IT have been covered in previous chapters. The Tucker IT manager was reactive and dictatorial. He would tell business managers what they would get. There was limited collaboration. Some business processes were supported; some were not. The IT manager stuck with terminals as opposed to PCs for several years and it was too late.

In a government organization, it was difficult to change the IT manager immediately. So the governance approach in Chapter 2 was put into place. The steering committees then began to direct IT resources. It was left for the IT manager to do the day-to-day management. Initiatives were begun in projects, planning, and technology. This created turnover in the IT organization. Several key IT positions were then filled not by the IT manager, but through direct involvement of members of the steering committees. The IT manager finally departed. However, a great deal of change had already been accomplished.

SHAMROCK AGRICULTURE

In Shamrock, IT was a small organization. They worked well on the projects, but they lacked some of the elements of direction. The following initiatives were taken:

- The state of the current technology was reviewed and new technology was identified.
- Key business processes were examined in terms of what could be accomplished to effect improvement and change.
- New projects were initiated using both external and internal resources after the above two items had been completed.
- A strategic IT plan was developed. This plan has been employed as a model for the business plan. The strategic IT plan has now been updated through several cycles.
- Informal communications between IT and the business were improved.
- A more organized formal project management process was implemented.

TACTICS FOR IMPLEMENTATION

There are some specific tactical moves that you can take. These have been gathered over the years in implementing changes in IT management.

- Don't announce changes or make them formal.
- Do not impose changes. If you do this, you will likely raise more resistance.
- Allow individuals to raise questions about the change. Be patient and address each one. If no one raises an issue, then you should raise some sample issues to get discussion going.
- Try to get people to adopt these changes as their own ideas.
- Make several small changes in parallel. This will keep people off-guard. Moreover, it will be harder for them to attack multiple changes without coming off as very negative.

PERFORMANCE MEASURES FOR IMPLEMENTATION

Figure 12.3 provides some questions that you can employ to track your progress in implementing changes. These measures apply to general changes. If you keep these questions handy, then you should refer to them before, during, and after changes.

- Do you have an overall sequencing for implementing improvements?
- Do you gather feedback from one change and then apply it to later changes?
- What is the general attitude of managers or employees after the changes are in effect? Are they more accepting of change?
- Do people volunteer different ways to implement change?
- Do individuals participate in how to define and how to measure the effectiveness of the change?
- Do employees or managers see the problems with the current situation in the same way that you did?
- Do people indicate and put forward additional improvements?
- How do people deal with individuals who raise issues and problems with changes? Do they support the individual or the change?
- After the change is made, does it stick? Or, do people attempt to revert to the old ways?

Figure 12.3   Performance Measurement Questions for Implementing Change

SUMMARY

In this book, some of the major challenges and problems that IT faces today have been presented. The reader probably can recognize and associate with many of these. For some the approaches that have been presented appear simple to understand and implement. Yet, experience shows that old ways are hard to change unless there is a major crisis as was the case at Supreme Oil. This book should provide you with a roadmap for you to improve the effectiveness of IT and the alignment of IT with the business.

For many years, systems and technology have helped out with much promise and benefit for business improvement. Yet, for too many organizations these visions have not come to fruition. Instead, there has been much frustration and exasperation with IT. The methods presented here have been successfully employed in a wide variety of organizations under a wide variety of political and cultural backdrops. They do work and yield both short- and long-term results.

Don't ever dismiss the political and cultural factors involved in IT. The growing importance and attention to technology and its impact have been accompanied with more politics in IT work. Politics cannot be avoided or discarded. The IT manager has to become a player, not a spectator in the politics. This is unavoidable. We wish you great success in your management efforts as well as humor and enjoyment. With over 70 years of IT experience between us, we have found IT challenging, but very rewarding. We, together with you, would not want it any other way.

Part IV

Address Specific Challenges

Chapter 13

Personnel and Staffing Issues

INTRODUCTION

In this part there are five areas of IT management that are considered in terms of key issues that are frequently encountered. For each issue, the following will be discussed.

- *Background.* How the issue arises and its importance are covered here.
- *Impact.* This is the effect on IT and management if the issue is not addressed.
- *Prevention.* In some cases, you can act ahead of time to head off an issue and prevent it from occurring.
- *Detection.* Tips are provided to help you detect signs that the issue is emerging.
- *Action.* These are steps that can be taken to address the issue.

Note that an entire chapter could be written about each issue so that there is no goal of providing a complete discussion. Rather, the purpose is to provide you with ideas and insight so that you can identify and deal with issues in IT management more effectively.

In this specific chapter, personnel and staffing issues are covered. From experience as IT managers, this is one of the most frequently encountered areas of problems. Part of this may stem from the lack or limited interpersonal skills that is present in some IT staff. As an aside, a technique that we have used with IT members is to openly address these and other issues—very untraditional from standard IT topics.

IT STAFF TURNOVER IS HIGH

BACKGROUND

This is most often encountered when times are good and IT skills are in high demand. It can also occur when there are substantial internal problems with IT. However, there can also be individual events with people's lives. Momentum then builds. Also, some IT people are constantly or regularly in touch with headhunters involved in personnel placement. A not uncommon practice has been to place someone in a firm and then after 2 years or so place him or her again someplace else.

IMPACT

Turnover in itself is healthy. Getting new people into IT means having access to different skills and knowledge. In addition, some IT people have skills and knowledge that are not local or specific to the firm. The impact is the worst if key programmers, supervisors, and other IT staff leave. Then the impact can be felt in projects as well as in maintenance and operations. Responses to user requests and work take longer. More people make changes to programs—potentially causing damage and increasing errors. What makes things worse is that the departures come without planning so that there is often at most only a 2-week transition. Documentation is not maintained. Knowledge is often not shared. Matters are made worse if the IT manager does not assume that turnover is possible at all times, but also at the worst of times.

PREVENTION

Obviously, you cannot prevent someone from leaving. However, you can minimize the damage by taking some sensible steps. One is to use the project meetings as a forum to transfer knowledge. Another is to assign joint tasks to two people. A third is to encourage sharing of knowledge about programs, design, etc., through lessons learned meetings. Milestone documents can also be presented. Again, you should assume that there will be some turnover.

DETECTION

Casual contact with individual IT employees without the supervisors is a good way of detecting problems early. Also, you should sit down where people eat or take breaks and listen to what they are talking about. If they never discuss work, then there could be a problem. If they do not talk about known issues and are silent, this could also mean problems.

ACTION

If you start to see some turnover, you don't want to overreact. However, you do want to get at the root causes of problems. Rather than ask what the problems are, you can ask, "Is there anything I can do to help?" If you find out that a head-hunter is raiding the staff, then you want to contact the headhunter as well as Human Resources.

When someone does announce that they are leaving, you should take actions to transfer as much knowledge as you can. You can institute walkthroughs of the program code. You can also have the person indicate what issues there are. If a critical person is leaving, then you may need to establish a limited consulting engagement with them to finish what they are doing. Do not assume that they are going to finish what they are doing. Their minds are already on the next job. Transfer the responsibilities as soon as possible. If you have a problem employee and they are working on sensitive material, then you should restrict access to what they are doing. In a few cases, we have had persons working entirely separately from the other IT employees at home.

IT MORALE IS LOW

BACKGROUND

There are many causes for low morale in IT. Salaries could have been frozen or capped for some time. The work assignments may not be interesting or appealing. People want more challenges. However, these causes are often less frequent than pressure on projects and fear of failure. An employee may be part of a project and may see that the project is behind schedule and in trouble. The person does not want to be part of a failed effort and so wants to leave. Another cause for morale problems is interpersonal problems between employees, supervisors, and managers. One bad IT manager can make life in IT a living hell.

There are also morale issues that can be generated external to IT. For example, if the IT manager places great importance on a specific project and then the project is not approved, morale can drop. How the IT manager conducts himself or herself is important here. Another factor is users or business managers who harass or make unreasonable demands on IT staff. This can be demoralizing as well. The general attitude of upper management toward IT is another factor.

IMPACT

The impact of low morale is not obvious or evident at first. People seem to be going about their normal work as usual. However, the impacts increase. It takes longer to resolve technical issues. Employees do not volunteer to work on issues or problems. There may be a general lack of initiative. Productivity suffers.

PREVENTION

One technique that we have used extensively is to institute more group work and discussions in meetings. Issues are discussed more openly and acknowledged. You also want to point out that the issues or problems that are depressing them have occurred many times in the past. Emphasize that they should put things into perspective. Focus more on accomplishments of the people. These steps help to keep the morale up. However, there will be times when morale will drop. This is natural and you may even want to label these times and indicate that morale will go up and down.

DETECTION

You should listen to what people are discussing. Detect their attitudes toward their work. Also, you want to watch how IT members deal with problems and issues. It is one thing for IT staff to criticize a user department as being backward or against change; it is another if this keeps up.

ACTION

If you detect low morale, you can begin to take action by accentuating the positive. Stress accomplishments. Also, keep an eye out for project pressures that can impact morale. If a project has an unreasonable deadline, don't just push the team members to perform. Start to look at the schedule. It is important for the IT manager to be directly involved and hands-on. Morale is an issue for all of IT, not just one group. We have also held some social events to help raise morale. If one person is very negative and the work they are doing now is not critical, encourage them to take a vacation. Consider sending them to a training class as well.

THERE IS POOR COMMUNICATIONS BETWEEN IT AND USERS

BACKGROUND

IT staff and business employees come with different viewpoints. What is important to an IT person may not be of interest to a department employee, and vice versa. You generally should assume that this will be an ongoing problem. How do IT and users communicate? In projects there are requirements, design, etc.? Communications problems here include misunderstood requirements, incomplete or partial information, etc. IT staff, on the other hand, may over promise what can be delivered. The IT person may want to please the user and so give an optimistic date. Then later it is changed and the users are upset since they made plans based on the original dates.

In operations and support, users may make unrealistic demands. They may exaggerate the importance of some problems to get attention. They may change requirements and requests as well.

IMPACT

The impact of poor communications may lead to more mistrust between the IT staff and users. IT staff may even ignore the information provided by some users. If the users are not clear as to what they need, the IT staff may make assumptions about what the users want and may create solutions that do not work in the real world.

One of the worst cases of poor communications led to the IT manager being directly involved in the work as an intermediary in transferring information. This was a temporary condition, but it solved the issue.

PREVENTION

One of the best means of prevention is to involve several people from both IT and the user department. This will reduce the possibility of miscommunications. Another step in prevention is to replay the information that is to conveyed so that it is validated.

We have found that the less communication there is, the greater the chance for miscommunications. Thus, it is important that there be regular communications—even if there is no issue.

Another technique is to involve the IT staff in the work of the user department. When they see and participate in the work that goes on, they are better able to communicate and understand. Conversely, it is good for users to see some of the issues first hand in meetings.

DETECTION

You can detect miscommunications if people indicate that they do not know what the users want. Track requirements and review communications to detect problems. You can also review the media used in communications in terms of e-mails and documents.

ACTION

If you detect miscommunications and problems, then you should freeze what is going on for a short time and review the work. Find out if what is being done is supportive of the real needs. Another tactic is to get more people involved. It may be that there is a personality conflict between two people.

TOO MUCH CRITICAL WORK DEPENDS ON THE SAME FEW PEOPLE

BACKGROUND

This is almost a permanent problem in both IT and in business processes. Over time certain people acquire knowledge and skills that cannot easily be transferred. Rather than force the transfer of information that might take time, managers just rely on these people more and more. In many IT groups, two or three people may hold critical knowledge for specific application systems.

IMPACT

These critical people may leave—creating a major problem. Another impact is that work results tend to slow down. The same few people get overworked and slow down. They get burned out. Productivity suffers. Users cannot understand since they may feel that the IT people have interchangeable skills and knowledge.

PREVENTION

The best prevention is to assume that they will happen. Review what people are working on and how dependent each system is on a specific individual. Consider assigning joint work and tasks to support the sharing of the knowledge. Some will resist this as it intrudes and threatens their informal power. Yet, your position is that it is in their self-interest to not be so critical.

DETECTION

One way of detecting this is to see who does not take a vacation. Who do people call on when there is a problem? Who do the users rely on when they have a problem? Answering these questions will help you to detect who is critical.

ACTION

You will probably have a situation where several people are too critical. Start to implement shared tasks. Encourage the critical employees to make more presentations to the other IT staff. Another step to take is to reassign work to other employees. You also need to review the deadlines for the work.

IT STAFF MEMBERS WORK IN ISOLATION

BACKGROUND

This is a major problem in many IT groups. People work alone doing programming, design, project management, and other work. They often only get together in project meetings where they review status. They do not make an effort to work together—in part because IT management by its actions does not encourage teamwork. Some IT managers believe that the greatest efficiency along with accountability is attained by assigning work to individuals. This attitude is also backed up by the history of IT where people worked in specialized areas.

IMPACT

There are many impacts to isolated work. If a person leaves, there is no one to readily take over his or her work. In addition, morale may be more of a problem since you may not hear about problems until it is too late.

Working alone people do not feel part of the IT group or the organization. They may begin to wonder if their services are really valued. This obviously creates more problems.

PREVENTION

The best prevention is to implement more shared work and tasks. Project meetings, as we have stated earlier, should be devoted to issues and lessons learned. IT meetings can do the same thing.

DETECTION

Detection is relatively easy. You can examine what people are working on and what tasks are jointly assigned. You can also observe how IT staff members interact at meetings. If they act surprised at information that they should have known, then you are seeing the problems of isolation.

ACTION

The long-term action is to get more teamwork going. The short-term approach is to change the meetings that are held within projects and IT overall. Here you want to encourage more participation. Another step that is more radical is to change the work layout so that two people work in one office or larger cubicle as opposed to individual cubicles.

SUPERVISORS LACK MANAGEMENT SKILLS

BACKGROUND

Many IT supervisors were promoted for doing good work in their technical job. Sometimes, the only way to get them more money is to promote them into being supervisors. In recognizing the job change, an IT manager may send them to one or more classes on supervision.

IMPACT

Many IT issues can be traced to the missteps and problems generated by IT supervisors. The supervisor may put too much pressure on his or her group. He may have high expectations because of what he or she can do. The people who were not promoted may have fewer skills and less experience. The overall impact can be lower morale in the group. Some employees may just want to give up and hand the work over to the supervisor.

PREVENTION

Experience has shown that individuals who are being considered for management and supervisory roles should see what the job entails. We have found that it is useful for them to work side by side with a proven, capable supervisor. Once they see what the job is like, they can either decide they do not want to do it, or they can develop better techniques for dealing with people. Another step is to have them handle some personnel and other nontechnical issues before they become supervisors.

DETECTION

On the surface a supervisor may be doing well. Work is going on. There are no visible complaints or signs of problems. However, underneath the employees may be seething and very unhappy. They may be intimidated. To see what is going on, you should attend some of the meetings of the supervisor and his group. Do this for all groups so that you do not appear punitive.

Another approach is to see how the supervisor handles issues. What role do they play? What roles and responsibilities do they assign to their employees? These will tell you a great deal about what is going on.

ACTION

If you see supervisors having problems, do not assume that they can be just sent to a class to improve their skills. You should consider doing some reassignment of work with other supervisors. Also, consider joint supervision of the work. You may need to have Human Resources gather feedback and evaluations of the group on the performance of the supervisor. We have found that this is a useful technique if employed uniformly across IT—much like standardized course evaluations.

Chapter 14

Systems and Technology Issues

INTRODUCTION

In Chapter 3, the assessment of current technology along with the adoption of new technology were covered. Here some common issues related to systems and technology are covered. While on the surface it might appear that once the issue was solved, the problem does not arise. Experience, however, reveals that these are repetitive problems. This is due to several factors, including management expectations, lack of analysis of the technology, and emergence of new technologies.

THE WRONG TECHNOLOGY IS SELECTED

BACKGROUND

The word "wrong" needs to be explained. You can acquire technology that is too difficult to use or install. New technology may not be as suitable to the business as was originally thought. Human resources are not available to work with the new technology. The technology may have unintended negative side effects.

How does this problem arise? One major reason is lack of analysis. The lure or hype of the new technology tends to minimize the amount of analysis performed. Another factor is that because other firms have used the technology, it should work in your organization. However, each organization has a unique combination of systems and technology architecture.

IMPACT

There is the obvious impact that more work will be required to implement the technology. If it is not suitable at all, then the technology fails and is put on the shelf. Even though this is a good time to learn lessons, many people don't because it is very embarrassing. Another impact is that it may turn management and IT off on new technology. Thus, good, new future opportunities may be lost. A third impact is the loss of resources from other projects and work that have to be poured into implementing the wrong technology. This occurs because many want to install it to save face.

In some cases, the wrong technology is installed and is attempted to be put to use. Then there are likely to be more issues. Support effort and costs begin to drain the IT staff. Other interfacing technologies have to be changed more than originally thought. In the user departments, people may have to invent work-arounds and shadow systems to deal with the new technology so that they can get their work completed.

PREVENTION

The best prevention is twofold. First, you want to implement an organized approach for assessing new technology with an emphasis on integration and on use in business processes. Hopefully, this will tend to head off some bad ideas.

The second part of the approach is to implement an active technology watch and monitoring program so that potential technologies can be examined before they get management attention. When you do this, you want to highlight not just potentially useful technologies, but also those that have shortcomings or problems.

DETECTION

The first sign of a problem is to review what analysis was performed in the evaluation and selection of the technology. Were other technologies considered? Was resource availability a factor that was thought about?

Next, if the technology has been procured, then you can examine the experience of those IT staff who were trained or brought up-to-date on the technology. What was their experience? Is there a list of potential problems that will have to be resolved to make the technology useful?

If the implementation has begun, then your attention should go toward the project plan and resolution of problems. How fast are the problems being resolved? What types of problems are outstanding? You hope that the problems are minor and involve the existing, not the new, technology. If they involve functions of the new technology which are beyond the control of the implementation team, then you could be in trouble.

ACTION

The tendency, when you have spent money and time on the technology, is to pour more resources into the implementation to make it work. This is frequently done. It can make matters worse. First, this approach detracts from other, needed work. Second, the technology may still not work.

A better approach is to create a list of problems that have to be addressed. Now, work with the implementation team, vendors, and users to see what should be done. Create two options in addition to the one of moving ahead with the installation. The first is to stop and kill the technology. The second is to place the installation on hold until conditions change or issues are resolved. You might want to wait for fixes by the vendor, or even for a new version of the technology. These alternatives serve you well politically. First, you are showing that you are neutral and not wanting to push ahead. Second, you can use this time to indicate what other work is needed in other areas with the same resources. By being neutral you can propose trade-offs and force IT and business staff to indicate their real feelings about the technology.

THERE ARE INTEGRATION PROBLEMS WITH THE TECHNOLOGY

BACKGROUND

Integration issues were given attention in Chapter 3. Let's begin by considering integration and interfaces. Technologies can interface through a network or hardware connection. This is normally not much of an issue. The major integration issue is the software. In one case many years ago, one of us had a Radio Shack microcomputer. The printer that came along was not specifically compatible with the microcomputer. It took over 3 months to write interface software between the two devices. This was a real waste of time.

Why do such integration problems arise? One reason lies with the current technology. This is usually based on technical developments that are now several years old. No one had envisioned the new technology then. Interfaces then were not considered. So there is no documentation or software usually to support the interface. If you contact the vendor of the existing technology, they are likely to indicate that this is not their problem.

Now turn to the new technology. It will likely be from a different vendor. It has many new features and capabilities. Typically, the new hardware or software was designed with some interfaces in mind. However, the vendor cannot ensure that all interfaces will work.

The integration issues arise most often where new software is acquired and is being made to interface to legacy systems. This presents a major challenge because of the limitations of the legacy systems.

IMPACT

The impact of integration problems is to create more work and eat up more time. Typically, the existing technology must be retrofitted through modification to interface to the new technology. In the case of interfacing new software to legacy systems, this can create many problems. First, the legacy system may have to change in major ways. As is common knowledge, if you make changes to old systems, you tend to introduce more errors and problems. The legacy system, which was stable, now becomes unstable. Alternatively, you may have to customize the new technology to interface to the existing one. This customization may later prevent you from installing upgrades to the new technology.

PREVENTION

You should be able to define what interfaces are required in advance. Then, after identifying the resources required, you should reallocate the staff to perform this additional work. It may help to either use the vendor or a consultant to support the interface effort due to their knowledge.

The integration effort should be managed as a separate project. This will give the work more attention. You will also have to be on guard to handle demands of other work during the integration effort.

DETECTION

Detection for potential problems begins early during evaluation. Here people often get excited about the features of the new technology. Don't get sucked into this black hole! Instead, focus on installation, troubleshooting, testing, and integration. These are the likely problem areas.

After the technology is installed and the people trained, the integration work begins. Look and spot the problems and questions that arise here. This will reveal what you are in for. If the questions are superficial, then experience shows that you can expect trouble.

ACTION

If integration problems arise, there is a tendency to apply more resources to push through the issues. This is generally not a good idea since you may not know the scope of the problems. Before pressing ahead, try to thoroughly understand the problems with the vendor.

THE TECHNOLOGY DOES NOT DELIVER RESULTS

BACKGROUND

It is amazing that people spend a lot of effort in evaluation, selection, and implementation of technology and then walk away. Why does this happen? Many times managers just assume that the benefits will accrue automatically. However, in many cases, people get the technology and systems, but the process does not change. Look at PDAs as an example. In some firms, literally hundreds were purchased with the view of improving scheduling and productivity. Yet, what happened was that upper managers did not put their schedules on the network. So employees were scheduling with thin air!

IMPACT

The immediate impact is discouragement that the benefits were not achieved. This may be followed up by a hunt for the innocent or guilty. Morale drops. People become very reluctant to embrace other new technology. Some firms actually become technology averse. Often, there are no lessons learned.

PREVENTION

The best prevention is to focus on measurement and on changes to processes. You want to measure the work before as well as after the new technology was put into place. By measuring the existing work, you can see what issues and problems that the new technology will not solve. This will help you to determine better if you want to go ahead with the new technology.

The other focus is process change. You should simulate how the new technology will function in the business process with the people it will be impact. The feedback you get will not only assist you in implementation later, but will also reveal to you where the potential problems will arise from.

DETECTION

You can detect problems first when you expose the new technology to the employees. Then you should listen to the questions that employees raise as to how the technology will be used. Note that some people will want to just embed the new system or technology into the process and not make any changes. They will want to warp any new process back to the old process that they know and love.

Problems can be detected during implementation and training. Here you will be covering how to convert over to the new process from the existing one. You should seek to identify the benefits that will accrue as well as any issues that have to be addressed with the change. Here, concerns that the new system will not address all of the users' needs will also appear. This seldom happens. There will still be loose ends.

ACTION

If the technology or system is implemented and there appear to be no benefits, you should look into the business process. Don't go after the vendor or implementation team. Try to see what is happening with specific transactions. In one case, there was supposed to be higher productivity. It did not happen. When the process was examined, it was found that people were writing down too many notes in the system. Why did they do this? Because in the old system and process they had to do this since some information was not correct. Well, it is now correct. So after retraining, productivity did improve.

THE TECHNOLOGY WAS IMPOSED ON US

BACKGROUND

This happens often with multinational firms and government agencies. Decisions about systems and technology are made by upper management without sufficient information or attention to implementation and the resources required. A regional or country office manager is then given the assignment of implementation. There have been many disasters from this approach. Local work does not get done. Resources are taken from normal work and applied to the implementation. Sales drop or costs rise.

IMPACT

The impact is that the local office must make quick decisions as to how to reshuffle resources to be divided between normal work and the implementation of the new technology. Since the pool of available and trained staff is very small, the burden falls on a few critical people in IT and the business departments.

Something has to give. Either some of the existing work gets put off. Or the implementation is stretched out. There is probably about a day in a week of flexible time without impacting the processes.

The inevitable result is that something suffers. Most often it is the current work in the office that pays the price. Then when complaints arise or the performance drop in the work is evident, people are put back on their regular work to catch up. It can become a struggle of going back and forth between the two areas.

PREVENTION

The best preventative step is to present the new technology or system to local management and have them identify issues and problems. Then an effort can be made to clean up processes and existing work to get ready to install the new system. When the implementation begins, there should be a weekly allocation effort between the regular work and the new implementation.

You should only consider 100% assignment of someone to the implementation if you have trained, backup resources available. Otherwise, the pressure on the key people will become too great. They may get burned out. This happened with a number of ERP installations.

DETECTION

If a local manager just accepts the new implementation and schedule without raising resource issues, then you can assume that there will be problems. The resource allocation problem will likely just be pushed down to lower levels in the local organization.

During implementation you can detect any problems present by reviewing what the key people are working on in any given week. Then you can detect stress as well as the impact of some work not being performed.

ACTION

If an implementation starts to slip, you want to start with the resource allocation method that is being used by the local office. There may be many other issues such as adapting the technology to the specific culture and country environment as well. However, resource allocation is usually at the heart of the problem. Don't push for "storming" the implementation with a dedicated effort. This will often not work because there is just too much to do. You may have to settle for installing part of the system or in delaying the full implementation of the system.

LEGACY SYSTEMS CONSUME TOO MANY RESOURCES AND ARE INFLEXIBLE

BACKGROUND

Legacy systems are almost always present. If a system, an automobile, or TV works, then why replace it? It is almost always easier to maintain and fix it. Typically, the IT group has resources dedicated to maintenance and support of the legacy systems.

As time goes on, legacy systems deteriorate. There are new interfaces to be created. There are enhancements to the system that make the system larger and more complex. There may be multiple programmers working on the system over time. Each one puts his or her own fingerprint on the code. There are normally never resources available to go in and streamline the legacy system. Moreover, with all of the changes made to the system, the system becomes more inflexible. It takes more effort and time to make changes.

IMPACT

Eventually, the people with the knowledge of the legacy system leave. The vendor stops issuing fixes and new versions of the software. The software becomes less efficient and less effective. Yet, management continues to insist that the legacy systems remain.

After some time, IT realizes that some changes cannot be made to the legacy system. They then start to build new, smaller systems that interface to the legacy system. More interfaces are created that have to be maintained. The nightmare gets worse.

PREVENTION

The best prevention is not to replace legacy systems. Instead, you should begin to measure the legacy system and the support effort. Here is a list of things to measure:

- Size of the system.
- Number and type of interfaces.
- Number of changes made to the system.
- Number of approved changes that are yet to be made.
- Extent of the maintenance and support effort.
- Average time to carry out a change.
- Staffing turnover and number of employees with knowledge of the system.

You should consider reworking the system in addition to beginning to define a new architecture that would replace some of the legacy systems.

DETECTION

The measurements that were identified in the previous section are a good starting point for detecting problems. However, you can also visit the user departments to see what they are doing. In some cases, they may have given up on requesting changes to the old system since these would take too long. They may then have developed workarounds and shadow systems to do some of the work. This is a good indication that a legacy system has outlived its usefulness.

ACTION

Rather than look at replacing the legacy system with a new software package, you should look at the business process. The process has probably changed and deteriorated since the legacy system was installed. There may be a need for an entirely new approach. If the legacy system is still meeting user needs, then you can consider selective rework on some of the modules of the old system.

THERE IS HIGH BACKLOG OF WORK

BACKGROUND

In most IT groups, user requests flow into IT and are examined. The approved ones are put in a queue to be worked on. The programmers and analysts may then bundle the requests based upon the part of the system that is changed. However, when all is said and done, much of the burden of the work falls on one or a few key people who know the old technology and system. This then creates a bottleneck and a backlog of work. Some IT people like having a backlog since it gives them a sense of job security.

IMPACT

If the users have to have the changes and they are not made due to the backlog, then they may improvise solutions. They tend to invent exceptions and shadow systems to handle the work. Meanwhile, in IT, work continues even though the need for the changes has evaporated due to the users finding other solutions. The impact is a lack of communication in addressing the backlog.

PREVENTION

Prevention of added backlog begins with considering requests in terms of what is really needed. Many times requests can be handled through process changes rather than through systems changes.

Another preventative step is to regularly review the backlog and see if the pending requests are still valid. In some cases, due to management change or process change, the need may have disappeared. Regular communications between IT and the users is necessary to sort out what is really needed.

DETECTION

You can identify which systems have backlog requests. Then you can go out to the user departments to see the impacts of not having the systems changes made. You may find that there is no impact. Alternatively, you may discover that the users are having to go through more steps in their work.

ACTION

The first action is to review the backlog with the user departments. Once you have eliminated some of the requests, then you are left with essential requests. Now you go into IT and find out if resources can be reallocated to work on these requests.

Management Issues

INTRODUCTION

Management issues are often some of the most time consuming and difficult issues for IT managers. They are beyond the scope of control of IT. Often, there are many external factors that the IT managers are not aware of. General managers also have a wide variety of styles that impact how IT is directed. Traditional technical and business training do not always provide the IT manager with the tools and experience to handle these issues.

Added to this are political factors. In the early days of systems, IT often reported to a vice president of finance or accounting. These people often took advantage of this relationship by imposing their own desires, will, and needs on IT. It is not surprising that in the late 1980s and 1990s that many CEO's were formerly heads of accounting and finance. IT gave the managers more information and through that contributed to their power. Today, the position of the CIO has become more common. The CIO often reports higher in the organization. But this change has not meant a decline in political factors. Rather, it has often been the opposite where political factors dominate.

MANAGEMENT IS NOT INVOLVED IN IT

BACKGROUND

Management involvement in IT is a matter of interest, importance, perception, and style. Some managers have experience in IT and want to be involved. Others understand IT generally, but do not want to get involved in the details.

Our experience is that having managers not involved in IT can be very beneficial. They tend to want to see IT issues and opportunities in straight business terms. This is more predictable. However, there is the potential downside where managers can misunderstand an IT problem and then take actions that appear to make little or no sense to IT managers.

IMPACT

One impact is that the IT manager is left more alone. If the IT manager is more technically oriented, this can result in problems in communications and misunderstandings. Presentations made to managers that have substantial IT jargon tend to turn these managers off. The managers may develop a distrust of IT and fear that they may be "snowed" by all of the IT words.

Another potential impact is that justification for new IT initiatives may take more effort. The general manager may not want to get involved in IT issues that quickly. The impacts of the issues can then grow.

PREVENTION

There are several approaches to deal with a manager who does not want to be involved in IT. One is to try and educate them through vendor seminars, presentations, and the like. This can speeden up the valuable time of the manager who may be wondering why they should know these things. After all, that is why they have IT and IT managers for.

A better approach is to follow the communications guidelines of Chapter 9 and keep in informal contact with the manager. The best communication instrument is through IT results and IT issues. A good general manager is used to and adept at handling problems. For one of the authors, this approach was used effectively several times. Eventually, the discussions became almost totally dominated by politics and political factors. Over time, we became more experienced with political issues. The manager enjoyed dealing with politics in a casual way. Bundling of issues and having very few formal meetings were also two useful guidelines.

DETECTION

How do you determine if there is a problem? One method is to assess the frequency and nature of contacts with the manager. If the contacts are infrequent and generated by you, then that is probably good. You also want to have at least half of the contacts avoiding issues. Otherwise, the manager may see you and think, "Here comes another problem."

Another sign to look for is how often the manager contacts you. Normally, if things are going OK, the manager will not contact you. He or she has better things to do. If the manager seeks you out, then typically someone has pointed out a problem and now the problem will fall on you.

ACTION

If you find that there are problems with a manager like this, there are several actions to take. One is to initiate informal contact where you present some positive results of IT work. You can also provide anecdotes and additional industry information. Another step to take is to point out some new technologies that you feel are not promising. This will show the manager that you are not into the technical side of IT and dazzled by the new technology.

SOME MANAGERS ARE OVERINVOLVED WITH IT

BACKGROUND

This can be a nightmare. We have seen several cases where the general manager was formerly head of IT. However, this was probably many years ago so that the manager is not up-to-date with what is current in the technology or the IT group. Remember too that you do not have a choice here. You have been placed in a situation where the manager is a given. You cannot change that.

IMPACT

One of more negative impacts that we have observed is that of the manager attempting to micromanage IT. He or she begins to want more detailed information about budgets, projects, and work. This can create a huge amount of extra work. Additionally, much of your time will go into meetings, presentations, follow up from meetings, and preparation for meetings. You end up watching over your shoulder and being second-guessed all of the time.

PREVENTION

To prevent problems, you want to assess how interested the manager is in IT. If you find that they are interested, then you should gather some issues and start laying them out for the manager. If they like involved with IT, then they will like participating in the issues. After you do this a few times, you can indicate how you would handle the issues. The manager has many other duties and so does not have time for these issues. If they start to see your way of thinking about issues, then they may develop more confidence in you and your problem-solving skills.

DETECTION

You can detect whether there is a problem by assessing how much the manager is involved in IT. More specifically, you can answer the following questions.

- Does the manager contradict your approach to problems?
- Does the manager demand more and more detailed information?
- How much of your time is spent in providing management with information?
- Does the manager seek to involve other people in directing IT?

Answers here can indicate that you have a major communications and relationship problem.

ACTION

If you find that a manager is constantly getting involved in IT, then you should start selecting the issues to be channeled to the manager. Try to make these technical. Then he or she is on unfamiliar grounds. They will start to back off on issues. At the same time, try to seek out the manager informally to bring them current on IT projects. This is passive information where they do not have to make a decision. This will also help them restore their confidence in you.

MANAGEMENT PLACES UNREALISTIC DEMANDS ON IT

BACKGROUND

This is a classic problem in IT and has been for many years. Over the years, people have been led to believe that systems and technology get better, easier, and more powerful. The software becomes more capable and so can do more of the work.

Unrealistic demands can also stem from management style. Some people like to pile on pressure and demands to see how their subordinates react. There can also be political factors at work where the manager sees that they can take credit if specific IT projects are finished ahead of schedule and under budget.

IMPACT

The IT manager takes the demands for performance in and then has to decide how to act. Many IT managers just pass the demands down to the IT supervisors and staff. They, in turn, become resentful of the IT manager. Communications and work problems start to proliferate. Unless the situation is changed, the demands grow and in the end cannot be met. Then there is a crisis. The person to blame naturally is not the general manager, but the IT manager.

PREVENTION

The best approach to this is to head it off with actions that dampen demands. As was stated earlier, the benefits of IT come not from IT work, but from what happens in the business after the IT work has been completed. So demands for benefits and results should be turned to the business.

There are then demands for schedules and costs. Costs in IT projects are more controllable than schedules except for labor hours. Schedules should be developed in advance with user departments. After all, the installation of a new system will be followed by process change and measurement. Thus, there should be more effort in negotiating schedules with end users prior to involvement by management.

DETECTION

You can easily detect the demands for benefits and schedule improvement or shortening. It is harder to detect more subtle demands for specific actions. Here you should review the communications—both verbal and written. You are looking for the words that can be interpreted as demands for action.

ACTION

If unrealistic demands are made, there are several options. One is to indicate immediately that the demands cannot be met. This will often be counterproductive. You risk being labeled as someone who is not on board as a member of the management team.

A better approach is to go away with the demand and work through why it is unreasonable. Look for some middle ground. Determine the best that can be done with the available resources. Then identify issues that prevent any further improvement. Go back to the manager after a "cooling off" period with the issues. Indicate that you want to meet the demands, but there are these issues to be addressed. Using this approach we have seen that some demands evaporate and disappear. Other demands are then changed.

MANAGEMENT FALLS UNDER THE INFLUENCE OF VENDORS

BACKGROUND

Vendors know that the real point where IT decisions are made is upper management. Thus, from the 1960s onward, leading vendors have sought to provide seminars, information, workshops, and free consulting to upper management on IT. Vendors have a number of advantages over the IT group. These include:

• The vendors present an industry view and can highlight trends and open management's eyes to new opportunities.
• Vendors have information on similar firms that are competitors to yours.
• Vendors have resources to create and deliver very slick, polished presentations.

It is no wonder that some managers become impressed and enthusiastic about some vendor products. They may ask the vendor in to review the IT group and the projects. As this is going on, the IT manager and staff continue to work on internal projects and work. They often don't have much time to gather similar information.

IMPACT

One potential impact is that management begins to question IT decisions and direction. They ask questions of IT. However, when IT provides answers, the manager cannot really understand them since the questions often came from the vendors. Distrust can grow. IT can see that their responsibilities and direction are under question—even when they have been performing well. If the snowball of distrust continues to roll downhill, then the vendor may be given an even larger role in overseeing IT.

PREVENTION

You have to assume that vendors will contact management. You should keep management informed of various vendor initiatives. Another measure that you can take is to build relationships with vendor managers and staff. They may be able to give you a heads-up warning of contacts. Keep the informal contacts up with management to detect when the vendors are making contacts.

DETECTION

You can detect that there is a problem if managers start to ask strange, what appear to be off-the-wall questions. They may pose questions that seem out of context. You may be asked to assess a specific vendor product. These are all signs of potential problems.

ACTION

If the issue arises, then you should be open to new ideas. Assume that vendor contacts will be made. A key idea is not to be defensive. This can be seen by management as being negative and too much in favor of the status quo. In fact, you might want to encourage some vendor contacts for hardware and networking components. These vendors are more likely to be on your side than standard consulting vendors or software suppliers.

MANAGEMENT CHANGES DIRECTION

BACKGROUND

You have an approved strategic IT plan. Projects are doing well. Life is good. Then out of the blue, management makes a decision or series of decisions that change the direction of IT. Why does this happen? In some cases, with strong executives, management may arbitrarily adopt some new method or tool. In other cases, management may be responding to business pressure. While it is infrequent, it is, nevertheless, a major challenge to IT management.

IMPACT

If the new management direction is taken at face value, then the effects on IT can be very damaging. All projects and programs could go into a state of review and suspense. Morale can drop. Uncertainty rises.

Even when not taken too seriously as an immediate threat to current work, there can be doubts raised about the direction of IT and what IT is pursuing. This can also be disruptive to IT.

PREVENTION

A critical factor for success here is to assume that there will be changes in management direction from time to time. Nothing, after all, remains the same forever. To prevent problems, you want to have an early warning system with informal management contacts. You may be tipped off or see signs early. This gives you time to think and prepare for what to do.

Another step to take is to analyze the IT projects and work and relate them to the business processes that are core to the business. Even if management changes direction, the basic business processes will likely remain intact. So the systems and technology will too. The real threat is to any work that is going on that is not related to either the IT infrastructure or to the key processes. These things could be changed or terminated. On a regular basis, you should review the work to see what falls in this category. Every now and then assume that there has been a change in direction and think about how you would change the IT work.

DETECTION

Management can indicate a change in direction by surprise. However, normally there are signs that things are happening. Management may be off-site often. There may be questions raised about some projects. A manager may ask you to go slower on a specific project. Don't ask what is going on. Because you probably will not be told.

ACTION

If there is a change in direction, then you should review the IT work and projects. Identify which will be untouched by the change. Then you should consider what new work is needed to support the new management direction. Become more proactive in considering what additional projects will be necessary. Also, think about how some of the current work can be terminated or changed. Use a change of direction as an opportunity to kill off some marginal projects.

MIDDLE LEVEL MANAGERS RESIST IT EFFORTS

BACKGROUND

Automation has touched many people in organizations. Most people think that it eliminates jobs at the bottom of the organization. In many cases, it tends to change these lower level jobs and make supervision and oversight easier. Supervisors and managers may receive more automated reporting on job performance, for example. Upper management is obviously not affected by systems except that they are provided with more information.

The real threats of automation in the past decade and for the future will be to king and queen bees, and middle level management. These people are affected because systems tend to automate specialized business rules. Exceptions tend to be eliminated or simplified. The allies of the king and queen bees are the middle level managers and supervisors. They have developed informal relationships over many years. For middle level managers, the threat is also that their positions will be made redundant. Outsourcing obviously is one generator of fear.

IMPACT

The effect of the perception of the threat from IT projects is to do anything to delay, change, or mitigate the results of the IT work. One method is to overwhelm project teams with exception transactions. The team cannot automate these within the schedule and project. The project may fail and then everything remains the same.

Another approach is for the middle level managers to behave and act as supporters of the project and change. Then on the side they may be telling employees that not much will change. After the project is over and the system is installed, the IT people will leave and they can go back to what they were doing and the same methods as they were doing it. If there is no measurement, they are often correct.

PREVENTION

You have to assume that there will be resistance to change. There will be a fear factor. What you should do is to get down to the people who are doing the work. These are the critical people you need to get on your side. Get them involved in the project and in designing how the new process will function with the new system. Then you can work with supervisors. If people begin to raise questions about the organization structure, roles, or responsibilities, then you can honestly state that these things would be addressed as the new process takes shape. Again, your allies are the average employees who see some political benefit from change.

DETECTION

You can detect a problem when some middle level manager is overly enthusiastic about the change. In their normal minds, change will mean more work and different methods. These are not things to get excited about.

Another sign of a problem occurs if the manager raises detailed issues and exceptions to the project team. This should normally be posed by the employees.

The fact that a manager is surfacing this should raise suspicion on your part. There is possibly a hidden agenda. Managers may also want to extend out the implementation as well.

ACTION

If you are getting resistance from managers, you may be tempted to raise the issue with upper management. This is not a good idea and should be a last resort. Many managers will think that you are not doing your job and are passing on your work to them.

A better approach is to sit down with the managers and give them a chance to vent their feelings and frustrations. Write down and investigate the problems and ideas that they raise.

Another technique is to get lower level employees to present some of the new process to middle level management. This tends to disarm criticism since their own employees are endorsing the new process.

Chapter 16

Business Unit Issues

INTRODUCTION

The roles and responsibilities of business units in IT projects and work has been a subject that has evolved and been debated for years. There is hard evidence through examples, experience, and surveys to indicate that effective end user and business unit participation are critical success factors for the overall success of the IT project.

Yet, issues related to business units and their employees continue to abound. Perhaps, a major source of the problem is that employees see participation in an IT project as work in addition to normal work for which they will not be rewarded. Instead, they feel that they are being placed at risk. They still have to do their normal work and are held accountable for it. On top of this, they are asked to participate in an IT project where they do not know much of what is going on as it appears too technical. During the project, they see some of the things that they do and why they do these things questioned.

ERP implementations brought these issues into the foreground. An ERP implementation gets into the detailed business rules. The elapsed time of the implementation is such that users cannot participate easily on a part-time basis. They have to be dedicated to the project. This created a number of problems. First, the users assigned to the ERP effort were often very senior so that the department employees had less guidance to do their work. Employees assigned to the project may have also felt that their jobs were at stake and that they would not be able to go back. On the project they were treated with more respect and given more attention. Going back to their normal work seemed boring and a let down. User issues persist and constitute a major challenge to IT in getting the work done and the benefits achieved.

THE WRONG EMPLOYEES ARE ASSIGNED TO IT WORK AND PROJECTS

BACKGROUND

In an IT project, the analyst or project leader assigned goes to a department manager and asks for one or more employees to be assigned to work on the project. What does the manager do? If he or she assigns the best people, the work in the department could be crippled. There could be impacts on the work if several average employees are put on the project.

What happens in some cases is that junior, less experienced people are assigned. Another type of individual that might be assigned is someone who is an outlier or loner. The manager may often assign someone whose absence will cause the least problems with the operations and processes in the department. Overall, planning for the personnel assignment is not carried well in many cases.

IMPACT

Getting the wrong people on the team can be a curse and sink the project. The person assigned may not have information on the details of the work. The IT staff asks them questions. Rather than appear as dummies, they answer with logical, but faulty statements. The IT staff then accepts this as the truth and creates requirements, design, and code around this information. Only much later is the real truth uncovered.

If senior persons are assigned, they may perceive the project to be a threat to their power. They are being asked to provide their specialized knowledge. This will be incorporated into the system. Their importance in the department after implementation may be diminished. As a result, they may try to sabotage the project by flooding the team with exceptions that occur rarely.

PREVENTION

In Chapter 8, guidelines were provided for getting effective user participation. To prevent the issue, the IT project leader should indicate that a number of different end users will be needed over time. This provides for greater user input and support for change.

In addition, the project leader should indicate that whomever is assigned initially will only be with the project for a limited time. When requirements are better understood, then a better choice of users will be possible. You want to avoid being stuck with one person throughout the project.

Another action is to limit the role of queen and king bees in the team. This is in the department's best interest since these people are critical to the exceptional work. For the team, this will prevent dealing with an excessive number of exceptions.

The project leader should target getting average users with energy and desire to move ahead. These people will likely benefit from the system implementation due to their knowledge and experience in the project.

DETECTION

How do you detect if you have the wrong people on the team? One sign is attitude. How do they view change? Do they think that improvements can be made in the way they currently perform their work? If they are defensive about their work and seem to like it as it is, then you have a problem on your hands.

The employees who are on the team will still be communicating with other employees and supervisors during the project. They will be giving off-the-cuff opinions and views to others. You should make regular visits to the end users to keep them updated on the project progress and work. You can also pick up some of their feelings based on what they were told by the user team members.

ACTION

If you have the wrong team member, one possible action is to keep them on the team and make the best of the situation. This can lead to more problems later. At the earliest sign of problems and issues, you should visit the department manager and indicate that it might be useful to rotate other end users into the team. Wider participation in the project will lead to wider understanding. You can schedule this with the department manager so that the work in the department is not disrupted.

EMPLOYEES RESIST CHANGE

BACKGROUND

This has been discussed in several chapters. Change management and coordination is becoming a part of an IT project and work. Employees and people in general often tend to resist change. They are comfortable with how things are now. The process works—perhaps, with some problems. But it does function. They may also feel that they are not being adequately compensated for the effort to make the change. They may not see change in their own self-interest. Then there is the fear of automation and the loss of jobs or diminution of pay that they see as potentially occurring.

IMPACT

One impact of resistance is to slow the project down. More exceptions and problems are brought up. The team assumes ownership of the issues as being addressed in systems. This occurs when many of these should be handled in the process.

Another impact occurs later after implementation. IT walks away from the end of implementation thinking that the project is a success. After all, it was completed within the budget and schedule. Too bad no one stayed around to ensure that (1) the process was changed and (2) the changes in the process were measured and managed. This is when the process reverts to some or all of its old form.

PREVENTION

The best prevention is to adopt the personnel approach discussed earlier. You want to place more importance on how and which end users are assigned to projects. You also want to be proactive in replacing team members on a regular basis.

But these steps are in the team. There is more work to be done out in the department. You should work to keep the department managers and employees informed as to what is going on. There should be regular visits to the department. Team meetings should be held in user departments.

DETECTION

Employees may actively resist change by raising problems and concerns. At a moderate level this is reasonable. But it can be excessive and tie the project up. They may ask, "How will the system handle …?" or "It does not seem that the system will be able to deal with …" The impact of this can affect the morale and progress of the team.

Other resistance can come in the form of passive resistance. Here employees do not openly criticize the project. Instead, they are often very, very quiet. They may be thinking that when IT leaves and project is done, they can go back to what they were doing. This is probably the most dangerous since it will lead to process reversion and deterioration later.

ACTION

When you encounter issues or problems raised by end users, take the time to get at the issue behind the problem. Do not assume or state that it will be handled in the project. All of the exceptions and issues are subject to later review with the department management and other employees. The fewer exceptions that you assume ownership for, the greater will be your chances of success.

THERE ARE TOO MANY EXCEPTIONS AND WORKAROUNDS

BACKGROUND

As was stated in Chapter 1, processes deteriorate over time. New types of work appear. New employees enter the department. Exceptions are generated as results. Most processes that are not highly automated have exceptions. In some cases, the volume of work generated by the exceptions can rival that of the normal work. For workarounds it is basically the same story. A workaround is generated when the system cannot perform the transaction directly.

Over a period of several years, the employees and supervisors tend to take all of this work in stride and treat it like normal work. It is just part of the workload. Most of the time the line management does not make a serious effort to change the process on its own. These comments apply to the case where process improvement was carried out several years ago as well.

IMPACT

Exceptions and workarounds cause many problems within the business department and with the IT project. For the department, exceptions and workarounds require more specialized knowledge of the work. This tends to reinforce the power of the king and queen bees. Moreover, the department staff tends to devote too much time to the exceptions so that normal work suffers. Look at what happens when you go into a bank branch with an unusual request. The teller has to call the supervisor, who may then in turn have to call the manager over. It can take three or four times more effort to deal with these exceptions.

For the IT project, you want to deal with workarounds since these are problems with the current system. Workarounds tend to be more easily identifiable than exceptions. The problems occur with exceptions. The problem is that an exception is often stated as another piece of work. If you don't ask about the frequency and history of the transaction as well as what knowledge is required, you may end up thinking that it is normal work. The project then becomes bogged down in exceptions.

PREVENTION

You cannot prevent dealing with all of the exceptions and workarounds. The key to success in dealing with these is to label all of the work at the start of the analysis. Do not plunge into detail for each transaction. Get an overview of what is going on. Prepare a table in which the rows are the transactions and the columns are skills required, frequency, volume, and time that the transaction has existed.

The next action is to then work on the normal and common transactions. Start negotiating with the department on what to do with the exceptions. Some can be eliminated through procedure changes; some should not have been created in the first place. Still others can be dropped by making minor changes to policies.

DETECTION

The best method to detect an exception is to ask what knowledge and steps are required to do the work. You should observe the work. This is still the best approach for gathering data—often better than interviewing. When you have found an exception, start looking at how much effort is required to complete the transaction. This can be a real eye opener and give you ammunition with the department to eliminate or simplify it.

ACTION

IT traditionally has assumed ownership of all of the transactions. The goal of the IT project normally was to automate as much of the work as possible. This changed with E-Business. In E-Business, you work toward total automation of the work. There are few, if any, manual steps. Thus, when you implement E-Business, you are forced to take a long, hard look at the exceptions. Use the same approach here.

THERE ARE SHADOW SYSTEMS IN THE DEPARTMENT

BACKGROUND

A shadow system is a manual or automated system that was developed within a department to help with their work. PC software such as database management systems and spreadsheets fueled the creation of many shadow systems. Many shadow systems have been created by junior employees and student interns. Departments quickly become dependent upon these systems.

While the shadow systems help the department do their work, they generate problems. Most of the time only people in the department know of their existence. IT is not aware of them until there is a problem. Shadow systems tend not to be documented. Only a few employees know how to work them. Some of the business rules in the software may be unknown to the current employees. These rules could be partially or totally wrong as well.

Shadow systems present a special challenge to an IT project. At first, the scope of the IT project is often to replace an existing system with one that has more functions and features. Then the shadow systems start to emerge from the woodwork and the scope of the project expands.

IMPACT

Shadow systems can slow a project down. However, they can also represent an opportunity to get more benefit from the IT project. If the shadow systems are ignored, then the department will face an inevitable dilemma. They will have to keep the shadow systems going since they were not replaced or covered by the new system. In addition, departments may have to modify them to accommodate the new system. The bottom line then is that the benefits that were anticipated from the new system will disappear.

PREVENTION

You cannot make shadow systems disappear. They are there and a fact of business life. You first want to inventory these shadow systems and determine how they are used. The shadow systems should become part of the requirements. They should become part of the new system. In one case, we were asked to help a firm select between two software packages. We carried out an investigation and found 12 shadow systems. The management did not believe this and undertook a thorough investigation and found 19 shadow systems. When these shadow systems became part of the requirements, an entirely different software package was selected.

DETECTION

How do you detect shadow systems? You almost always have to observe the work. Ask to be trained as well. When you uncover a shadow system, you should determine what types of transactions are supported. If the shadow system supports normal work, it belongs with the requirements. If it only supports exceptions, then you bundle it in with the exceptions discussed earlier.

ACTION

The action for a shadow system is based upon what transactions it supports. For those supporting normal work, you have to look at the code and business rules. These will become part of the requirements.

For those that support exceptions, do not spend too much time on these. Deal with the exception overall. This will take care of the shadow system.

SEVERAL BUSINESS DEPARTMENTS DO NOT GET ALONG

BACKGROUND

The conflicts and problems between IT and departments are well known and have been extensively researched. Those between business departments have gotten much less attention. Business departments often have to compete for power and resources. They also compete for management attention. Some departments are more powerful than others.

This impacts IT projects because often you have to address a process that spans several departments. As you collect data and coordinate team members from multiple departments, you can sometimes sense the tension in the air.

IMPACT

If business departments do not get along in regular work, their conflict will carry over to an IT project. When a question or problem surfaces, different departments may stake out conflicting positions. The project leader does not have the authority or power to solve these issues. The issues then rise up to upper levels of management. When this happens several times, management starts to question the value of the project. They sometimes do not deal with the underlying department conflict.

PREVENTION

You cannot prevent or solve the conflicts between departments. You have to ask the question, "Where is the conflict likely to be the least?" The answer is in the lower levels of the organization. Here people are too busy doing their everyday work to participate in the politics. At the supervisor and middle management levels there is more time and opportunity for politics. Therefore, you should concentrate your effort with the lower level employees who are doing the work. With them you should acknowledge that the departments may not get along. However, you also point out that the purpose of the project is to improve the process, not to solve some political problems between departments.

DETECTION

In order to detect conflicts, you might observe how work is being passed between departments. If one department creates manual logs and makes notes before passing on the work, then you can sense that there is a problem.

Another step to take is to gather data from each department separately. Then compare the stories and information that you receive. This can also indicate the problem.

ACTION

You cannot solve the problem. Instead, you should focus on the work. If the conflicts surface, you can acknowledge that there are problems. Then you turn the focus back on the work. The truth in terms of requirements is out there (like the *X Files*), but it is in the detail.

THERE ARE PROBLEMS WITH THE BUSINESS RULES AND POLICIES

BACKGROUND

In any business process, there are policies that govern how the work is to be performed. Then there are specific business rules, procedures, and guidelines that actually implement the policies. The problems arise because over time the rules and procedures have gotten out of sync with the policies. After awhile employees tend to focus on the procedures and rules rather than on the policies. In most cases, business departments do not check to see if there is consistency between the policies on the one hand and the rules and procedures on the other.

IMPACT

The impact on an IT project is to create a problem. If you carry out the procedures and rules as they are performed, you violate the policies. Unfortunately, problems and inconsistencies that are not visible in the old setting suddenly become open to all when you automate them. If the team accepts the rules and procedures without further investigation, they could end up implementing what is there, but not what should be there. This can cause extensive rework.

PREVENTION

The best approach for preventing this problem is to gather the policies along with the rules and procedures. Then have a subteam of the project team examine these for consistency and completeness in implementing the policies. If there is consistency and completeness, then all that it costs is some small amount of time. This is a small price to pay compared to potential major problems later.

DETECTION

Take some sample transactions and write down the procedures and business rules. Select some common work that is frequently performed. Next, go to the supervisors and collect the policies that govern the work. You may find that there are few written policies and that the situation has become very informal. In this case, sit down and examine the rules and procedures and extract policies that would be supported by the rules and procedures.

ACTION

The main action to take is to prepare a table of policies, business rules, and procedures. Get these reviewed by the department staff. Create policies if there appear to be none present. These actions should be part of the requirements analysis.

Chapter 17

Vendor and Outsourcing Issues

INTRODUCTION

Outsourcing management is complex because there are multiple organizations involved with distinct cultures, methods, and ways of doing business. Vendors have to spread their resources across multiple clients. The demands of a specific client, the conflict for resources, and the limited pool of qualified technical and management staff lead to many issues.

VENDOR PERFORMANCE IS POOR

BACKGROUND

This may be either a real or perceived problem. The word "poor" is relative to the specific situation. Poor vendor performance can mean some or all of the following:

- The vendor is not addressing issues that they have been given on a timely basis.
- The vendor staff assigned to the work is not as qualified as you thought or expected.
- The work products produced by vendor staff are not acceptable.

There can be many factors behind vendor performance. One is the availability of qualified vendor resources. Another common factor is misunderstandings generated by the lack of communication or poor communication. A third factor may be high client expectations created during the marketing of outsourcing.

IMPACT

In today's IT environment, organizations depend upon outsourcing for major and significant IT activities. Vendors may support daily operations, the help desk, system development, software maintenance, computer and network management, and software package implementation to mention a few activities.

Poor performance impacts the schedules for the work and projects and can also create operational problems. When these problems arise, the client firm may be forced to consider alternatives. If an entire function has been outsourced, then there are no internal resources to take over. Even if there are internal resources, there will likely be a learning curve required for internal employees to get up to speed.

When problems occur, the tendency is for the business managers and staff to blame IT. Yet, IT may not have even been responsible for the outsourcing. It could have been imposed by upper management.

PREVENTION

The best way to prevent problems with vendors is to identify potential issues at the start of the outsourcing engagement with the vendor. This will create an awareness of what will be looked for. Next, beginning with the start of the vendor work, there must be a close tracking of the work, issues, and potential problems. A key lesson learned is that you don't want to wait until problems are major.

Another part of preventing problems is to institute common issue tracking. That way, both the vendor and the client are working off the same list. Issue reporting goes both ways. The client is also dealing with issues that may hold up the vendor work.

DETECTION

You can often detect problems early. If there is reduced contact with the vendor, then you might become concerned. If there are misunderstandings evident in meetings with the vendor technical staff, then this could be a sign of problems. If there is no direct communication between the vendor workers and the internal employees, then there can be misunderstandings. This arises when the vendor inserts a project manager to act as an intermediary with the internal staff. Then there is the potential for translation problems.

You can also detect that there may be major problems if it is taking too much time to resolve smaller, more minor problems. These minor problems tend to fester and get worse. Impacts grow.

ACTION

If there are problems in performance, the client managers and staff need to make a list of all outstanding issues—assigned to both the vendor and client. These need to be discussed internally in terms of importance and impact. Then you should institute multiple, regular meetings on the unresolved problems. Insist that some progress be made soon. If people make promises regarding problems, these should be documented and circulated.

In general, the more regular and consistent the contact you have with the vendor, the better the performance will be. Lack of contact and persistence may give the vendor the sign that the issue is not important. That is why you clearly have to indicate the impact and importance of the issue.

THERE IS SUBSTANTIAL TURNOVER OF VENDOR STAFF

BACKGROUND

Vendor turnover is natural—the same as that of internal employees. However, it tends to be more pronounced since the vendor is using the same people with other clients and in marketing efforts to get more business. If the best people were constantly assigned to one client, the cost might be prohibitive.

In consulting, there are often junior- and senior-level consultants. Once the work has begun with a client, there is sometimes a tendency for the vendor to pull out the senior people and leave the junior ones. This makes sense to the vendor as they are leveraging off their resources. However, when problems arise, the junior people may not be knowledgeable or capable of dealing with them. Moreover, getting the senior people back after sometime results in them having to come up to speed and learn the situation all over again.

IMPACT

The major negative impact is that the new vendor employees take longer to gain knowledge about the systems and situation. The client is paying for this time.

It is not just the money involved, but also the impact of delays in schedules. Work performance may also be affected since the new people may not be as experienced as the former workers.

Another impact occurs in business units. If the vendor employees have been working with the business employees closely, they have established working relationships. When new vendor employees appear on the scene, then the relationship has to be rebuilt—taking more time and costing more money.

What makes this worse in IT is that there is a great deal of local knowledge about specific people, policies, procedures, and systems. It is not like turnover in a call center where junior people can be replaced more easily. IT knowledge is more precious.

PREVENTION

At the start of the vendor relationship and work, guidelines should be given about replacement of people. Specific items to be addressed include the following:

- How new employees are selected for the client work.
- How there will be overlap between the old and new employees to share information.
- How specific information will be transferred and conveyed to the new people.

Documentation of the work should also be addressed. However, there is a problem here. Most of the time, the documentation does not cover all situations or possible problems. Another factor to review is how the former vendor staff can be brought back to solve specific problems that the new people cannot handle.

DETECTION

Absence is a good indicator that turnover is possible. The vendor staff may be pulled out to support a marketing effort. So you must keep tabs on when the vendor staff is present and what they are working on when present.

You can also ask the internal IT staff who are interfacing with the vendor staff if they have picked up any sign of turnover. The vendor employee may mention other customers or potential customers, for example.

In the case where the vendor staff is working remotely in their offices, you should visit the vendor site and see what is happening and who is doing your work. You want to determine how dedicated they are to your work.

ACTION

If you are experiencing turnover, then you want to sit down with the vendor managers or coordinators and go over staffing and assignments. Revisit the rules that were established for turnover of work.

Also, in the vendor meetings, go over which vendor staff is working on what tasks. This should be carried out even if there is no problem. The benefit here is that it gets the vendor to expect that you will be monitoring the vendor staffing.

MULTIPLE VENDORS ARE FIGHTING

BACKGROUND

In a number of cases, there will be multiple vendors involved in different, but interfacing activities. An example is one software vendor and a consulting firm that is assisting in implementing the software package. Another example is a network support vendor and a separate help desk vendor.

Problems often arise because the client assumes that the vendors will work out their problems jointly without client involvement. After all, they may feel that that is what they are paying for.

Different vendors may have different perspectives on what the scope of their work is. It is unlikely that two vendors will have identical views. Thus, the vendors may perceive that they are responsible for the same thing. Alternatively, they may feel that the area lies with the other vendor. This can leave some areas that are not addressed.

Impact

When vendors have different views of their work, there is a potential for vendor conflict. Conflict, either open or covert, requires the client firm staff and management to play a more active role in overseeing the work. In essence, the IT group now has to act as a system integrator and manager at a more detailed level. We have seen where this oversight is often more than the work of doing one of the vendor's jobs themselves! A major problem that was not planned for or anticipated.

If the conflict is not resolved early, then there can be work left undone. Additionally, there can be more rework and fixing later. These factors can affect the cost, the schedule, and the work quality.

PREVENTION

At the start of considering outsourcing, you should identify how many different potential vendors you will need. Then you can identify the interfaces that will be required between the vendors. You should now proceed to determine what common tasks and what knowledge will be needed to be shared. It is also useful to get ahead of issues by creating a list of potential issues that could arise between vendors.

When you go to evaluate and select vendors, you want to make sure that vendor interfaces and working with other vendors are part of the evaluation criteria. Ask each vendor what problems they have encountered. Also inquire as to how they identify, work on, and resolve issues that they have with another vendor.

It does not stop there. When the vendors begin work, pull out the interfaces as a separate project and piece of work. This will give it more attention. Organize meetings with multiple vendors in which joint issues, problems, and opportunities are discussed. This will assist you in dealing with problems early and not waiting for them to arise before establishing a problem-solving approach.

DETECTION

Detecting a multiple vendor problem means that you have to look for signs. One sign is that one vendor expresses surprise at some situation. See how they respond. If they do not assume ownership and indicate that another vendor is responsible, then you can start to see that there will be more problems coming.

Another technique is to see how vendors behave with each other in joint vendor–client meetings. Watching body language and listening to tone of voice can reveal a lot about what is under the surface.

When vendors do not address interfaces and problems directly, they may be making assumptions as to their relationship. This can be dangerous since each vendor may be making different assumptions. A real danger sign.

ACTION

When you see a conflict or disagreement between vendors, then you must take the "bull by the horns" early. Get all of the problems out on the table with each vendor separately. Analyze these problems and then get the vendors together. It is important not to play the "blame game" or try to determine who is guilty. You have to solve the problem and move on. Remember too that you are going to continue to be dependent on these multiple vendors in the future.

THE VENDOR IS NOT MANAGING THEIR WORK

BACKGROUND

This sounds at first like an unlikely issue. However, it can easily arise because the vendor may be assuming that you will be doing the oversight and direct management of the vendor work. Some vendor staff we have encountered like to take advantage of the situation and play off the client against their own management.

Remember that the vendor managers and leaders are likely spread thin among multiple clients. They cannot be there at every meeting and contact. This can give rise to misunderstandings about the tasks and the work itself.

IMPACT

If the vendor staff is not being managed by the vendor, they may be drawn off on additional tasks that are requested either by IT staff or business employees. Much of this additional work may be well intentioned. However, it will lead later to disagreements on costs and scope of work.

Another impact of lack of management is that internal IT management may have to step into the gap and assume direct responsibility for oversight. This can lead to more problems since the vendor may later say that "Well, you were managing them and telling them what to do. You assumed this role. So you have to assume the consequences."

PREVENTION

How the vendor staff and work are to be managed should be one of the first things that are addressed in the negotiations with the vendor before work begins. The vendor needs to state specifically what they will be responsible for in management. In addition, an escalation process needs to be determined for dealing with management issues related to the vendor work.

DETECTION

You can detect that there is a problem if you begin to see that you or other IT managers are becoming more involved in directing the vendor staff. This can start very subtlety and then grow over time. It often starts because of expediency since the vendor manager is not available.

Another sign is to see if the vendor leaders are present in the major meetings. If you find that they cancel meetings or are "no-shows," then this is another sign of the problem.

A third way to detect problems is to compare what the vendor staff is saying versus what the vendor leaders are saying. If the vendor leaders have information that appears out-of-date, then you know that there is, at a minimum, a communication gap within the vendor organization.

ACTION

You could fill the management gap and take over the direction of the work. This might be useful in the short run, but it has many problems over the longer term. Moreover, it will become harder for vendor management to reassert itself.

A better approach is to have regular meetings with the vendor leaders. In these meetings, you should openly address the direction of the vendor employees. At these meetings, you can also identify any specific problems that have arisen.

THERE IS A DIFFICULTY IN TRANSFERRING KNOWLEDGE FROM THE VENDOR

BACKGROUND

Vendors are performing work for you. It is natural to assume that the vendor employees will be communicating and sharing knowledge with internal employees. But this often does not happen. The vendor staff may solve a network problem. The fix worked and life goes on. They may not have an opportunity to explain the fix to the internal staff.

The problem also arises because in many outsourcing arrangements, there is a lack of provision for transferring knowledge. The focus in the contract and in planning is for the performance of the work itself.

IMPACT

Lack of transfer of knowledge means that you are more dependent upon the vendor experience and knowledge. This will make it harder for you to get a grasp on the details of what is going on. It also makes it more difficult to either take the work over or, alternatively, to turn it over to another vendor.

The impact grows with longer outsourcing arrangements. Over time, the vendor staff has collected a large body of knowledge that has not been conveyed.

Much of this has not been documented. This increases the cost of any eventual transition.

PREVENTION

For prevention you want to build in knowledge transfer as part of the vendor agreement. This goes beyond documentation. It also includes regular meetings where problem solving and other vendor actions are discussed. The vendor may be reluctant to do this since it means extra work. However, you should insist on this.

Another measure is to go to the internal IT staff and ask them how much of the vendor work they are aware of and knowledgeable in. Ask them "If they had to take over, could they do it?" Also, ask "What additional information they need to understand the work?"

DETECTION

You can detect that there is a problem if a situation arises that the vendor cannot address. Then you can see how the internal employees react. This is a good sign of what knowledge was transferred.

Another method of detection is to measure the extent of vendor communication in which information was provided. This can be through meetings and documentation.

ACTION

If you find that information transfer is not occurring, then you want to carry out two steps. First, for future work you want to establish the regular meetings and more documentation, if possible. Second, you should go back over what the vendor has done and ask the internal employees what additional information they would require to do the work themselves. You may also have to review code, logs, and other results of vendor work.

THERE ARE PROBLEMS IN VENDOR COMMUNICATIONS

BACKGROUND

Vendor managers and staff have many contacts across the IT organization, amongst themselves, and with business employees. With these extensive contacts, it is not surprising that there is substantial miscommunication.

In general, vendor communication has been a subject of less attention than vendor contracts, review of work, and other activities. Yet, it is a precursor to many of the problems that arise between vendors and customers.

A simple example will highlight the problem. Sam, who works for the vendor, meets with Brenda in a user department. Brenda indicates a new requirement to Sam. Sam takes this information back to the vendor headquarters and relates it to Bob, the project leader for the vendor. Bob then translates this requirement into additional work. Bob contacts Richard who is responsible for overseeing the vendor work. Now Richard has to verify the requirement with the IT staff, with the business manager, and with Brenda. That is a lot of communication and a major opportunity for miscommunication.

IMPACT

There might seem to be no immediate impact of poor communication. Yet, very soon after there is a miscommunication, the problems begin to grow. People take actions and make assumptions based upon the information that is communicated. These then can result in extra work, conflict, and more problems.

Another impact is that as a result of communication problems, distrust between the vendor and customer staff can grow. This can lead to more conflict and disagreements.

PREVENTION

Early in the contract work you want to establish how communication will be handled. You can also review communication as the work progresses. Consider having a communication plan and a review method with the vendor as well.

DETECTION

Look for communication problems in terms of what you are told by different people. Remember to include the internal employees as well as the vendor employees. Look for inconsistencies. Be sensitive to people presenting old information. This can reveal a lack of communication. Another step is to be aware of the source of issues. You want to know how the problem came into existence. You will often find it was communication based.

ACTION

When you see signs of communication, you should get people in a meeting to discuss how communication is being carried out. Review the communication with examples where there have been problems.

You should also point out specific issues that were caused by communication problems along with the impact of the problems. This will indicate the importance of communication.

THE VENDOR HAS A CLOSE PERSONAL RELATIONSHIP WITH A SENIOR MANAGER

BACKGROUND

Vendors want to establish good relationships with customers. It is natural that the vendors will want to make contact and build relationships with the people in the client firm who can make decisions. Thus, contacts with upper management are viewed not only as important, but also as essential to getting and retaining business.

Having relationships with a senior manager also helps the vendor by helping them get problems handled. A high-level manager can force decisions and actions down on the internal employees.

IMPACT

One effect of this direct contact is that the IT management and staff may feel very uneasy in dealing with the vendor. They may be reluctant to share information since that information could be misused and abused through later contacts between the vendor and upper management.

Another impact is that the vendor may sense that they have a great deal of power. They may use the relationship with the upper-level manager to communicate his or her wishes directly to the IT staff. The IT staff have no access to upper-level management so it is difficult for them to sort out what is truth and fiction from what the vendor is saying.

PREVENTION

You cannot easily prevent the vendor from contacting upper-level managers. Nonetheless, there are several actions you can take. One is to indicate to upper-level management that they should expect some contact with the vendor. Ask them how they want to handle this three-way communication.

The second action is to sit down with the vendor and address this three-way communication. Indicate that there have been problems in the past or at other firms. Also, emphasize that you want to prevent any of these problems. Finally, tell them what you might do in some cases to validate what they tell you. This will help put the vendor on guard that you are alert to any potential problem.

DETECTION

One sign of a problem is when the vendor starts to quote what the upper-level manager says. This is a sign to you that they are now using the relationship—either positively or negatively.

Another indication of a problem is when the upper-level manager comes to you with information and actions that could only have come from the vendor. Now you are starting to see the signs of the relationship from the other perspective.

ACTION

Obviously, you cannot kill off the contact between the vendor and manager. You will have to live with it. However, you can work on the vendor in terms of raising questions with the information they are communicating. The vendor should be your major focus since you likely have little opportunity for upper management contact on a regular basis.

You want to point out to the vendor that it is their best interest to have a healthy working relationship with the IT group to get the work done. After all, if they have wonderful contacts with upper management, but are not getting the work performed, they will suffer the negative fallout along with you.

Appendix A
Magic Cross Reference

Area	Topic	Pages
Areas of change	Failure	3–5
Business processes	Characteristics	5–6
Communications	Formal presentations	174–175
Communications	Informal communications	173–174
IT	Roles and responsibilities	32–33
IT direction	Business unit IT strategy	148–149
IT direction	Process planning	145–148
IT direction	Roles of business units	142–146
IT governance	Approach	10–11
IT governance	Business vision, mission	33–35
IT governance	Definitions, discussion	6ff
IT governance	Planning tables	37–38
IT governance	Trends and challenges	7–9
IT management change	New roles for IT	203–204
IT oversight	Goals	22–23
IT projects	Evaluation	89–91
IT projects	Origination	85–87
IT projects	Setup	94–98
IT projects	Tracking	99–101
Outsourcing	Approach	158–159
Outsourcing	Strategy	159–160
Outsourcing	Vendor evaluation and selection	161–165
Software packages/development	Process evaluation	189–191
Software packages/development	Requirements analysis	190–194
Steering committees	Levels	30–32
Strategic IT plan	Problems	73
Strategic IT plan	Resource management	76–78
Strategic IT plan	Steps	66–68

Area	Topic	Pages
Strategic IT plan	Tables and outline	70–72
Strategic IT plan	Updating the plan	78–79
Technology	Cost elements	47–48
Technology	Myths	49–51
Technology management	Critical success factors	55–56
Work management	Assess methods and tools	123–125
Work management	Issues management	128–129
Work management	Milestone review	125–128
Work management	Work review	122–123

Appendix B
References

Cassidy, A., *A Practical Guide to IS Strategic Planning*, Saint Lucie Press, New York, 1998.

Lientz, B.P. and K.P. Rea, *On Time Technology Implementation*, Academic Press, San Diego, 1999.

Lientz, B.P. and K.P. Rea, *Breakthrough Technology Project Management*, 2nd ed., Academic Press, San Diego, 2002.

Luftman, J.N., *Managing the IT Resource: Leadership in the Information Age*, Prentice-Hall, Englewood Cliffs, 2003.

Post, G.V. and D.L. Anderson, *Management Information Systems: Solving Business Problems with Information Technology*, 3rd ed., McGraw Hill, New York, 2002.

Sage, A., *Systems Management for Information Technology and Software Engineering*, John Wiley & Sons, New York, 1998.

Thompson, R.L. and W. Cats-Baril, *Information Technology and Management*, 2nd ed., McGraw Hill, New York, 2002.

Appendix C
Websites

@Computer Weekly—computerweekly.co.uk—management and technical articles.
Bit Pipe Knowledge—bitpipe.com—gives a good listing of articles and features from various sources.
CIO Insight—cio.com. This is a regular magazine that gives case studies, examples, and technology management articles.
eWeek—techupdate.zdnet.com. This is a magazine on E-Business related to management.
IEEE publications—computer.org.
Information Week—informationweek.com. This magazines gives applications, examples, and case studies of technology use.
Intelligent Enterprise—intelligententerprise.com. This gives a number of IT articles.
IT Magazine—itmagazine.com.
Outsourcing Center—outsourcingcenter.com. This is an excellent source of information for IT and process outsourcing.
Technology Evaluation—technologyevaluation.com. This magazine gives assessments of new technology from a management view.
Tech Republic—techrepublic.com. This is an excellent source of information and has different groupings for IT management, professionals, and consultants.

Index